BUT FIRST,
CHAMPAGNE

BUT FIRST,

CHAMPAGNE

A Modern Guide to the World's Favorite Wine

BY DAVID WHITE

Foreword by Ray Isle
Photography by John Trinidad

Skyhorse Publishing

Skyhorse Publishing books may be purchased in bulk at special discounts for sales promotion, corporate gifts, fund-raising, or educational purposes. Special editions can also be created to specifications. For details, contact the Special Sales Department, Skyhorse Publishing, 307 West 36th Street, 11th Floor, New York, NY 10018 or info@skyhorsepublishing.com.

Skyhorse® and Skyhorse Publishing® are registered trademarks of Skyhorse Publishing, Inc.®, a Delaware corporation.

Visit our website at www.skyhorsepublishing.com.

10 9 8 7 6 5 4 3 2

Library of Congress Cataloging-in-Publication Data

Names: White, David, 1982- author.
Title: But first, champagne : a modern guide to the world's favorite wine / by David White.
Description: New York : Skyhorse Publishing, [2016] | Includes bibliographical references and index.
Identifiers: LCCN 2016035626 (print) | LCCN 2016040068 (ebook) | ISBN 9781510711440 (alk. paper) | ISBN 9781510711457 (ebook) | ISBN 9781510711457 (Ebook)
Subjects: LCSH: Champagne (Wine)
Classification: LCC TP555 .W45 2016 (print) | LCC TP555 (ebook) | DDC 641.2/224--dc23
LC record available at https://lccn.loc.gov/2016035626

Cover design by Jane Sheppard
Cover photo by Françoise Peretti - Collection CIVC.

Print ISBN: 978-1-5107-1144-0
Ebook ISBN: 978-1-5107-1145-7

Printed in the United States of America

Wine demands to be shared.
So this book is dedicated to everyone with whom
I've pulled (or popped!) a cork.

CONTENTS

PART TWO: DIGGING DEEPER IN CHAMPAGNE

AUTHOR'S NOTE

There's never been a better time to explore Champagne.

Of course, the region and its wines have always been associated with prestige and luxury. And knowledgeable wine enthusiasts have long talked about top champagnes with the same reverence they reserve for the finest wines of Bordeaux and Burgundy.

But everyday consumers kept champagne way back on the high shelf. And too often, when bubbles were poured, they were shoddy imitations like

Exploring the Champagne Bollinger cellars.

André. Real champagne was, for most, more of a symbol than a beverage to be savored.

Today, that's changing.

Sommeliers, retailers, and wine enthusiasts everywhere have become passionate ambassadors for "grower" champagnes, which are made by the farmers who grow the grapes. Champagne's biggest houses—producers like Louis Roederer, Pol Roger, and Taittinger—are making better wines than ever before. Across the world, people are beginning to appreciate champagne as an affordable luxury. Indeed, global champagne sales hit a record in 2015.

This book is designed as an approachable guide to all things Champagne. The first half reveals the region's exciting history. Throughout the text, sidebar essays attempt to answer any questions that may arise. The second half explores Champagne's various sub-regions, discussing geography and terroir. This section also profiles Champagne's leading producers, from the smallest growers to the largest *négociants*. If you come across any words you haven't seen before, consult the glossary on page 280.

Communicating effectively about wine doesn't demand an encyclopedic knowledge of rare fruits and bizarre aromas, so this book isn't a collection of tasting notes. Nor is it an academic exercise, so don't expect a comprehensive guide. While great sparkling wine can be made in many regions, the focus here is exclusively Champagne.

As a style note, I've reserved "Champagne"—with a capital "C"—for the region. When a lowercase letter is used, I'm talking about the wine.

David White
September 2016

FOREWORD

Champagne is the wine that everyone knows, and that no one knows. Millions of bottles are drunk throughout the world every week, at parties, at restaurants, at clubs, at social events. Weddings are toasted with champagne; birthdays are celebrated. It is inarguably the wine that brings the most pure delight, thanks to its bright effervescence, celebratory pop, and—might as well say it—extraordinary, centuries-long marketing campaign, to the most number of people in the world.

At the same time, champagne is one of the great *wines* of the world. The best champagnes age as long or longer than great Bordeaux and Burgundies; they have the same nuanced complexity and profound depths. And yet, partly because of champagne's success at promoting its festive image, only a very tiny percentage of the millions of people who drink it realize that.

Certainly I didn't for a very long time. I don't recall the first glass of champagne I ever had, but I clearly recall the first bottle. It was a bottle of Moët & Chandon White Star, back when the house's basic brut bottling was called that, and my parents gave it to me to celebrate the opening of a play I'd written (at my college theater, just to ground this in reality). I have zero memory of the wine, which I drank with my girlfriend, but I do recall being impressed by the gift. We were not a champagne-drinking family in the slightest.

If you land in the wine business, though, you inevitably realize that there is much more to champagne than its all-purpose fizzy gift-worthiness. First comes the realization that the wine is not monolithic, and that the different houses bottle vintage wines, *tête de cuvées* and other more obscure cuvées along with those basic bottles that every restaurant serves (Laurent Perrier's bone-dry Ultra Brut, the first modern zero-dosage wine, was my personal eye-opener in this regard). Next, perhaps, some friend opens a bottle of vintage champagne that's been sitting in a cellar for ten or twenty years— well, *that's* pretty amazing, you think. And then, roughly in the late nineties and largely thanks to the importer Terry Theise, a large number of people (again mostly in the wine business, initially) started to realize there were champagnes out there beyond what the big houses made—small producers, working from individual estates, working to define the region's wines in a very different way. I got lucky in terms of the first grower champagne I tasted. It was in 1999, and I was at an after-work dinner with a bunch of wine salespeople at a place called Grand Szechuan International on 9th Avenue in New York. We'd all brought wine, and as we were putting them on the table a fellow named Mike Wheeler pulled a champagne I'd never seen before out of his wine bag. It showed two faces in profile, and was called Substance; the producer was Jacques Selosse. "What's that?" I said. "That is the best fucking champagne on the planet," he said. Admittedly there was a certain amount of sales guy bravado in the statement, but after a couple of sips, I began to wonder whether he was actually right.

My point is, we all know to a degree what champagne is, but it's that voyage of discovery into everything else that champagne is that makes it such a compelling wine. Its history is fascinating. The technique used to make it, and how history and location brought that technique into being is fascinating. There a great stories even in the historical footnotes of champagne. I had no idea, for instance, before reading David White's book, that the charismatic champagne ambassador and entrepreneur, Charles Heidsieck (or "Champagne Charlie," as he was known in the US) was accused of being a Confederate spy during his travels and thrown into a malarial swamp-situated prison outside of New Orleans. That alone is a novel waiting to be written.

Which brings me to David White's smart, entertaining, and valuable book. I doubt there's a wine writer in the business (or a wine anyone in the business) who doesn't rely on his Terroirist wine blog for daily insight into more or less everything being written about wine. What his blog does not give away is the energy and liveliness of his storytelling, and the crisp appeal of his prose. *But First, Champagne* covers the stories of champagne with great verve; the technical aspects of champagne with accuracy; and the producers, grand marques, and growers alike, with clarity and depth. It's one of those rare wine books that should appeal to people just getting into champagne and longtime champagne obsessives (there are more than you think) alike. In fact, it should probably best be read with a glass of champagne in hand—as to which one, well, read on.

Ray Isle
Executive Wine Editor, *Food & Wine* magazine
New York, April 2016

Introduction

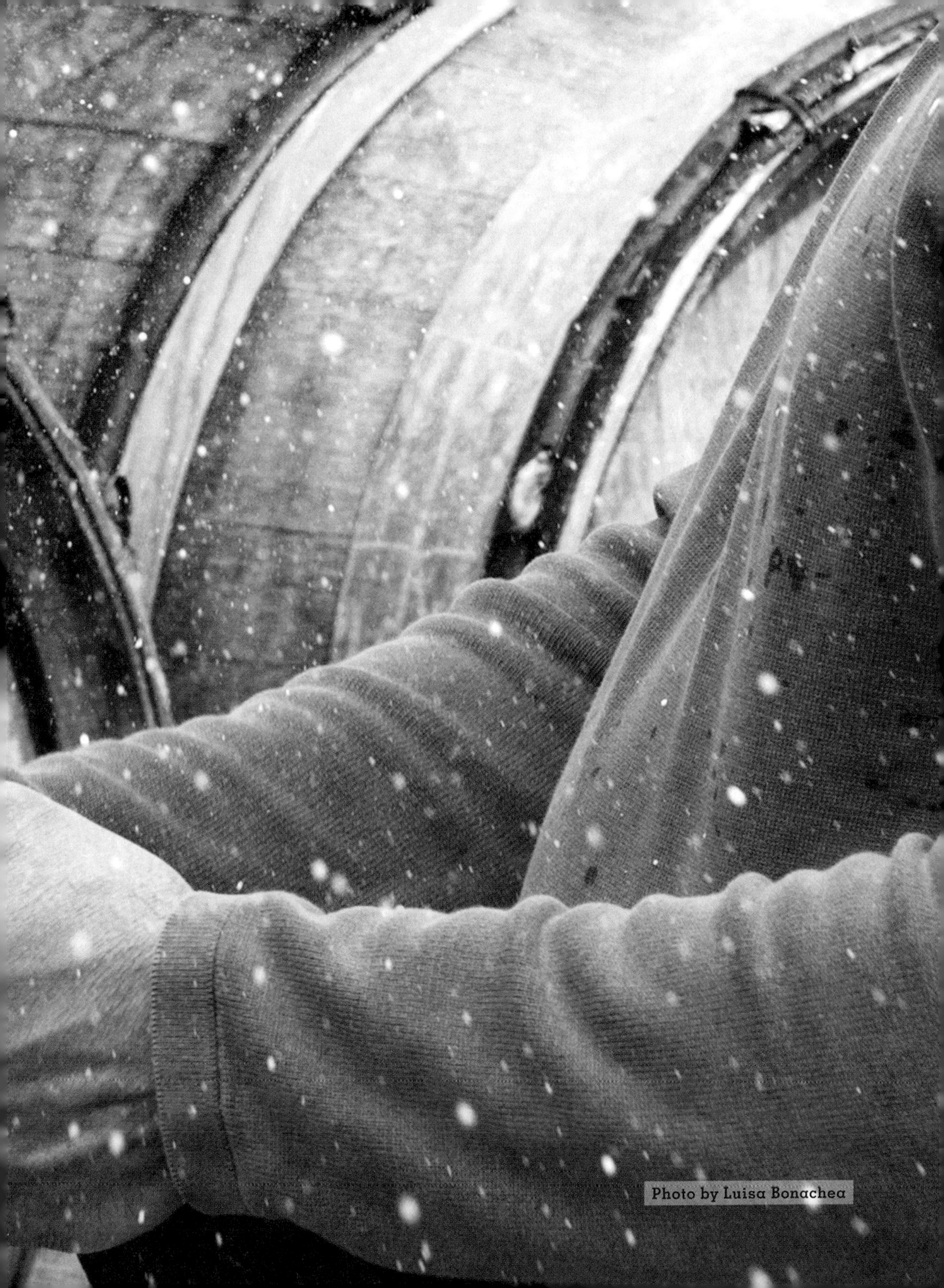

Photo by Luisa Bonachea

SEARCHING FOR AUTHENTICITY

Life is worth celebrating. This profound realization hit me while chatting with Terry Theise, a well-known wine importer.

Moments after sitting down for dinner, Theise ordered us a bottle of champagne made by Marc Hébrart, a small French producer he'd brought into the United States. As the sommelier filled our glasses, I was momentarily transfixed by the bubbles. And that's when it hit me: life *is* worth celebrating.

And what do we celebrate with? Bubbles.

Every bottle releases shimmering millions that seem to defy gravity, floating up to the drinker. They're seductive and sensual, and the gentle foam they create is explosively aromatic. Most people don't know those bubbles are quite literally intoxicating. Because carbon dioxide delivers alcohol more directly into the bloodstream, champagne delivers a quicker buzz than still wine. As Theise joked a few weeks after we first met, "drinking a half of a glass of champagne on an empty stomach is like having nitrous oxide without having to go to the dentist."

Pleasure is contagious—and no drink is capable of providing more pleasure than champagne. The very word has come to inspire euphoria and trigger an emotional release. That fabled "quick high" inspired Theise to visit Champagne in 1995, a year he was also celebrating a high of his own making. He had just started dating Odessa Piper, the well-known restaurateur and chef. When they first connected, Piper lived in Wisconsin while Theise was settled in Washington, DC.

"As happens in long-distance relationships," he explained, "you have a lot of misery and heartbreak when you're apart. But when you come together, it's a big celebration. So we quickly ran through all the grower champagnes that were available in the US market and I found myself thinking, 'Is this really all? There have to be more good growers than this.'"

Theise had become focused on "grower champagne" because he was—and still is—fascinated by terroir. This French term captures the idea that great wines invariably express time and place by translating a distinct vintage year, the unique soil in which they're harvested, and the weather in which they're grown. Just as a Virginia apple tastes different from the same variety ripened in Massachusetts, Chardonnay produced in Sonoma tastes entirely different from Chardonnay produced in Burgundy. Theise's obsession with terroir inspired him to begin his wine business by importing wines from small vineyards in Austria and Germany in the 1980s. And it's why he had no interest in supporting large champagne producers. Big houses like Moët & Chandon, Veuve Clicquot, and Taittinger purchase grapes in bulk from growers across Champagne and rely on blending to produce a consistent product year after year. But Theise had little interest in wines that were just consistent. So he planned a trip to France with Piper to look for growers who were interested in celebrating the wonderfully explosive chaos of different soils and different weather patterns.

Champagne vineyards outside the town of Polisot in The Aube.

"This was all personal," he continued. "At first, all I wanted to do was to buy some champagne to ship back to myself so I'd have stuff in the cellar to open up with Odessa. We visited dozens of producers. And I came away with my mind expanded—I had not realized the profound degree to which champagne was a wine of terroir, just like every other wine of northern Europe."

By the conclusion of his trip, Theise decided to add champagne to his import portfolio. But convincing American consumers to try more varied, off-the-beaten-path champagne was an uphill struggle. While the region and its wines were always associated with prestige and luxury, only serious wine enthusiasts knew that the best champagnes could be as diverse—and spectacular—as the finest offerings from Bordeaux and Burgundy.

Moreover, the good champagnes were spectacularly expensive for the wallets of Main Street Americans—suited for the high times but often lost in the clamor of whatever celebration was going down. Gushing Champagne bottles were the image of post-game euphoria and rap-star debauchery. As for the "by-the-case" imitation champagne served at weddings—think Cook's "California Champagne" and cheap Spanish cava and Italian prosecco—well, the less said the better.

That was the cultural knot; Champagne in America was a symbol, not a real wine.

But slowly, Theise worked around to the back of the champagne cliché and built a discerning market for his new growers. Home consumers appreciated the fact that Theise wines literally sparkled with personality—and they had the additional cachet of not being available at corner outlets or big-box racks. Sommeliers at chic, "farm-to-table" restaurants jumped at the opportunity to bring the distinctive experience of terroir champagnes to sophisticated diners.

Today, there's little doubt that Theise fundamentally reshaped the global champagne market. While growers accounted for just 0.62 percent of the America's Champagne imports in 1997, they now account for more than 5 percent. That percentage continues to rise.

It was one of the wines from the Theise portfolio that reshaped my own taste for champagne.

In the winter of 2010, I was spending the last week of the year in Colorado with family and friends. At Christmas dinner, we popped a bottle from Laurent Champs, the fifth-generation proprietor of Vilmart & Cie.

Since 1890, Champs's family has made champagne from their own vines, refusing to sell grapes to big-brand blenders.

I'd had plenty of great champagne previously; I fell in love with wine three years earlier and immediately—as is my habit—went deep by planning tasting trips across the world, taking classes, and reading every wine book I could find. My new-found wine geek friends had regularly talked up champagne, but with the Vilmart, something finally clicked. The nose was explosive, offering aromas of white flowers, sandalwood, and fresh baked bread. The palate was outlandishly rich but somehow weightless. This wine drinker saw the light in the bubbles.

I couldn't help but wonder how such a deceptively simple beverage could have such an alluring bouquet and taste so good.

At once, I set out to fill in the obvious gaps in my knowledge base, tasting as many as I could to expand my experience of champagne. And over and over again, the wines just knocked me out. Finally in July 2014, I headed to Champagne to visit some of the producers whose wines had left me searching for superlatives.

My first stop was Krug, the legendary champagne house founded in 1843 and located in Reims, the main city in Champagne. The property is open by appointment only. To gain entrance, I had to check in with a security guard at a solid metal gate that looked like it could stop a tank. A relic, perhaps, from World War I, when Reims was indeed a battleground and locals sought refuge in Krug's cellars. Once inside, a receptionist urged me to make myself comfortable in the winery's opulent living room. She poured a glass of Krug's Grand Cuvée and encouraged me to sign the leather-bound guest book. Minutes later, the impeccably dressed hospitality manager came out to lead me on a tour.

Krug was definitely the high end of tradition, but luxury tastings in luxury settings weren't what I was after. Like Theise, I was far more interested in down-home conviviality and nose-to-the-soil local producers than exclusivity and extravagance. So I moved on.

Early the next morning, I drove to Ecueil, a small village in northern Champagne with just 300 residents. I had an appointment set up with Frederic Savart, a local vigneron whose popularity in the United States has surged over the last couple of years. Gaining access to the winery was easy; I simply pulled into the driveway of Savart's home. Wearing boots, jeans, and a military jacket, Savart was out unloading barrels from a van, making room

for them in the glorified shed where he produces about 35,000 bottles of wine each year. We toured and tasted, but only after he handed over the morning's task of labeling bottles to his young daughter.

After leaving Savart's, I drove 30 minutes South to Cuis, a village with a whopping 400 residents, to visit Didier Gimonnet. The Gimonnets have been growing grapes in Champagne since 1750 and making wine since 1935, when Didier's grandfather, Pierre, began making his own. Upon my arrival, Gimonnet emerged from his vineyard covered in mud, and quickly disappeared to change. We then tasted through his full

Frederic Savart.

lineup and chatted in his living room, where he remembers playing on the floor as a toddler while his dad was out tending to the vines.

This was the champagne I was looking for. Krug's wines are delicious—and worth every penny. But I went to Champagne to seek out winemakers like Frederic Savart and Didier Gimonnet—authentic, mud-on-the-boots farmers who believe that great wines should be a unique representation of the vineyards in which they're grown.

After a quick dinner in Épernay, Champagne's second largest city, I headed to the small village of Avize, where I had a room booked at the small hotel owned by Anselme Selosse, a winegrower who has had a larger impact in Champagne than anyone since Dom Pérignon. The next morning, we met to walk around his cellar.

"Nature is larger and bigger than all of us; it's crazy to think that man can dominate nature," Selosse explained. "Wines must show the characteristics of the place. Illuminating the vineyard is my obsession."

Didier Gimmonet.

Anselme Selosse.

For Selosse, wine should be enjoyed, yes, but it should also perfectly capture the characteristics of the soils in which it's grown. Waxing poetic about the production of wine, of course, pervades the industry. Every winemaker today will repeat some version of how "wine is made in the vineyard." But when Selosse took over his father's winery in 1974, this wasn't yet a cliché. In fact, if truth be told, in the Champagne of the old days, output and market price routinely trumped talk of the mysteries of terroir.

There were exceptions, obviously. But most of the large producers that dominated the region sought simply to deliver a consistent—and consistently growing—product each year. They purchased grapes from thousands of growers across Champagne and paid by the ton. So growers sought to "dominate nature," maximizing yields by utilizing fertilizers, herbicides, insecticides, and fungicides. The results were predictably atrocious, but it didn't matter. For most producers and virtually every consumer, champagne wasn't about wine; it was about luxury. So Selosse's philosophy wasn't just unusual, it was subversive and, given the market, more or less irrelevant.

But Selosse had learned to care deeply about the quality of the fruit underneath a wine in Burgundy, where he was inspired by the vignerons at celebrated properties like Domaine Coche-Dury, Domaine Leflaive, and Domaine des Comtes Lafon. These are some of Burgundy's most legendary producers, and year after year, they prove that wines can, indeed, express the characteristics of their vintage and the soils and climate in which they're grown.

Shortly after taking over his father's vineyard holdings back in Champagne, Selosse began moving towards organic farming and obsessing over his land, never sacrificing quality for yield. Pursuing perfect ripeness in his grapes was no easy task in the unpredictable climate of northern France.

In the cellar, Selosse chose to focus on his *vin clair*—the still wine that's created before champagne producers initiate a secondary fermentation to create bubbles—because "[it] shows that all the flavors are there; bubbles are just an accessory."

Although soft-spoken, Selosse speaks with the fervor of a believer and the charm of a practiced storyteller. As we chatted in his cellar, Selosse talked at great length about the microorganisms that live in a vineyard's soil—and the unique characteristics they bring to his wines.

By way of illustration, he pointed towards the ceiling where the hindquarters of several pigs were hanging, slowly curing. For Selosse, the difference between Prosciutto di Parma and Jamon Iberico can be explained entirely by the flora, fauna, and fungi the pigs fed on. He quickly extended the argument to cheese, milk, and sake. A moment later, Selosse pulled out a cigarette lighter, found a piece of paper, and lit it on fire. Within seconds, all that remained was a small pile of ash. All living things resolve to little more than carbon, he said, and the "signature" of everything we consume comes ultimately from the ground.

"Nowhere else in the world can you make wines with the flavors we have here," he explained, bringing it all back to champagne. Scientific? Perhaps not. But with wines that are so extraordinarily expressive, I'm certainly a believer.

Selosse's impact can't be overstated. He has inspired a whole generation of growers in Champagne to pursue the ideal of terroir. And together with other wine influencers, he has helped educate today's consumers to recognize champagne as a vessel fully capable of expressing a vineyard—just as they do for other wines.

Olivier Collin (Champagne Ulysse Collin) apprenticed with Anselme Selosse and makes terroir-inspired wines from Congy in the Sézannais.

Of course we all want the pleasure wine offers. But those of us who obsess over what we drink aren't looking for taste alone; we're looking for an experience, the deeper and richer story that wine can tell. And champagne has one of the best.

There is something obviously unique to champagne; it's what we reach for at big moments. It's how we christen ships, start new years, welcome babies, and celebrate Super Bowl victories. Yes, the big brands have spent millions to make that connection for us, but there's an unnecessary limit to their message.

Terry Theise often laments that large champagne producers have relegated their wines to "beverages of ceremony," because such marketing presumes that such celebrations are few and far between. Celebrations—and champagne—should not just come once a year. As he explained, "there can be weekly, if not daily celebrations in life."

From dinner with friends to a child's laughter or a lover's embrace, every day has moments worth the warmth of reflection—and worthy of a toast. No other drink can so effectively take us out of the ordinary and help us connect to one another. And the more we can appreciate the sun and soil of wine, the more we can appreciate the textures which comprise our own terroir—linking us to our pasts and futures.

In its greatest moments, champagne provides far more than pleasure; it offers a window into life. Romantic? Sure, but champagne is there to nourish the romantic in us all.

Life is worth celebrating. And that's why champagne matters.

Part One:

Champagne Through the Ages

6

Chapter One:
On the Trail of the Bubbly

Today, champagne sparkles at celebrations the world over. The heavy, dark bottle, the wire cage, the iconic pop of the cork, the foam, the bubbles, the toasts—and that first, bright taste of communal joy that champagne has come to represent.

Everyone knows—and doesn't know—the real story of champagne, although it's been written about and aggressively marketed, as both legend and fact, for generations. And of course, good "old" champagne has changed almost beyond recognition from what it once was, when it began. All experts agree that what the contemporary world now calls champagne was first produced in chalky soils of the northeast of France, close to Paris, close to what is now the German border. The region—war torn for centuries—of Champagne.

Legend would have us believe that an oenophilic Benedictine monk, Dom Pérignon, "invented" champagne in 1697. Good for local glory. But in fact six years before Pérignon even began working as a cellar master at the Abbey of Saint-Pierre of Hautvillers, an English scientist named Christopher Merret was adding sugar to wine to create a second fermentation—*et voilà*—palate-tingling bubbles. Even worse for *la belle champagne*, we know that monks in the French Pyrenees were purposefully producing sparkling wine as early as 1531.

Pinning down a date for champagne's first bubble is one of those academic crusades perhaps best left to teetotalers. Fizzy wine has been

A statue of Dom Pérignon in front of the cellars of Moët & Chandon.

around for as long as wine has graced our tents and our tables. The Bible in Proverbs 23:31 lays down one of the first government warnings: "Do not look at wine when it is red, when it sparkles in the cup and goes down smoothly." As usual, a command not universally followed.

For most of human history, though, those sparkles were considered a flaw—something you'd want to eliminate, not enhance. In fact, it's highly likely that pious Pérignon actually dedicated his time to ridding his wines of those nasty bubbles. Indeed, a 1713 inventory of his Abbey's wines shows that most were red—and none were sparkling.

Bubbles—though "natural" to the winemaking process—were slow in being accepted. Even the sophisticated French didn't get the tingle for a long time.

THE EARLY DAYS

The region of Champagne is one of the rich and prosperous heartlands of France. It's a central hub of confrontation and communication. With river valleys leading from the English Channel in the north to the Mediterranean in the south, Champagne has played an important role in French history since ancient times.

The town of Avirey-Lingey in the Côte des Bar.

While there's evidence to suggest that wine was made there before the first century BC—and conclusive proof that the Romans planted vines in the region shortly after their victorious legions arrived in 57 BC—any history of Champagne's wines should begin in 496. That year, the region's wine was singled out as a celebratory beverage.

Those were heady times for the Gauls. Clovis, a Frankish ruler, had finally succeeded in driving the weakened and reeling Romans out of what is now France and uniting the notoriously bristly Frankish tribes. But immediately, a confederation of Germanic tribes—the Alemanni—came crashing into Clovis's new kingdom. The Franks were hard-pressed by these newcomers and it looked as though Gaul would exchange Roman overlords for Germanic pagan rule. But Clovis's wife, a devout Christian from Burgundy, urged her husband to ask for God's help. He obliged, promising to convert to Christianity if victorious.

And win he did. On Christmas day after his stunning and unexpected victory, Clovis arrived at the Christian basilica in Reims—in the heart of Champagne—for his baptism. So many people crowded round for the ceremony that the bishop couldn't get to his vial of holy oil. Miraculously, a white dove swooped down and carried the oil to the bishop. A lavish celebration followed the baptism, and naturally, wines from Champagne flowed freely.

A REGION AND A WINE

Champagne is a historic region in northeastern France, beginning about 100 miles east of Paris. Best known for the sparkling wines that bear its name, the region is divided into four wine-producing districts: Montagne de Reims, Vallée de la Marne, Côte des Blancs, and the Aube.

Reims is the largest city in Champagne, with nearly 200,000 residents. Épernay, which sits just 15 miles south of Reims, has a population of only about 25,000 residents but is considered Champagne's "wine capital" since about 90 percent of the city's population works in the industry and several large producers are headquartered there. Troyes, a town of about 60,000 residents 65 miles south of Épernay, is Champagne's third commercial center. Troyes hosted many of the famous Champagne fairs of the 12th and 13th centuries.

THE WINE-GROWING REGIONS OF
Champagne

MASSIF DE ST. THIERRY

MONTAGNE DE REIMS

VESLE

VALLÉE DE LA MARNE

VESLE ET ARDRE

REIMS

MONTS DE BERRU

VALLÉE DE LA MARNE RIVE DROITE

GRANDE MONTAGNE DE REIMS

GRANDE VALLÉE DE LA MARNE

VALLÉE DE LA MARNE OUEST

to Paris

ÉPERNAY

SARMELIN

VALLÉE DE LA MARNE RIVE GAUCHE

CONDÉ

COTEAUX SUD D'ÉPERNAY

CÔTE DES BLANCS

MARNE

PETIT MORIN

VAL DU PETIT MORIN

GRAND MORIN

CÔTE DE SÉZANNE

CÔTE DES BLANCS

VITRYAT

N

GRAND CRUS

· LEGEND ·

1. SILLERY
2. PUISIEULX
3. BEAUMONT
4. VERZENAY
5. MAILLY
6. VERZY
7. LOUVOIS
8. AMBONNAY
9. BOUZY
10. AŸ
11. TOURS-SUR-MARNE
12. CHOUILLY
13. OIRY
14. CRAMANT
15. AVIZE
16. OGER
17. LE MESNIL-SUR-OGER

AUBE

MONTGUEUX

TROYES

AUBE

BAR-SUR-AUBOIS

CÔTE DES BAR

PARIS

Champagne

SEINE

BARSÉQUANAIS

Illustration by
Katherine Messenger

From that day onwards, divine coronation at Reims became *de rigueur* for French kings—and toasting the event with champagne became a part of the ritual.

Clovis's dynasty—the Merovingians—ruled much of Western Europe over the next 200 years. Though rule *was* warfare during those dark ages, for the rich countryside of Champagne, it was, oddly enough, a period of relative peace and prosperity.

Vineyards flourished. It was largely monks who tended to the vines. The converted Frankish nobility—the warriors—funded abbeys and monasteries in hope of redeeming their bloody souls. In 650, the wealthy Archbishop of Reims founded the Abbey of Saint-Pierre of Hautvillers, which

The Reims Cathedral sits on the site of the ancient basilica where Clovis was crowned.

quickly became the most expansive and important Catholic enterprise in the whole of Champagne.

The wine the monks produced bore little resemblance to today's champagne; most was light red and cloudy. But quality steadily improved as the pious fathers honed their skills—making wines for the holy mass, to treat the sick, welcome guests, and thank their noble benefactors.

Merovingian rule came to an end in 752, but Christianity survived and the Catholic Church continued to cultivate and extend its vineyard holdings. The reputation of Champagne's wines spread far and wide.

One factor was the election of Urban II as Pope in 1088. Surprisingly, the man who became the head of the Roman church was the son of a winegrower from Châtillon-sur-Marne in Champagne. So it's not surprising that bishops, priests, and deacons from across Europe knew they could gain favor with the Pontiff by bringing him wine from his home vines.

Abbaye Saint-Pierre d'Hautvillers.

Urban II was the Pope who launched the Crusades. Strangely enough, as nobles in their thousands marched off to fight in the Middle East, northern Europe enjoyed a period of relative calm and prosperity.

Peace brought trade. Champagne was becoming a bustling entrepôt of northern European commerce. The region's counts soon were providing protection for visiting merchants and organizing "Champagne Fairs" where leather, lace, blankets, fur, gold, olive oil, and more were bought and sold. Merchants in Champagne specialized in wool, and around 1200, they began pushing wool deals—and perhaps loosening wallets—by offering free wine. One of the world's oldest sales tactics worked for wool—and it also brought recognition and renown to the region's wines.

The French monarchy also played a role in publicizing the vineyards of Champagne. Philip Augustus, who ruled France from 1180 to 1223, would only serve wine from the Abbey of Saint-Pierre at his royal table. Soon the wines from Champagne were the most popular in Paris, then Europe's largest city. The other great wine-producing regions of today's France were out of the running in those days. Bordeaux was ruled by England from 1152 till 1453 and Burgundy was an independent Duchy from 1032 till 1477.

The caves of Moët & Chandon, established in 1743. Photo by Luisa Bonachea.

France was on the ascent as a major power in Europe and by the turn of the 14th century, Champagne was flourishing. But centuries of prosperity came to an abrupt end in 1315 when the wrath of God seem to descend on France.

DEVASTATION, PLAGUE, AND ENDLESS WAR

In the spring of that fateful year, rains were exceptionally heavy and long. Soaked crops didn't ripen and there was no food for livestock. Without sun and warmth, salt could not be evaporated, so it became extraordinarily difficult to preserve meat. The first disastrous growing season was followed by two more years of flooding, compounded by unusually brutal winters.

Three successive years of crop failures sent all of northern France—and especially Champagne—into chaos. Disastrous animal and human epidemics followed. Eighty percent of Champagne's livestock was wiped out, and over ten years, it's estimated that northern Europe lost between 10 and 25 percent of its population.

The monarchy and civil order were strained. In 1328, France's 33-year-old King, Charles IV, died without male heirs. By ancient Frankish law, the throne couldn't pass to his one-year-old daughter, Mary. So it went to his cousin, Philip of Valois.

But the critical issue of succession soon brought war—over 100 years of war—between the rulers of France and England over claims to the crown of France. Charles IV's nephew, who had become King Edward III of England, maintained that he was entitled to the French throne as well through the female line. His mother was Charles IV's sister and Edward argued that ancient Frankish law only forbid passing the crown to a woman, not *through* a woman. That "small" point of succession was the flashpoint that set off what became known as the Hundred Years War, a war that impoverished England and ravaged France.

In the midst of the wars, plague struck. In the three years after the Black Death arrived in 1348, it killed more than half of Champagne's population.

The wars, however, continued. In 1356, the English captured France's king during the Battle of Poitiers. Though kingless, the nobles continued to impose ever-increasing taxes and military levies on the peasantry who finally rebelled in 1358. In Champagne there were weeks of pitched battles, reprisals, and atrocities known as the "Jacquerie" after the term the nobles used for resisting locals.

English armies swept into Champagne. On the feast day of Saint Andrew in 1359, Edward III approached Reims intent on a traditional French coronation. His troops besieged the city but its inhabitants were able to withstand five straight weeks of bombardments and assaults. The English remembered this affront and, when they returned to Champagne in 1369, they burned and pillaged with a vengeance.

It's hard to imagine the destruction of a "local" war that goes on for decades. Besides the back and forth of military campaigns, deserters and bushwackers—known as "routiers"—made the countryside a war zone by attacking travelers and supply convoys. They even took over villages. One notorious routier bragged that his men "drank the cellars dry" in Attigny, a hamlet not far from Reims.

When the Hundred Years' War finally wound down around 1453 and a semblance of order was restored, Champagne was in shambles. Entire towns were abandoned. Farms were barren. Cellars were empty. France controlled Aquitaine—the southwestern region of Bordeaux—but the English remained entrenched in Calais, the major northern port city.

The Krug caves. Photo by Luisa Bonachea.

THE HUGUENOT WARS

But within a century, savage dynastic conflict across northern France was replaced by equally savage religious wars. Rebellions against the power of the Roman Catholic Church began in the patchwork of principalities and city states in Germany and Switzerland in the years after 1525, and sects of fervent religious non-conformists—which often looked unfavorably on the consumption of liquor—took root in the Netherlands and France. While the German states—which had no all-powerful German king—often sheltered and supported Lutheran "heretics," the French nobility tended to remain solidly Catholic. Tensions soon led to general violence and repressions across France. In 1562, Catholic soldiers killed worshippers at a Huguenot service in Wassy, a village in Champagne, and went on to massacre most of the town's residents. Atrocity led to atrocity, and continuing conflicts between the Huguenots and Catholics—which were to last until 1598— soon devolved into full-scale wars of religion which ravaged all of France, but especially Champagne. Opposing what they saw as the luxury and debauchery of the monasteries which controlled much of the agricultural land, Huguenots attacked and sacked them, as they did the Abbey of Saint-Pierre in 1564, driving out the monks, clearing out the cellars, and burning the Abbey's archives.

The entire European continent was swept up in wars of the Reformation, but clearly religion was not as important as machinations for European supremacy. Catholic France declared war on Catholic Spain in 1635 and on the Catholic Holy Roman Empire in 1636.

France was not yet decisively unified behind the king. Years of war had produced armies of seasoned soldiers who were primarily loyal to their generals. Those armed leaders traded favors with the monarch and, for long periods, opposed his rule. A vicious civil war known as the Fronde swirled over Champagne between 1648 and 1653 until the king's complex alliances put down the rebellion and the French, exhausted from fire and carnage, almost welcomed the absolute rule of the great unifier king, Louis XIV.

WHAT THE SUN KING DRANK

Louis XIV was the first of a long string of "star endorsers" of champagne. He first tasted champagne in 1654 at what was then the grown-up age of 15. From that day onwards, he rarely drank anything else. And if the king endorsed champagne, the court followed.

The chalk caves of Champagne Charles Heidsieck.

Louis XIV proved to be a genius at consolidating the power of the monarchy and ruling absolutely from Paris, and later Versailles. Upon the death of his chief minister, Cardinal Mazarin, in 1661, he took full control of the French government, surprising his council by announcing that he would govern alone.

To begin, he reorganized the nation's finances. The treasury had brought France to the verge of bankruptcy through uncontrolled spending, haphazard tax collections, and chaotic borrowing. By establishing a clear taxation system and imposing strict rules on borrowing, Louis XIV quickly brought down the nation's deficit.

Oddly enough, Louis exempted the nobility from paying taxes. But it was a calculated move that paid off in that he made the nation's noble houses more dependent on the king and more willing to relinquish their power bases in the provinces. Essentially he was taking apart the old feudal order, which might sooner or later threaten his rule. Nobles, now living on the largesse of the crown, were encouraged to live "the good life" at Versailles. Originally a hunting lodge, Louis XIV turned it into a sumptuous royal palace where his court could prance, and become powerless.

He professionalized the French military and established centralized control so the troops were loyal only to the state and the king. No more private armies reporting to generals who could threaten him.

The public supported these moves; generations of conflict had left the French people eager for stable, orderly rule. The bourgeois, especially, backed Louis XIV's efforts to depose the feudal order. He worked to gain their support—and their tax payments—with intelligent efforts to encourage commerce and trade. He promoted fashion and tapestry weaving, boosted industries like silk and marble, and invited leading artisans—painters, glassmakers, furniture makers, goldsmiths, silversmiths, and more—from across Europe to work in France. His obsession with luxury elevated France to the global arbiter of good taste, helping reduce imports and expand French exports.

Champagne's wine industry benefited enormously during Louis XIV's reign. Since the king's preference for champagne was well known, royal attendants regularly brought champagne to Versailles to gain favor. Even wealthy nobles in the provinces would stock their own tables with champagne, emulating the glitter and grandeur of Versailles. Elites in other nations, especially Russia, also began drinking champagne to show off their own good taste.

CHAMPAGNE GETS BETTER

Just as Louis XIV was increasing demand for champagne, a Benedictine monk named Pierre Pérignon set out to improve the wine's quality.

Born in 1638 in Sainte-Menehould, a village 50 miles east of Reims, Pérignon grew up amidst the vines; his father's family owned vineyards in Champagne. In the tradition of wine mating with religion, Pérignon entered the Benedictine Order at the age of 17, and in 1668, the monk who knew the grape was sent to the Abbey of Saint-Pierre of Hautvillers to take over its growing wine operation. Ransacked during the French Wars of Religion, the Abbey was gradually rebuilt in the mid-1600s and its vineyards replanted. Under Dom Pérignon's 47-year tenure, the Abbey regained its reputation for producing the best wines in Champagne.

With the help of Dom Thierry Ruinart, a scholar at the Abbey, Pérignon explored and documented improvements in growing, harvesting, and processing that other winemakers in the region soon adopted.

Vineyards bordering Hautvillers. Photo by Luisa Bonachea.

In the vineyard, Pérignon pruned in the spring, recognizing that pruning immediately after harvest left vines more vulnerable to winter frost damage. He pruned aggressively, because excessive growth led to a crowded canopy and too much shade, which slowed ripening. Timing the ripening had always been a problem in northerly Champagne. At harvest, Pérignon picked early in the morning, because he saw that cool temperatures helped keep the grapes intact. And he transported his grapes with mules and donkeys, since horses were more likely to damage the delicate grapes.

Pérignon was similarly thoughtful and selective in the cellar, emphasizing quality over quantity of output. He rejected bruised, broken, underripe, overripe, and otherwise imperfect grapes. At the time, this was revolutionary, since producers traditionally dumped everything that could be pulled from the

CHAMPAGNE'S MANY STYLES

If a champagne is simply described by its sweetness level (e.g., brut), it's almost certainly a non-vintage blend of Chardonnay, Pinot Noir, and Pinot Meunier. But champagne comes in many other styles:

Blanc de Blancs: Translated as "white from whites," this designation is used when a champagne is made entirely of white grapes. Almost always, a *blanc de blancs* is 100 percent Chardonnay.

Blanc de Noirs: Translated as "white from blacks," this designation is used when a champagne is made completely of Pinot Noir and/or Pinot Meunier, Champagne's only approved dark-skinned grapes.

Rosé: In Champagne, pink wine is produced in one of three ways.

In the first method, a small amount of red wine is added to a white wine to dye the juice pink. Although the most popular way to make rosé in Champagne, this method is actually against the law in most European wine regions. These champagnes are sometimes labeled as "rosé d'assemblage."

In the second method, the juice from dark-skinned grapes is bled off its skins after a short period of time, typically a few hours to a few days. These champagnes are sometimes labeled as "rosé de saignée."

In the third method, which is essentially a hybrid of the first two, a rosé de saignée is blended into a white wine.

Vintage: If a vintage, or *millésime*, is listed on the label, 100 percent of the grapes inside come from that particular year. A vintage champagne can be in any style—a blend of different grapes, a *rosé, a blanc de blancs*, or a *blanc de noirs*.

vines into the vats. He also pressed gently to separate the juice from the skins, thus producing the first white wine from red wine grapes.

Pérignon was also a celebrated blender, recognizing that different grapes could provide different aromas and flavors to wine. He was particularly fond of Pinot Noir, believing that the region's other grapes—Pinot Blanc, Pinot Gris, Pinot Meunier, Chardonnay, and more—were more likely to become unstable and produce bubbles, a perpetual problem in Champagne.

ARE BUBBLES BAD?

The fact is, all Pérignon's efforts were going into the perfection of the Abbey's *still* wines. Everyone—or at least everyone French—thought excess gas was neither healthy nor healing, though it bubbled up in wines from Champagne all the same. And just at that time, across the Channel, English wine connoisseurs were falling in love with the tingle of those unintentional bubbles.

In the early 17th century, wine was released for transport and sale within months of harvest, much like modern-day rosé. It was carried to market in wooden casks. In England, merchants would transfer the wine from the casks into glass bottles under corks since the English were already producing stronger, more durable glass in new coal-fueled ovens.

In winter, Champagne's wine regions were so cold that so-called primary fermentation would often pause, leaving behind unconverted sugar and yeast. Fermentation would subsequently resume in the spring. But in England, where the wine had been transferred to corked glass bottles, the spring warm-up bubbles would be preserved. (Today, those early efforts from Champagne would correspond to wines which are *pétillant-naturel*—naturally sparkling— because the wines are bottled before primary fermentation has finished.)

Some English merchants even began adding molasses to wines prior to bottling to increase the likelihood of effervescence. Indeed, English dramatist George Etherege wrote about "sparkling champagne" in his 1676 comedy, *The Man of Mode*, noting that it "makes us frolic and gay, and drowns all sorrow." (The addition of molasses helped catalyze the secondary fermentation, a tactic that winemakers in Champagne would master in the 1830s and quickly claim as their own. This method became known as the "*méthode champenoise*" and is now known as "*méthode traditionelle*.")

By the turn of the 18th century, bubbly wines were a hit in England. And the French soon acquired "the English taste." That odd reversal happened just in the nick of time.

A VINOUS RIVALRY

The region of Burgundy was officially incorporated into France proper way back in 1477. Inhabiting one of the world's great wine-producing terroirs, the vintners of Burgundy had long resented their royally privileged northern rivals. Champagne, after all, had a monopoly on coronation ceremonies and dominated the king's wine cellars. That rivalry almost led to trouble in the final years of Louis XIV's life.

Davy Dosnon apprenticed in Burgundy before launching his eponymous champagne. Photo by Luisa Bonachea.

Throughout the 17th century, both regions marketed their wines by touting endorsements from prominent physicians and publicizing the preferences of the elite. Champagne had the advantage among aristocrats— after all, Louis XIV introduced the world to French luxury and exclusively drank champagne. But Burgundy had the advantage among health-conscious doctors.

Towards the end of his life, Louis XIV developed a number of ailments. While the royal doctor, Antoine d'Aquin, continued to support the king's champagne habit, a prominent physician who had befriended the king's mistress, Guy-Crescent Fagon, began blaming the king's failing health on his excessive consumption of champagne. Fagon urged Louis XIV to drink Burgundy, and in 1693, he became the royal physician.

This news only escalated tensions between Burgundy and Champagne. By the turn of the 18th century, the two regions were inundating Paris with pamphlets containing incendiary claims and denunciations about the other's wines. Many feared the war of words would escalate into actual warfare.

The feud, fortunately, died on its own as Champagne began moving away from still, red wines and toward clear, effervescent wines.

HOW CHAMPAGNE IS MADE

The process of making Champagne has essentially remained unchanged since the mid-19th century.

Because of the region's cool climate, grapes are typically harvested with relatively low sugar levels and relatively high acid levels. Unless the producer is making a rosé, the juice of those grapes is then quickly pressed off to keep the wine white. This juice is then fermented, with yeast converting the sugar into alcohol and carbon dioxide, which is allowed to escape. This produces a traditional—albeit highly acidic—dry wine, which serves as a "base."

A traditional champagne press in the cellar of Champagne Marie Courtin.

If the producer is making a "single-expression" champagne, utilizing grapes from a single vineyard, a single variety, and a single vintage, the base is now complete so it can be bottled. Typically, though, the producer will now assemble a blend, combining this base with other wines from various vineyards and various vintages. The resulting blend is then bottled.

Champagne bottles sealed with crown caps in the cellar of R. H. Coutier.

Once the wine is bottled, a second fermentation is launched by adding a mixture of yeast and sugar called the *liqueur de tirage*. At this point, the wine bottle is temporarily capped (typically with a crown cap, but sometimes with a traditional champagne cork) and stored *sur latte*, or on its side. Because this fermentation takes place inside a bottle, the carbon dioxide is captured. Non-vintage champagne must age on its dead yeast—called "lees"—for at least 12 months. Vintage-dated champagne is required to mature on its lees for at least three years. Many producers age their wines *sur lie*—"on the lees"—for much longer.

After aging, the dead yeast is gradually forced by gravity to the bottle's neck over a period of 8-10 weeks through a process called "riddling." Once the lees have been collected in the neck—and the wine is standing sur pointe—the winemaker "disgorges" the wine by removing the temporary cap and surrounding sediment, ideally without losing much liquid. This process can be automated by freezing the neck so that the sediment turns into a solid pellet.

The wine is then topped off with a small amount of wine and cane sugar—a mixture called *liqueur d'expédition*—in a process called "dosage." (A few small

The effect of riddling as lees collect in the bottle neck.

growers instead dose with *moût concentré rectifié*, or concentrated and rectified grape must, contending that it's more neutral.) This step is only required if a winemaker wants to sweeten his wines, and these days, it's fashionably avoided.

Finally, the wine is resealed with a more permanent closure.

Riddling in the cellars at Champagne Bollinger. Photo by Luisa Bonachea.

Chapter Two:

Bubbles Sweep the World

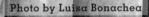
Photo by Luisa Bonachea

When Louis XIV died in 1715, the dozen-plus children he fathered through various mistresses weren't eligible for the crown—and most of his immediate family had perished. So the crown went to his five-year-old great-grandson, Louis XV.

The King was too young to rule, obviously, so his great uncle, Philippe II d'Orléans, became Regent of France. Philippe preferred Paris over Versailles, and governed from the Palais Royal, where he opened his gates to artists, musicians, writers, and other intellectuals. Under his rule, the Palais Royal became a center of hedonistic diversion. The regent's nightly *petits soupers*—debaucherous, orgiastic dinner parties—quickly became the talk of the town. These parties always started with the new effervescent champagne, so fashionable elites in Paris began seeking fizzy wine for their own gatherings.

If they want bubbles, we'll give them bubbles. Winemakers in Champagne followed the money and began moving away from still wine. But getting just enough and the right kind of bubbles wasn't easy. Each grape harvest was different and cellar masters didn't yet know enough chemistry to generate bubbles with precision. They knew, though, that the bubbles were best captured in glass; whatever bubbles you could capture in a big cask would dissipate shortly after the bung, or stopper, was removed.

So glass, but not just any glass. English glass was clearly superior since French glassblowers were only beginning to transition away from lower-temperature wood-fired ovens. Most French bottles weren't strong enough to withstand the high internal pressures of fizzy wine.

Transporting wine in bottles, however, was against French law, since authorities believed bottles—more difficult to tally—hindered tax collections. Finally, in 1728, King Louis XV gave his consent for wines from Champagne to be shipped in bottles and in an instant, vast new markets opened for the region's sparkling wines.

The first person to take advantage of the decree was Nicolas Ruinart, a wealthy fabric merchant in Épernay. His uncle, Dom Thierry Ruinart—who had worked alongside Dom Pérignon—inspired his nephew to make wine. So in 1729, Ruinart launched a winery dedicated to sparkling wines. At first, the plan was to simply give the wine away to top clients. By 1735, though, demand was so strong that Ruinart was able to abandon the cloth trade and concentrate exclusively on the burgeoning champagne trade. (It should be noted that while Ruinart is the oldest champagne house, Gosset is the region's oldest winery, founded in 1584.)

Other operations opened. In 1734, Jacques Fourneaux, a wine merchant, established the company that would eventually become Taittinger. In 1743, a wine merchant who was accredited to serve the royal court, Claude Moët, established another sparkling wine house.

The same year Ruinart abandoned the cloth business, King Louis XV issued another decree impacting the branding of champagne. He decreed that every bottle of champagne contain one "Paris pint" (equivalent to 750 milliliters, today's standard wine bottle size) and be tied down with "three-threaded string, well twisted and knotted in the form of a cross over the cork." Since bottles were still made by hand, milliliter uniformity was a long way off. But even quasi-consistency in bottling helped make Champagne a clearly recognizable product.

For the next three decades, the region boomed. Ruinart, who produced just 3,000 bottles of wine in 1731, was producing 36,000 bottles annually in 1761 and selling them across Europe. Other producers courted clients in Russia and North America. Delamotte, Lanson, and Veuve Clicquot Ponsardin launched their operations over this period.

One of the Veuve Clicquot's press locations in the Côte des Blancs.

Keeping champagne quiet in the bottle was still touch and go—and quite dangerous. Bottles exploded so frequently that springtime visitors to Champagne's cellars were issued metal masks. Exploding bottles added to the cost and complexity of the production process, which helped create a unique relationship between growers and producers that continues to this day. In Burgundy and most other wine regions, small estates and monasteries could produce wine in place. But in Champagne, merchants—production specialists known as *négociants*—began buying grapes from smaller growers and selling the resulting wines under their own names.

As pioneers like Claude Moët and Nicolas Ruinart laid the foundations for this new industry, revolution brewed.

LIBERTÉ, ÉGALITÉ, FRATERNITÉ

On January 5, 1757, Robert-François Damien, an unemployed domestic servant, rushed past guards at the gates of Versailles and stabbed Louis XV. The wound was minor and Damiens was arrested on the spot. It was a harbinger of a malaise that would eventually lead to revolution.

The French had good reason to be angry. During the Seven Years' War, which was fought mostly between 1756 and 1763, the nation lost virtually all its colonies. This didn't just hurt French pride; it aggravated the nation's debt, which led to new taxes that were shouldered entirely by the commoners.

The Champagne Bollinger cellar.

When Louis XV died of smallpox 1774 and was replaced by his grandson, Louis XVI, the nation's dissatisfaction with its monarchy—and disgust at monarchy's continued extravagant lifestyle—reached a fever pitch. Louis XVI was young and lacked self-confidence, but the monarchy he inherited was already vulnerable.

Louis XIV's extramarital affairs were well known. Philippe II d'Orléans's nightly orgies were the talk of Paris. Louis XV spent more time hunting and womanizing than ruling. Enlightenment thinkers along the way had step by step undercut the king and the church by questioning the moral authority of both institutions. Louis XVI was in trouble from the day of his coronation in 1774.

By 1776, France was hurting. Even though a number of Champagne houses had opened over the previous decade, things were particularly bad in Champagne. Warm weather in early 1776 caused about 90 percent of the region's sparkling wines to explode in the cellar. Meanwhile, thanks to the American Revolution, Champagne lost access to a quickly growing market when Britain's navy enforced embargos on the upstart colonies.

The French people were also frustrated by Louis XVI's decision to support the American war for independence. The irony was huge, since American colonialists were fighting to *rid* themselves of a monarch. And who would pay? Certainly not the Americans. Louis XVI was borrowing the monies, and he would have to raise taxes to repay those loans.

Within France, things got steadily worse over the next decade. Harvest after harvest was poor. French livestock herds were plagued with diseases. Food prices skyrocketed. By 1788, commoners were spending half their income on bread. And after a severe hailstorm, France experienced the worst harvest in 40 years.

Meanwhile, back in Paris, the Estates-General—which represented the clergy (First Estate), the nobles (Second Estate), and the common people (Third Estate)—gathered in May for the first time in 175 years. Summoned by Louis XVI to solve the government's fiscal crisis, the Assembly came to an impasse over whether they should vote by estate or all together. In response to the impasse, the Third Estate decided to form its own parliamentary body.

The King hadn't authorized or approved of the assembly and began positioning troops around the city. When, on July 13, a rumor spread that the King's army was going to disband the new assembly, the city erupted in open rebellion. Angry crowds stormed the Hôtel des Invalides to loot firearms and canons, which were stored in its cellars. They then headed to the Bastille for gunpowder. The French Revolution had begun.

The news traveled quickly across France. In Reims, peasants and artisans took to the streets to celebrate. Estates were looted. The vineyards at the Abbey of Saint-Pierre and other monasteries were confiscated. The revolution took its chaotic course. In 1791, Louis XVI was recognized in Sainte-Menehould, a village in Champagne about 50 miles east of Reims, on his attempted flight from France. He was captured and taken back to Paris shortly thereafter.

The next year—with France seemingly at war with itself—Austrian and Prussian troops invaded. In a desperate rally of national pride, rapidly raised French revolutionary forces turned back the invaders. On the day after the decisive battle, a constitutional convention in Paris proclaimed the First Republic.

But champagne producers could not rest easy. Their product was a symbol of luxury, of everything that the revolutionaries hated. Nobles were drinking champagne as they came to the guillotine, but winemakers were losing their best clients. During the Reign of Terror, which ran from June 1793 to July 1794, the guillotine killed as many as 40,000 people. Producers surreptitiously edited sales records to hide the names of buyers. Most of the big houses managed to survive, but Champagne marketing—to this day—still sometimes needs to skirt the image of privilege and wealth.

THE EMPEROR'S REIGN

Napoléon Bonaparte was born in Corsica, but he considered Champagne his real home. That's because in 1779, just before his tenth birthday, he was enrolled at the Royal Military Academy of Brienne in the south of Champagne. He came on a scholarship; the school admitted 120 children, half of whom came from wealthy families and half of whom were chosen from the poor aristocracy.

At first, he hated it. His French was poor and colored by a thick Corsican accent. School life was rigid, discipline was harsh, and the cool climate was not what he was used to. School rules did not allow cadets to communicate with their families. But he buried himself in his drills and books and gradually fell in love with Champagne.

One reason? His friendship with Claude Moët's son, Jean-Rémy. They met when Moët visited the military academy soliciting champagne orders.

Stained glass backdrop to the entrance to the Moët & Chandon cellar.
Photo by Luisa Bonachea.

Even though they were ten years apart in age, the two developed a deep friendship that would last both their lifetimes.

When the revolution began, Bonaparte, who by then was serving in the army, threw his support behind the revolutionaries. He spent most of those early years in Corsica engaging in battles with loyalists and Corsican nationalists. In 1793, he was banished from the island by Pasquale Paoli, a leading Corsican nationalist.

A cask of port from Napoleon Bonaparte sits in the cellars of Moët & Chandon. Photo by Luisa Bonachea.

When Bonaparte returned to France, he rose rapidly in rank after he almost singlehandedly saved the young French government in 1795 by suppressing a royalist insurrection in Paris. It wasn't long before the young officer shot up to become commander of the "Army of Italy," a French military force stationed on the Italian border and used for operations in Italy.

In Italy, Bonaparte's lightning successes against the Austrians and their Italian allies made him a national hero. He subsequently led French armies into Egypt and Syria to disrupt Britain's trade with India. He seemed unstoppable.

Returned to France in 1799, Bonaparte led a coup and then formed a new government—the Consulate—which he headed. Within five years, he was crowned France's first Emperor. Then, facing down the British, the Russians, the Austrians and the Spanish, France's now imperial armies proceeded to plant the tricolor, as the French flag is colloquially known, all across Europe.

Many producers in Champagne welcomed Bonaparte's wars. Before each campaign, legend has it that Bonaparte would visit the Moët cellars to pick up champagne for his troops. Wherever those troops went, one could almost always find a champagne salesman close behind, with wine for troops and an order book for the newly conquered. Jacquesson, which supposedly made Bonaparte's favorite wines, and Henriot were both founded during this period.

In 1811, famously, Charles-Henri Heidsieck, whose uncle, Florens-Louis Heidsieck, had launched Heidsieck & Co in 1785, rode a white stallion from Reims to Russia in advance of Bonaparte's army.

But the end came rapidly. Bonaparte's disastrous invasion of Russia led to the destruction of his fabled army and, eventually, his own fall from power. After Bonaparte's exile to Elba, Russian soldiers occupied Champagne. They imposed enormous fines in retaliation for the ones they suffered under Bonaparte and plundered the region's cellars. Moët alone lost more than 600,000 bottles.

Through all this, Champagne gained a rich new market. Russia became—and would remain—one of the region's largest buyers. Jean-Rémy Moët predicted this outcome, telling friends, "all of those soldiers who are ruining me today will make my fortune tomorrow. I'm letting them drink all they want. They will

Charles Heidsieck's cellars. Photo by Luisa Bonachea.

A BRIEF HISTORY OF SABRAGE
(WITH A HOW-TO GUIDE!)

Flamboyant or distinguished? Ostentatious or noble? Regardless of where you come down, sabrage—the ceremonial art of opening champagne with a sword—is one hell of a party trick.

The tradition traces its roots to the Napoleonic Wars that followed the French Revolution. As Napoleon Bonaparte swept through Europe, he relied on his light cavalry—the Hussars—to lead the charge. For Bonaparte's fans and foes alike, the Hussars were seen as a symbol of the empire's early invincibility. The horse-mounted troops were always armed with brass-hilted sabers, and historians credit them with inventing sabrage.

The precise details, though, are murky.

Some suggest that as these young cavalrymen rode off to battle, townspeople would toss them Champagne for the journey. Others suggest that when the Hussars returned home, inevitably victorious, townspeople would celebrate by offering bottles of Champagne. Perhaps both were traditions.

Others trace the tradition to the vineyards of Barbe-Nicole Ponsardin, better known as Veuve Clicquot. After Ponsardin's husband died in 1805, Napoleon's soldiers would frequent the young widow's estate, eager to impress her. Legend has it that Madame Ponsardin would welcome the men and hand out Champagne as they left for battle.

Opening a foil-wrapped cage and pulling out a cork while mounted on a horse is difficult, obviously, so the Hussars used their swords to pop open their wine.

Take your pick of which story to believe—and share it with your friends the next time you see an easy opportunity to behead a bottle of bubbly. Most sparkling wines will do, but make sure the bottle is thick with prominent seams.

Sabrage carries some danger, of course. While most drinking games only threaten the liver, using a sword to dramatically open a bottle of Champagne puts, well, virtually everyone within a 30-foot circumference at risk. And there's nothing fun about broken glass. Sabering takes a bit of practice, but once mastered, it's quite simple.

How to Saber

1) Acquire a saber. While a brass-hilted sword looks impressive, you don't actually need one; any sturdy instrument will do. Most performers simply use the back of a chef's knife.

2) Remove all the foil and paper around the neck of the bottle, but leave on the cage.

3) Chill the bottle. Then chill it some more. You'll want the champagne to be ice cold, as the low temperature will help calm the bubbles, ensuring you don't lose much wine.

4) Locate one of the bottle's two vertical seams and remove the wire cage.

5) Hold the bottle at a 45-degree angle, pointed away from people, pets, and anything breakable.

6) With confidence, run your blade flat along the seam, striking the lip of the neck ring. Make sure you follow through! The top should come right off.

7) Bask in the glow of your success.

8) Drink!

be hooked for life and become my best salesmen when they go back to their own country."

WINEMAKING BECOMES AN INDUSTRY

Following the collapse of Bonaparte's empire, the early 19th century was a period of relative peace and prosperity for France, although governments came and went in bewildering succession. In Champagne, the winemaking evolved through huge technological advances. The number of champagne houses exploded with producers like Perrier-Jouët, Laurent-Perrier, Billecart Salmon, G. H. Mumm, Bollinger, Deutz, Krug, and Pol Roger all opening their doors between 1811 and 1849.

The Verznay windmill, an iconic landmark for G.H. Mumm.

The first major processing innovation took place in the cellars of Veuve Clicquot. At the time, sparkling wines were inevitably full of sediment. Bubbles, after all, depend on the presence of yeast and sugar—and winemakers had no good system to remove dead yeast from bottles. Since sediment left wines cloudy and susceptible to off flavors and aromas, champagne was typically decanted or poured into fresh glasses throughout service. Some producers devised ways to lessen sediment, but these processes were always labor intensive—and often involved the use of harsh clarifying agents.

The lack of clarity annoyed Widow Clicquot. In 1806, she thought of a stunningly simple idea: Rather than storing bottles on their sides, she wondered if storing wine bottles on their necks would concentrate the sediment, thus allowing for its easy removal. Clicquot cut holes in her kitchen table large enough to hold bottlenecks and brought it to her cellar. Over the next few weeks, she turned and tapped the bottles each day—and was amazed at how easily the sediment collected in the neck. By quickly pulling the corks on these bottles, the sediment came shooting out—and little wine was lost.

This new system, called *remuage*, or riddling in English, enabled Clicquot to produce clear wine. It also enabled her to easily top up her wine with *liqueur d'expédition*—a mixture of wine and cane sugar, and sometimes brandy—to tailor its alcohol and sweetness. This practice is known as *dosage*.

Riddling in the caves of Champagne Bollinger.

In 1818, Clicquot's cellar master, Antoine Müller, perfected the system of sediment removal. By connecting two heavy, rectangular boards to form an inverted "V"—and cutting 60 holes on each side, all at a 45-degree angle—Müller dramatically improved the efficiency of Clicquot's system.

Word quickly spread and by the 1820s producers across the region were setting up their own riddling systems with Müller's device, called a *pupitre*. Corks were also improving, and around this time the first corking machines were developed. Production accelerated quickly.

Riddling racks in the caves of Champagne Charles Heidsieck.

In 1836, champagne took another leap forward when a pharmacist, Jean-Baptiste François, created a simple device—called a *sucre-oenomètre*—that enabled producers to measure the amount of sugar in their wines. Since the bubbles in sparkling wines were still the result of unfinished primary fermentation, the device helped winemakers better predict whether the sugar they added would produce more pressure than bottles could withstand. This greatly reduced the loss of wine. Prior to François's invention, champagne producers regularly lost 30 percent or more of their wines to bottle breakage. The sucre-oenomètre brought breakage down to about 10 percent. This also made the production of champagne far safer; with so much glass exploding, cellar workers routinely lost eyes in the early 19th century.

In 1844, the sucre-oenomètre led to the invention of a reliable dosage machine. Most sparkling wine was already sweet; virtually every bottle of champagne was sweetened just prior to shipping. But thanks to the widespread adoption of riddling and the dosage machine, producers could finally top off their wines with precise amounts of liqueur d'expédition.

In the 1850s, glassmakers finally began producing bottles that could withstand the pressure inside bottles of champagne, virtually eliminating

The caves of Champagne Bollinger. Photo by Luisa Bonachea.

breakage. And in 1857, Louis Pasteur discovered the role of yeast in fermentation, thus enabling scientists to isolate yeast. This soon led to the creation of *liqueur de tirage*, a mixture of sugar and yeast that enabled winemakers to reliably spur secondary fermentation.

Just as champagne makers were perfecting the production of sparkling wine, the French railroad system linked Reims with the rest of France, better connecting Champagne to Paris, the seacoast, and more distant markets. This boosted sales both across Europe and in dynamic new markets like the United States.

Production surged. Between 1844 and 1868, champagne sales nearly tripled, from 6.5 million to 15 million bottles. Producers also began pouring large sums into publicity and advertising. The United States, for example, became a major consumer in the 1850s thanks in part to the flashy marketing efforts of Charles Heidsieck, who became known across America as "Champagne Charlie." (Heidsieck learned the value of showmanship from his father, Charles-Henri Heidsieck, the man who rode a white stallion from Reims to Russia in 1811 to market his uncle's wines.)

Veuve Clicquot and Moët, meanwhile, led the industry in recognizing the impact of luxury branding. In 1866, for example, Moët commissioned George Leybourne, a well-known British entertainer, to perform songs extolling champagne as a reflection of taste. The company also paid Leybourne to drink nothing but champagne in public. Advertising posters started to flood Paris. G. H. Mumm promoted its wines with the slogan, "Nothing but Quality."

As the world fell in love with champagne, Paris became the "City of Light." In the 1860s, thanks, in part, to two decades of economic growth, the city installed 56,000 gas lamps. That boom, though, would soon experience a brief but serious setback.

A MOST VIOLENT YEAR

In 1866, Prussia—a kingdom that included parts of present-day Germany, Poland, Russia, Lithuania, Denmark, Belgium, and the Czech Republic—emerged as a leading European power after defeating the Austrian Empire in the Seven Weeks' War.

Political leaders in France, led by Napoleon III, viewed Prussia's victory anxiously, concerned it upset the delicate balance of power that had resulted in fifty years of relative peace. They were right.

CHAMPAGNE CHARLIE SEDUCES AMERICA

In the 1850s, the United States welcomed Charles Heidsieck with great fanfare. In the 1860s, the United States threw him in prison—and almost killed him.

Iron work from the Charles Heidsieck wine caves.

Heidsieck founded his eponymous Champagne house in 1851 after splitting off from the family business. The European market was fiercely competitive, so Charles looked west, visiting the United States in 1852.

He immediately saw the market's potential, so partnered with a New York importer to facilitate sales. Heidsieck's wines became a huge hit, with fans from Boston to New Orleans.

When Heidsieck returned to the United States in 1857, he was welcomed with lavish receptions in every city he visited. Newspapers up and down the eastern seaboard published glamorous profiles of the goateed wine merchant, dubbing him "Champagne Charlie." During his nine-month stay, Heidsieck became a fixture at society parties.

By the eve of the American Civil War, Heidsieck was selling 300,000 bottles to the United States each year. But his life in America would soon become complicated.

When Heidsieck learned of the escalating conflict between the North and the South, he hastily headed to New York to try and collect from his accounts.

When he arrived, his importer claimed, falsely, that a new law absolved northerners of their debts.

Desperate for payment, Heidsieck headed to New Orleans to visit other accounts. Merchants there were struggling—the Civil War was taking a steep toll—but one offered to pay in cotton. Since cotton was in high demand across Europe, Heidsieck accepted and chartered two boats out of Mobile, Alabama. But the Union Army had blockaded all routes out of the South—and successfully sank one of Heidsieck's ships.

Heidsieck promptly decided it was time to get home, with or without his money. However, that would prove an even bigger challenge; all routes out of the South were sealed by blockade. So Heidsieck hatched a plan to charter a boat from New Orleans to Mexico or Cuba.

Just before departing from Mobile, Heidsieck visited the French consulate to mail his wife a letter. While there, the consulate asked Heidiseck to deliver some documents to New Orleans. Those documents contained evidence that French textile firms were breaking the blockade and supplying the Confederate army.

By the time Heidiseck arrived in New Orleans, the Union had gained control of the city. When troops searched Heidiseck, they discovered the documents—so they arrested him, charged him as a spy, and sent him to Fort Jackson, which was an alligator-filled, disease-ridden prison in the swamps of the Mississippi.

The arrest caused quite a diplomatic rift, with Napoleon III appealing directly to President Lincoln for Heidiseck's release. Champagne Charlie was freed after just seven months, but by then, he was broke and in poor health.

Fortunately, Heidiseck's luck would soon improve. Shortly after returning home, he received a letter from the brother of his New York importer. Ashamed of his brother's behavior, he offered deeds to 127 different parcels of land in Denver—about a third of the city—in the hopes of making amends. Denver had become one of the American West's wealthiest cities, so the windfall enabled Heidseick to pay off his debts and re-launch his Champagne house. It would soon become one of the world's most popular brands.

On July 16, 1870, after a series of provocations, the French parliament declared war on Prussia. Hostilities began just three days later. The Prussian army, still fresh from the Seven Weeks' War, mobilized more quickly than the French and quickly collected a series of victories in northeastern France. After pushing through Alsace and Lorraine, German troops marched directly through Champagne on their way to Paris. Yet again, the vineyards became battlefields. Entire villages were burned.

Mercifully, the conflict ended quickly. On May 10, 1871, the Treaty of Frankfurt brought the Franco-Prussian War to an end. It would go down as one of the bloodiest conflicts of the 19th century, with nearly 900,000 men killed, injured, or captured. More than 85 percent of those losses were on the French side.

THE BELLE ÉPOQUE

The Franco-Prussian War brought France to its knees. For two years, champagne sales plummeted. But by 1874, the region's wine industry was back on its feet thanks to a burgeoning love affair with a new product—dry champagne—the now iconic *brut*.

Champagne Bollinger barrels. Photo by Luisa Bonachea.

UNDERSTANDING SWEETNESS LEVELS

Champagne's sweetness doesn't come from the wine itself—the "base" wine of every champagne is dry. Rather, the sweetness comes from a small amount of wine and cane sugar—called *liqueur d'expédition*—that's added just before corking during a process called "dosage."

Without this mixture, most champagne would be too acidic to enjoy. After all, Champagne is a very cold region, so the grapes don't ripen as much as they do in other regions.

Sweetness preferences have changed over time. In champagne's earliest days, quite a bit of sugar was added. Today, it's fashionable to avoid dosage entirely and leave wines bone dry. The most common level of sweetness is "brut," which provides just a touch of sweetness.

Sweetness levels are below. They're certainly confusing; "Extra Dry" champagne is noticeably sweet and "Dry" champagne is extremely sweet! For reference, Coca-Cola contains about 110 grams/liter (g/l) of sugar.

Brut Nature: 0-3 g/l Residual Sugar (RS)
Extra Brut: 0-6 g/l RS
Brut: 0-12 g/l RS
Extra Dry: 12-17 g/l RS
Dry: 17-32 g/l RS
Demi-Sec: 32-50 g/l RS
Doux: >50 g/l RS

Dry champagne got its start in 1846. That year, a British wine merchant visiting Épernay fell in love with Perrier-Jouët's *vin clair*, the still wine that serves as the base for champagne. Two years later, he asked the winery to ship him that 1846 wine without any dosage, believing that his customers would actually prefer dry champagne since Port, cream Sherry, and Madeira dominated the "sweet" market. Perrier-Jouët obliged, but the experiment was a failure. The wine was criticized as too "brute" and the merchant had to return most of it.

In 1857, Veuve Clicquot sent Britain a champagne that was quite a bit drier than normal—and unlike Perrier-Jouët's, this one was a hit. By 1865, a handful of other producers in the region were experimenting with drier wines, but they were still a novelty—and typically tart and underripe.

One of those pioneers was Alexandre Louis Pommery. She recognized the importance of doing something different and believed that the English market would prefer drier wines. Such wines, though, would depend on a rich, ripe base. In the 1870s, she began asking her growers to push the ripeness levels of their grapes—promising to pay for their losses if the risks of volatile fall weather led to a wipeout. A perfect growing season came in 1874, and the resulting wine was a hit; it became the most expensive champagne in London. Within just a few years, the entire English marketplace had shifted away from sweet champagne and towards the drier style perfected by Pommery.

WHY ARE SHIPS BLESSED WITH CHAMPAGNE?

When a newly built ship is launched into the water for the first time, it's almost always "blessed" with a sacrificial bottle of champagne that's smashed over its hull.

The tradition of ceremonial ship launching is ancient. In the third millennium BC, Babylonians sacrificed oxen upon the completion of new water vessels. Other cultures practiced similar rituals; the Ottomans sacrificed sheep.

These sacrifices were always about asking the gods for protection at sea. The Greeks would go on to call on Poseidon, the Romans on Neptune. In the Middle Ages, priests would board British ships before their maiden voyages to sprinkle holy water and pray to Christ.

By the 17th century, sacrificial animals and holy water had been replaced with wine at most ship launchings, religious and secular alike. Typically held in a large goblet, the wine would first be shared by ceremony attendees and then poured on the deck or over the bow. The goblet would then be tossed into the sea. This quickly became expensive, especially since those goblets became more impressive as time went on. At first, the goblets were collected and reused. But by the late 17th century, the ritual was simplified—and the modern-day tradition of breaking a bottle over the bow became the norm.

The sacrificial wine wasn't always champagne—in fact, Madeira was probably the most popular choice in this ritual's early days. Towards the end of the 19th century, though, champagne became the standard choice, almost certainly because it had become the noblest wine. The tradition continues today.

The world was clearly falling in love with champagne. In 1882, celebrated British journalist Henry Vizetelly published a book entitled *A History of Champagne* in which he noted, "We cannot open a railway, launch a vessel, inaugurate a public edifice, start a newspaper, entertain a distinguished foreigner, invite a leading politician to favour us with his views on things in general, celebrate an anniversary, or specially appeal on behalf of a benevolent institution without a banquet, and hence without the aid of champagne, which, at the present day, is the obligatory adjunct of all such repasts."

Champagne sales also saw a boost in the late 19th century thanks to the *Syndicat du commerce des vins de Champagne*, a small group of top producers that came together to promote and protect the region and its wines. In 1887, the group sued producers in the Loire Valley who were marketing their sparkling wines as "champagne." The highest court in Angers found in favor of the *Syndicat*, ruling, "Henceforth the term 'Champagne' or 'Champagne wines' shall refer exclusively to wine produced in, and sourced from, the ancient province of Champagne, an area with specific boundaries that shall neither be extended nor contracted."

Champagne vineyards in the Côte des Blancs.

LES GRANDES MARQUES DE CHAMPAGNE

Within a year of its 1882 launch, the *Syndicat du commerce des vins de Champagne* represented 22 champagne producers. By the end of the 19th century, the group had grown to 60 members, thus representing most champagne houses. All members called themselves grandes marques, or big brands.

While the syndicate didn't enforce any formal regulations, it advertised a shared "respect for traditional rules of production" and spoke as a powerful, unified body for the entire industry. Importantly, it fought to protect authenticity in labeling, a battle that was becoming increasingly important as producers outside Champagne—and even outside France—began advertising their sparkling wines as "champagne" in the mid-19th century.

As an industry trade group, the syndicate's impact was diluted in 1912 when smaller houses broke off to form the *Syndicat des Négociants en Vins de Champagne*. Its impact was diluted again by the creation of the *Comité Interprofessionnel du Vin de Champagne*, which represented both growers and producers, in the early days of World War II.

In 1992, the group was rocked when Christian Bizot, director of Bollinger, took public issue with the fact that many grandes marques were pushing production by purchasing low-quality grapes and using too much "pressed" juice. (With white wine production, the initial crushing process releases only about 65 percent of a berry's juice. The remaining juice is extracted through the use of a "press"—and as extraction becomes more aggressive, the resulting juice becomes more astringent and bitter.) Bizot also alleged that some grandes marques were purchasing bulk, cooperative-produced champagne—*sur latte*—and affixing their own labels to it. He proposed a set of guidelines for the grandes marques to follow.

Quality standards had been discussed in 1964 when the trade group reorganized and rebranded itself the *Syndicat des Grandes Marques de Champagne*. At the time, though, the group refused to adopt any formal rules.

But Bizot's public accusations gained attention. So in 1993, the group was renamed the *Club des Grandes Marques* and began enforcing minimum quality standards. Bizot's public accusations opened a pandora's box. In 1997, a British journalist approached every *Grandes Marques* to ask if membership in the *Club des Grandes Marques* should convey superior quality and, if so, if other producers that adhered to such standards should be able to join.

Only Bollinger answered yes to both questions. In response to the obvious and growing schism, the *Club des Grandes Marques'* chairman, Louis Roederer's Jean-Claude Rouzaud, pledged to create stricter quality standards and to open up the group to more producers. But the grandes marques couldn't agree on any new standards so the group was disbanded.

However, the phrase "grandes marques" is still used informally to reference Champagne's biggest brands.

Champagne was also assisted, in at least some small way, by the phylloxera epidemic. A grape pest, phylloxera hit Bordeaux in 1869 and the Rhone Valley a year later. It quickly spread, devastating vines in Burgundy in 1878 and destroying most vineyards in Europe shortly thereafter. However, it didn't reach Champagne until years later in 1890—and barely spread in the region until 1897. Consequently, Champagne's producers were able to provide libations for those who couldn't source Bordeaux or Burgundy. And by the time phylloxera moved into Champagne, researchers had discovered that grafting *vitis vinifera* (the European grapevine) onto the rootstock of *vitis labrusca* (the American grapevine) stopped the louse. In Champagne, replanting virtually kept pace with vine destruction.

As champagne embedded itself into popular culture, production continued to become more efficient. In 1884, a Belgian inventor named Armand Walfart noted that if the neck of a pre-disgorgement champagne bottle was dipped into a shallow pool of below-freezing liquid, the sediment would turn into a frosty pellet, so could be expelled with virtually no loss of wine. Both Moët and Perrier-Jouët adopted this system, called *dégorgement à la glace*, in 1891. It quickly spread.

When the Eiffel Tower was completed in 1889 for the World's Fair, Western Europe was booming—and France was its hip and happening epicenter. The economy was growing and prosperity was expanding. Automobiles were on the road, women and men obsessed over fashion and the arts, and urban sophisticates took food and wine seriously. It was the *"Belle Epoque."* And Champagne, which had become a part of France's national identity, was thriving.

In 1909, nearly 40 million bottles of champagne were sold across the world. Alas, the numbers of that triumphal year wouldn't be matched again for nearly three decades.

Chapter Three:

Joy, Wine, and War

As a new century began in 1900, everything was changing. Advances in communications, travel, science, medicine, manufacturing, weapons, cities, food, education, and more transformed the world. The very air was different. News had become truly global. Markets were broader and deeper. As new fortunes emerged, so did new classes. The structures of government and the inherited rules of society were increasingly coming under question.

The Champagne region, though still overwhelmingly rural, felt these tides. Insofar as its wines had gained worldwide acclaim, this pastoral corner of France was being lured towards the huge opportunities—and huge risks—of expanded markets for its signature product.

An agricultural factory, so to speak, Champagne's output depended on the volatile variables of sun, rainfall, and weather. But more ominously, the region lay on the border of the populous, militarily powerful, and ambitious state of Germany, which since the Franco-Prussian War of 1870 had emerged as the arch-enemy of France.

Across "new Europe" and in great cities around the world, cosmopolitan elites were celebrating their successes and extravagant wealth with the luxury elixer of the age: champagne. The sparkling bubbles that crowned their lavish parties perfectly captured the spirit of an age oblivious of what was to come.

Sadly, Champagne—the bountiful source of so much joy and conviviality—was to suffer more than almost anywhere in Europe in the series of disasters that followed.

IF IT'S PROFITABLE, MAKE MORE

For the grape growers and wine producers of Champagne, the surge in demand was like striking gold. Of course, planting and harvesting grapes in an unpredictable climate remained a risky business, but the explosive growth of markets for a unique product was hard to resist. It turned the region into a kind of boomtown. Fortunes were there to be made—and were. Profits seemed so easy that soon the established champagne houses faced upstart competition. A new railroad hub in Reims, opened in 1862, had connected landlocked Champagne not only to the rest of France but to markets around the world. But rapid transport cut two ways. You could export wine efficiently. But unscrupulous producers could also import cheaper grapes and wine stocks and brand the resulting product "champagne." It was all perfectly legal. The established houses had "names," but there was little quality control beyond tradition. Champagne might contain grapes from the Loire Valley or the Languedoc, from Germany or even Spain.

France did have a law that 51 percent of a wine must come from grapes grown in the region named on the label. But the other 49 percent could come from anywhere—and be anything. Rumors abounded that less reputable houses were pressing apples, pears, and even rhubarb to turn a quick profit.

Imitators could fake the contents, the labels, or both. Leon Chandon and Victor Clicquot launched houses in Champagne with labels that were nearly indistinguishable from their more famous neighbors. "Champagnes" could be produced and labeled virtually anywhere. A German company was caught selling sparkling wine adorned with labels based on bottles of Deutz and Veuve Clicquot. In those days, the creativity of market scams was endless. In New York, the Great Western Wine Company, which made sparkling wine, convinced the US Postal Service that its production facility should have a special post office branch—named Rheims, of course.

What was to be done? How to ensure quality and maintain upmarket pricing? In a world before effective intellectual property laws, producers were in a quandary as to how to protect their brands. Local growers of higher quality grapes became increasingly angry when cheap imported grapes forced prices—and profits—down. There were no safety nets.

WHAT'S IN A WINE?

The tension was tolerable when the harvests were decent. But in the first decade of the 20th century, Champagne suffered a series of calamitous harvests. Not only were local growers battered by rains which destroyed their crops, imports of grapes from other regions threatened to put them permanently out of business. Some producers used plummeting grape prices to force confiscatory, multi-year contracts on growers and colluded to drive prices down even further. Tons of grapes were secretly imported to be branded as "champagne." In 1909, even if growing conditions had been perfect, Champagne didn't have enough acres under vine to produce all the bottles that supposedly came out of the region.

Battles erupted over soils and origins. Growers in the villages of northern Champagne, around the Marne river, believed that only they grew "true" champagne grapes. Marne vineyards sit on chalk, a soil that drains easily, holds a constant temperature, and is loose enough for vines to grow

The town of Cumières and the Marne river.

freely and deeply. In the Aube, which begins more than 65 miles south of
Épernay, the vineyards root into gray, limestone-rich Kimmeridgean soil
that's nearly identical that what's found in Chablis. Aube growers were just
as much soil snobs as their northern neighbors. They had every right, they
claimed, to call their wines authentic champagne, since Aube's main city,
Troyes, had been the capital of Champagne for nearly 1000 years, from the
end of the ninth century until the French Revolution.

France being France, the government realized that the locals might
not work their disputes out amicably. Moreover, French rulers had a long
tradition of rearranging the world by Decree of Law. So in 1908, the
government stepped in to resolve what might seem to be a commercial
problem with a politically complicated solution from on high. Let there be
appelations. The first pass defined the specific geographic areas permitted to
call their wines "champagne." Those areas included only northern districts
around the Marne. The Aube was excluded.

Everyone was unhappy. Marne growers knew that many now officially
certified producers would continue to buy grapes from outside Champagne.
And growers in the Aube were furious they could no longer use the iconic—
and very profitable—champagne label.

WHY DOES SOIL MATTER?

Winemakers—and those obsessed with all things vinous—often sound like geology professors.

With wine, soil matters. Climate, elevation, and style decisions like whether or not to utilize oak impact the aromas and flavors of a wine, of course, but soil might be the most important factor in a wine's final expression—especially in Champagne.

At the simplest level, soil has the biggest influence on how much water a vine can retain. Access to too much water means vigorous leaf growth, but water-packed—and thus diluted—grapes. Access to too little water means a dead vine. Ideally, a vine will be slightly stressed. In those situations, the grapes will be concentrated and flavor-packed.

Dominique Moreau of Champagne Marie Courtin crafts wine from vines planted in kimmeridgian limestone sub soils from the Côte des Bar.

Champagne is best known for the chalky soils of the Marne. There, thanks to ancient earthquakes, vineyards are packed with belemnite fossils. The belemnite chalk moderates soil temperature, as it absorbs heat throughout the day and gradually releases it at night. It also allows for exceptionally good drainage. In the Aube, most vineyards sit on Kimmeridgian clay with a surface layer of gravelly limestone. The topsoil helps moderate temperature, but not as effectively as chalk. Kimmeridgian clay drains well, but again, not as effectively as chalk.

Both areas, though, can create stunning—albeit different—wines.

Despite decades of serious research, scientists still struggle to explain exactly why soil impacts a wine's flavors and aromas. We do know, though, that serious wine enthusiasts are more likely to talk about "minerality"—think saline and stones—in wines from the Aube and "chalkiness" in wines from the Marne.

The growing storm turned violent in 1910. Seemingly endless rain brought mold and mildew to grape crops across the region, and late hailstorms destroyed whole vineyards. Many growers were totally wiped out.

Yet, amazingly, champagne houses continued to process wine, since they were able to import grapes from elsewhere in France. This was an agricultural class war. Impoverished growers looked at the thriving champagne producing houses and took to the streets. In October of 1910, more than 10,000 growers marched through Épernay in protest. Protests soon turned violent.

THE WRATH OF GRAPES

On January 17, 1911, a truck carrying wine base from the Loire arrived in Épernay. Word spread quickly and more than 2,000 growers armed with hoes and hatchets intercepted the truck and dumped its contents into the Marne. They then marched five miles west to the cellars of M. Achille Perrier in Damery, where they found another truck loaded with nearly 2,500 bottles of outsider wine. That truck's cargo, too, was dumped into the river. Rioting growers ransacked Perrier's cellars, destroying 7,000 bottles of wine and emptying 42 casks.

By the next morning mobs had attacked other cellars rumored to use non-local wine. More barrels were thrown into the Marne. In Aÿ, a commune just three miles north of Épernay, winemakers' homes and champagne warehouses were looted and set on fire. More than 40 buildings burned to the ground.

The rioting ended as growers dispersed back into the countryside. No one had been killed, but the ferociousness of the uprising stunned France. Growers maintained that they were enforcing the law and that honest producers, like Bollinger, had not been touched. But some presumably honest houses like Ayala had fallen victim to the general mood and been destroyed.

The government took the matter very seriously, dispatching 40,000 troops to ensure order. It was clear that policymakers would have to work with vineyard owners and wine producers to redo the boundaries that would define authentic champagne.

It took nearly six months, but by June lawmakers produced a bill dividing Champagne into two sub-regions: "*Champagne*," which was comprised only of the communes that made it into the 1908 decree; and "*Champagne Deuxieme Zone*," which was comprised of villages in the Aube and Seine-et-Marne.

The measure also created a rating system for the region's villages—the *Échelle des Crus*—to scale prices paid to growers.

The 1911 initiative just salted old wounds. Growers in the Marne resented the Aube sharing the Champagne name—and many objected to their position on the scale of location-determined grape pricing. Growers in the Aube didn't like being relegated to second-class status. Luckily, the fall of 1911 produced a strong harvest and tensions, for the moment, subsided.

But producers, growers, and lawmakers alike recognized that the measure was a temporary fix. Moreover, everyone knew that any solution made for Champagne would affect how *appelations* would be devised for France's other wine regions. The geography of wine was no small issue for a nation of passionate wine lovers and a major wine industry. Globally, France produced one in every three bottles of wine in 1911.

Finally, in the summer of 1914, lawmakers introduced a measure that they hoped everyone could get behind. But before both houses of French Assembly could vote, the guns of August rocked all of Europe into the nightmare of world war.

The cellars at Champagne Pierre Moncuit.

WAR COMES TO CHAMPAGNE

On June 28, 1914, a bomb thrown by a Serbian nationalist in Sarajevo killed Archduke Franz Ferdinand, the presumptive heir to the Austro-Hungarian throne. With Russia maneuvering to cut Austria's influence in the Balkans, the Austrians decided to use the assassination to confront the Tsar. Having secured tacit support from Germany, Austria-Hungary delivered harsh terms to Tsarist-backed Serbia. When the Serbians vacillated, Austria-Hungary declared war.

Germany, knowing the Russians were mobilizing and trying to cut off a two-front war, slashed into Luxembourg and Belgium with the intention of delivering a knockout blow to France. France retaliated with its own declaration of war. The German invasion of France eventually stalled on the Marne even as German troops on the Eastern front mauled the Russians. England and Italy mobilized. Europe, the Atlantic, the Middle East, and even the Far East became war zones. It was the first "world" war.

Champagne, on the border between France and Germany, bore the brunt of the German offensives. Initially, *les citizens* responded with anti-German ardor. Train stations in Reims and Épernay filled with young men eager to defend *la Patrie*. Wives, girlfriends, and parents cheered them on.

Within weeks, though, the mood changed. More than 160,000 French soldiers died in the first battles. On September 3, Germany swept into Champagne, taking Reims almost immediately and Épernay within days. On September 7, the Germans crossed the Marne. With the German army just 30 miles east of the Seine, no one knew if Paris could hold.

But hold it did as the French mounted a last-ditch defense. The Germans bogged down in the marshes of Marais de Saint-Gond and a mutual slaughter ensued. The First Battle of the Marne, as it became known, involved nearly 2 million men and resulted in 500,000 killed or wounded.

Ultimately, the Germans were forced back. Épernay and Reims came once more into French hands, as massive collisions between mobile armies soon settled into a horror of static warfare. Both sides dug deep and almost impenetrable trenches along a meandering line stretching from the North Sea to the Alsatian foothills. Hundreds of opposing divisions supported by thousands of artillery pieces pounded weak points and commanding heights in search of costly but limited victories. The front hardly changed, though soaked with blood, for the next four years.

Fort de la Pompelle, a key point in the defense of Reims during the First World War.

Across Champagne, the initial year of conflict was devastating. Countless structures, including the Ruinart champagne house, were completely destroyed. In September of 1914, the German army set up a hillside position four miles from Reims and started shelling the city. The Reims cathedral, where so many kings and queens had been crowned, was pulverized. Surrounding villages were reduced to unrecognizable piles of rubble. Anything forward observers suspected of being military—a truck, a school, a bridge, a church tower or a massive old stone winery—was instantly targeted. Yet out in the vineyards, grapes continued to grow and were harvested, often at night. In the midst of a battlefield, wine production continued.

In fact, the 1914 growing season was extraordinary. Beyond the trenches, most of the vast green fields of Champagne were not militarized. Under the sun, against the sounds of shelling, the harvest matured. Almost all of the local men had joined the French army, so the tasks of gathering grapes and processing wine fell to women, children, and those deemed too old for war. In Champagne, maintaining tradition was not a luxury, but survival. It was life. Keeping the wine "alive" became a kind of symbol for defending France itself. Though thousands of soldiers were dying in hopeless assaults against dug-in machine guns, their farms had to survive. It was a bizarre tradeoff—and monstrously costly.

Notre-Dame de Reims, better known as the Reims Cathedral.

Maurice Pol Roger, the mayor of Épernay and proprietor of Pol Roger, saw the spirit of France in the resistance of people of Champagne—and in the survival of champagne itself. He coordinated a clandestine network to ensure production could continue. It was no easy task to slip barrels, presses, and other equipment to vineyards and wine houses without alerting the Germans. He arranged for innocuous-seeming runners and cyclists to alert vintners to when secret shipments would be arriving. And, since bank notes weren't readily available, he even printed a special currency for Épernay, assuring growers, producers, and other harvest workers that the scrip could be converted to real money after the war.

Despite the rich harvest that year, actual wine output was less than half of what it had been in 1913. But Pol Roger and others knew that the 1914 bottles were not just something to be proud of—they contained a spectacular vintage. What better way to celebrate the hoped-for victory than with a bottle of champagne produced under such dire conditions?

THE MACABRE DANCE OF WAR

As 1914 drew to a close, French commander Joseph Joffre decided to launch a major offensive in the hope that a breakthrough victory might still be possible. German defenses in Champagne, however, proved impenetrable. French *poilus*—the infantryman—were mowed down *en masse* in frontal assaults against German positions. Artillery fire, rain, and freezing temperatures turned contested areas of Champagne's green garden into a nightmare of white, sticky mud that jammed weapons and turned trenches and shell holes into murderous quagmires.

The results were horrendous, and largely concealed from the French public—100,000 French casualties and virtually no gains. With the grim logic of attrition warfare, Joffre launched another offensive into the same deathtrap of trenches six months later, sacrificing another 145,000 men in just six weeks of fighting. Yet the front was only displaced—in places—by 2.5 miles. Attrition was rapidly decimating the French army.

The Germans continued their shelling. On one day—February 22, 1915—more than 1,500 shells fell on Reims. Just as Londoners during the Blitz took shelter in subway tunnels, the population of Reims descended into the vast limestone cellars where champagne houses stored their wines. They were an ancient retreat. Almost all of these caves began as chalk quarries excavated by Roman slaves. In the middle ages, monks discovered that they offered cool, stable temperatures that made a perfect environment for storing wine. Expanded and

Surrounded by vineyards, La nécropole nationale de Villers-Marmery, in the Montagne de Reims, is the resting place of over 520 French soldiers from the first World War.

connected, these multi-level wine cellars now offered protection against the impact of German shells in the city above.

The whole city went underground. Some 20,000 of Reim's inhabitants set up schools, churches, medical clinics, and even cafés so life could continue. Dressmakers, watchmakers, and cobblers continued their crafts. Bakers made bread and butchers carved meat. Even City Hall was reestablished in subterranean quarters. As the war went on, the

Finding shelter in the Krug cellars during World War I. Photo courtesy of Champagne Krug.

French military expanded the caves so troops could move from the bombed city to front line—a multi-mile trek—without ever going above ground.

In the spring of 1915, the introduction of poison gases at various points along the front created a new crisis. Soon troops were attacking and defending using rapidly developed gas masks. Released at first from cylinders to be carried against the enemy by the wind, gases would often descend and hang, like fog, over the ground. In the aftermath of these attacks, women, children, and old men would actually use primitive gas masks when they emerged from Champagne's cellars to pick grapes by night.

Both sides used gas as the war continued. Countermeasures evolved, but gas burns were horrendous. On the western front, the war of attrition produced no victors and an ever-mounting sacrifice of lives. The German advance at Verdun, a battle that began in February of 1916 and lasted for 10 months, claimed more than 700,000 military casualties. The Allied advance at the Battle of the Somme, which was fought from July till November, claimed more than 1.3 million.

It's bizarre to talk about a growing season in Champagne in 1916 while the war was raging and even the soil was poisoned with gas. But it came—and was not a good one. In the fall of 1916, heavy rains—disastrous for the troops—brought mildew and rot to the vineyards and prevented grapes from ripening. The outlook was dismal—nothing but mud, death, and devastation.

Though the war was being fought almost entirely within France, Germany was damaged, too. Also engaged on two fronts, the Germans had schemed to force Russia out of the war from the beginning. Conditions in Russia were horrible, and in March 1917, army mutinies and home front riots broke out there. The Tsarist government collapsed, and Lenin's new Communist regime soon pulled the country out of the conflict to consolidate its own power. Germany, despite attacks born of desperation—and the realization that America might soon come to the aid of the allies—was too exhausted at that stage to press its advantage with breakthroughs in the west.

THE AMERICAN EXPEDITION

Outrage over German submarine attacks against American ships—ships that may have been aiding the allies with war supplies—convinced President Woodrow Wilson to ask Congress to declare war against Germany on April 2, 1917. Within days, the United States was committed to the European war.

The Americans were not prepared to fight thousands of miles from home. The US Army had fewer than 140,000 men. Hundreds of thousands had to be recruited, trained, supplied, and transported to France. The mobilization, coordinated through unprecedented war powers granted to the government, was massive. But it took time.

Although an advance contingent of 14,000 American soldiers reached France in June of 1917, they were not battle-ready and were hampered by inevitable logistic delays of the Atlantic crossing. US General John J. Pershing, commander of the American Expeditionary Force, first had to establish training bases, communication infrastructure, and supply chains for the oncoming influx of US units.

American troops were gradually committed to the front lines, although at first they didn't make much of a dent. It wasn't until March of 1918 that 300,000 American soldiers were in France. But then the American mobilization moved into high gear and 200,000 troops began arriving each month. The tide was obviously beginning to turn and despite the Russian collapse, the Central Powers were desperate.

The Germans decided that if they were to have any chance for some kind of negotiated settlement, they'd have to take Paris before the Americans reached full strength. On July 15, they began another "final" offensive through Champagne. The sound of German shells falling on Épernay could be heard in Paris. But what became known as the Second Battle of the Marne was not to be a German breakthrough. Within three days, it became clear that the French would hold.

By early August, the Germans had given up hope of retaking Champagne and moving on to Paris. They pulled their battered forces back to fortified lines. There would be more offensives in 1918, but the course of the war now favored the allies.

WAR ENDS, WINE BEGINS AGAIN

Germany was exhausted. Fresh American troops and mountains of war materiel flooded into French and English sectors. The grey legions were finally falling back. On November 11, 1918, Germany agreed to an armistice stipulating an immediate end to hostilities, a withdrawal of German troops, a return of Allied prisoners, the imposition of reparations, and the scrapping of the German high seas fleet. Final terms of the peace—the fateful Treaty of Versailles—took another six months to hammer out, but the Armistice ended the war.

WHAT'S IN A NAME?

French courts began protecting the name "champagne" in the mid-19th century as producers in the Loire Valley and elsewhere in France began advertising their own sparkling wines as "champagne." These various decisions were affirmed by France's highest court in 1889.

Two years later, a number of nations gathered in Madrid to create an international system to protect trademarks. The "Treaty of Madrid," as it became known, gave international recognition to brand champagne. Among the Treaty's signatories, at least, "champagne" could only be affixed to sparkling wines from the Champagne region in France.

The Treaty of Versailles, which brought an official end to World War I, reaffirmed international recognition of trademarks. During the negotiation process, France inserted language requiring other nations "to respect any law, or any administrative or judicial decision given in conformity with such law . . . defining or regulating the right to any regional appellation in respect of wine or spirits produced in the State to which the region belongs."

French policymakers were mainly working to prevent Germany from deceptively marketing their wines and brandies. But accordingly, all nations that signed the Treaty were required to recognize that "champagne" could only be used to describe sparkling wine originating in Champagne. In subsequent international trade deals, European Union agreements, and the like, French policymakers and industry representatives would continue to fight for Champagne's recognition—and sue whenever such stipulations were violated.

The United States didn't sign the Treaty of Madrid or the Treaty of Versailles, though. So wine producers in America were allowed to label their sparklers as "champagne." In 1983, the United States and the European Commission began a series of conversations about the wine trade. These negotiations would take more than 20 years, but in 2005, American officials agreed to end the use of "semi-generic" names like Champagne, Chablis, Burgundy, Chianti, and Sherry—with the exception that a producer already using one of those names could continue to use it—in exchange for looser trade restrictions on US wine.

Because of that grandfather clause, Korbel, Cook's, and André still get away with calling their offerings "California Champagne" and many cheap, US-manufactured jug wines are still labeled as "Chablis," "Burgundy," and "Chianti."

World War I had claimed more than 17 million lives, of which some 10 percent came from France. Millions more were maimed and disabled.

When the guns at last fell silent, large swaths of Champagne were scarred with trenches and blasted earth. Constant shelling had reduced Reims and countless villages to unrecognizable piles of rubble. Where lush forests had been, there were only eerie fragments and charred splinters. Soils were contaminated by poison gas, and treacherous with bunkers, craters, and unexploded mines. Human bones lay under shreds of barbed wire. The region had lost about half its population, with every village having young men who would not return. Out across the landscape, more than 40 percent of Champagne's vineyards had been destroyed.

Yet the sun shown in 1918. The weather was good. Thousands of rows of grapes, though poorly tended through the days and nights of war, did survive and bear fruit. The Champenois emerged from their cellars and claimed the harvest. The vintage was not only good; it was great. However, the output of 1918 was but a fraction of what it had been in the prosperous pre-war years.

Those battle wines of 1914 to 1918 would forever be tied to the war, representing to the victors the triumph of determination over adversity. The Champenois buried their dead and set about rebuilding their vineyards and their lives.

Chapter Four:

A Changed World

Photo by Luisa Bonachea

The markets for champagne in the immediate postwar years were meager. France, England, and Germany were exhausted. Far fewer people could afford champagne.

Russia, where the pre-war aristocracy had routinely lavished millions of rubles on champagne, was reeling through revolution and civil war. The high-living nobility were dead or in flight. Lenin's government repudiated contracts, refused to honor bills, and vilified champagne as decadent capitalist luxury. Popping a bottle could get you denounced—and shot. Almost overnight, a hundred-year-old market for 10 percent of Champagne's production dried up.

In the wealthy and exuberant post-war United States, the single-issue temperance movement finally succeeded in closing down the bars and curtailing the parties. The 18th amendment to the US Constitution prohibited the production, transport, and sale of alcohol anywhere in the country. It took effect in January of 1920, and officially, at least, ended French champagne sales to the United States.

Champagne was down, but not out. European markets slowly but surely came back to life. In Paris, London, Berlin, and New York, young people—the survivors—celebrated new freedoms and a release from the horrors of the war years with roaring twenties lifestyles. The here-and-now exuberance of drinking champagne became a mark of the times. In France, growers, producers—and policymakers—began laying the groundwork for champagne's rebirth.

The search for profits remained critical to the French. The same quality, naming and pricing issues that had brought riots to Champagne in 1910 had not gone away. So immediately after the war, the French government picked up where it had left off, issuing politically complex decrees as to how champagne could be produced and sold.

In 1919, policymakers finalized the *Échelle des Crus* first outlined in 1908, a scale or ladder of grape pricing based on locality. The system was essentially government imposed price controls on the supply side of wine production. The government rated the quality of each village's soil and the value of the grapes that could be produced on that soil. Villages in Champagne were assigned a quality rating of 22.55 to 100. Every year, a joint committee of houses and growers would assess market conditions and set fixed prices for a kilogram of grapes—and individual vineyard owners would receive a percentage of that price, depending on their village's *echelle* rating.

Twelve villages were awarded *"Grand Cru"* status, so were awarded 100 percent of the price. About three dozen villages were ranked between 90 and 99 and awarded *"Premier Cru"* status. Those in villages ranked between 22.5 and 89 couldn't designate their grapes as *"Grand Cru"* or *"Premier Cru"* and were paid according to their specific ranking. The scale was later adjusted to a Cru floor of 80. This pricing system persisted until 1992. The *echelle* ratings were officially abolished in 2007, but the terms *Grand Cru* and *Premier Cru* are still used by those who source grapes and produce wine from Champagne's top villages.

Policymakers then turned their attention to the geography of the unique Champagne label. Who could call their product champagne? The region was expanded by bringing the second-class *deuxieme zone* into the fold. Grapes of the Aube could be used to produce "real" champagne. These pricing and *appellation* rules were finalized in 1927, and the 84,000 acres specified are essentially today's boundaries. Legislators also detailed policies on grape cultivation, authorizing seven grapes: Pinot Noir, Chardonnay, and Pinot Meunier, which remain dominant today, along with Arbane, Petit Meslier, Pinot Blanc, and Pinot Gris, which even then were relatively obscure. An eighth grape, Gamay, was authorized in the Aube—so long as growers agreed to uproot those vines by 1942. (That deadline was later pushed back till 1962 due to World War II.) Eight years later, legislators went on to issue rules on pruning and harvesting and finally codified the specifics of sparkling wine production.

Advances in planting and growing techniques progressed apace. Growers replanted their vineyards with phylloxera-resistant rootstock and approached vineyard management more systematically. With an eye toward raising quality, they analyzed the impact of wind, sunlight, and soil on vineyard location and vine orientation. Producers, meanwhile, began moving toward the drier *brut* style favored by the British—long a major market and trend setter.

Producers also worked to perfect blends. Champagne traditionally employs a unique production model. A handful of large merchants buys grapes from many small growers and sells the resulting wines under their own now-famous house names. Since producers source from different vineyards in different villages—and utilize multiple vintages in their cellars— the goal of most producers is the creation of blends that deliver a consistent experience year after year.

One notable exception proves the rule. Eugène-Aimé Salon, a native of Champagne who had become wealthy selling fur in Paris, reversed

APPELLATION D'ORIGINE CONTROLÉE

The rules that were finalized in 1927 codified more than just Champagne's geographical boundaries. They also established the first set of quality rules for a wine region, thus catalyzing the push to create France's *appellation d'origine controlee*, or AOC, system.

France had long recognized the importance of designating origin for wine. But such designations, called *appellation d'origine*, ignored the importance of grape varieties and viticultural processes.

In 1906, Joseph Marie Capus, a professor of agriculture in Bordeaux, began urging wine industry leaders to push for the suffix "controllée" after "appellation d'origine." For Capus, a designated origin was worthless without quality standards. His suggestion was mostly dismissed, though, as producers didn't want to invite bureaucratic interference.

After World War I, Capus gained a powerful new ally when Pierre Le Roy de Boiseaumarié, a celebrated fighter pilot who directed a wine estate in Châteauneuf-du-Pape, joined his effort. By 1925, they had convinced top wine producers across France to support mandated quality rules.

Most winemakers continued to resist, but in 1935, the French parliament created a new regulatory body and tasked it with managing and issuing wine production rules. The new group—the *comité national des appellations d'origine*—was comprised of government officials and representatives from viticulture syndicates. It promptly created the *appellation d'origine contrôlée system*, and by the end of 1937, Bordeaux, Burgundy, Champagne, and the Rhône had their first set of AOC regulations. These rules became a model for other nations in Europe.

The CNAO, which is today known as the *institut national de l'origine et de la qualité*, would go on to issue rules for a variety of other agricultural products, including cheese and butter. It covers 300 French wine regions today.

In Champagne, AOC regulations dictate the region's boundaries, approved grape varieties, vineyard practices like pruning methods and yields, the winemaking process, and even labelling and packaging.

THE GRAPES OF CHAMPAGNE

More than 99 percent of Champagne's vineyards are planted to only three grapes: Chardonnay, Pinot Noir, and Pinot Meunier. Most champagnes are a blend of all three grapes.

Pinot Noir accounts for 38 percent of Champagne's plantings and is the predominant variety on the Montagne de Reims and in the Aube. In blends, Pinot Noir is credited with providing backbone and structure and offering aromas and flavors of red berries.

Pinot Meunier accounts for 32 percent of Champagne's plantings and is the predominant variety in Vallée de la Marne. Viticulturists long assumed that this grape was genetically related to Pinot Noir, but recent research has challenged this assumption. So today, the grape is often referred to as "Meunier." In blends, Meunier is credited with rounding out wines by offering moderate acidity, unctuous aromatics, and bright fruit flavors.

Chardonnay accounts for 30 percent of Champagne's plantings and is the predominant variety on the Côte des Blancs. In blends, Chardonnay is credited with providing finesses by imparting acidity, floral aromatics, and flavors of green apples, citrus fruits, and hazelnuts.

The four other permitted grape varieties—Arbane, Petit Meslier, Pinot Blanc, and Pinot Gris (also called "Fromenteau")—together account for just 0.3 percent of vineyard plantings. These grapes are curiosities, to be sure, but some of Champagne's hottest producers have embraced them—with stunning results.

Laherte Frères, a small producer in the Côte des Blancs, planted a small parcel with all seven grape varieties in 2003 and today makes a wine from the site called "Les 7." Tarlant, a grower-producer in the Vallée de la Marne, makes a blend of Pinot Blanc, Arbanne, and Petit Meslier called "BAM!" Likewise, Cedric Bouchard, a grower-producer in the Aube, makes a Pinot Blanc from a 21-acre vineyard of 50-year-old vines called La Bolorée.

the Champagne *modus operandi* at the turn of the 20th century. He purchased 2.5 acres of vines in Le Mesnil-sur-Oger. Believing that the best Champagne would be singular in its expression—made from one village, grape variety, and vintage—Salon produced his first wine in 1905. At first, these wines were held solely for private consumption. But their popularity grew. So Salon began purchasing fruit from 20 other small parcels in Le Mesnil, and in 1921, just as the global economy started to surge, Salon began offering his single-village, single-vintage, single-variety wine commercially. The success was immediate, in part because Salon became the house champagne at Maxim's, one of Paris' most fashionable restaurants. Salon would remain virtually alone in the pursuit of singularity for the next several decades, but his focus never wavered. As of 2016, Salon has released just 38 vintages since that first public offering.

THE ART OF BLENDING

More than 85 percent of all champagne produced is "non-vintage." At big champagne houses, especially, vintners are expected to rely on their sensory memories and experiences to produce wines that deliver a consistent experience to consumers each year. The process of combining wines from different grapes from different vineyards from different vintages to create a perfect blend is called "*assemblage*."

This is a highly imaginative process, to be sure. But the mythology surrounding blending is a bit overblown. With most non-vintage offerings, 85 to 90 percent of the base wine comes from a single vintage. Each champagne house has its own vision and style, of course, but savvy consumers know to expect less from a non-vintage offerings when the base is from a less-than-stellar year.

Entrance to Champagne Salon.

The Clos du Mesnil.

LES ANNÉES FOLLES

The mid-twenties were a boom time for champagne. Economies recovered. Stock markets soared and new money shaped new tastes. Young people left the countryside in droves for the opportunities and glitter of cities. Cars got faster. Skirts got shorter. Movies, airplanes, and jazz took off. It was breakout of youth, excess, and euphoria.

Paris, especially, became a symbol of all the new life could be. Artists, expatriates, and the wealthy rushed to the city, and champagne flowed freely. Wine that had been stored in the barricaded caves of Champagne during the war—including the great vintages of 1911, 1914, and 1918—were pushed into the limelight to the applause of eager customers.

Prohibition in America hardly slowed the rush. When the 18th amendment finally took effect in January, 1920, the champagne houses worried about losing that immense market. But America was still celebrating and still thirsty. The French found plenty of smugglers—gangsters who made fortunes by moving illegal liquor—willing to slip champagne into the United States. The runners collected their cuts, of course, but the French producers discovered that there were no import taxes to be paid on wine that "didn't exist." The routes were roundabout. Shipments of illegal champagne moved through Canada, Mexico, or the Caribbean and were offloaded in America at night from blacked-out trucks or fast boats. There were turf wars and murders over the shipment of wine, but about 70 million bottles of champagne made it to the States during prohibition from 1920 to its repeal in late 1933.

American consumption was almost mythic. Its wealth and tragedy were immortalized in F. Scott Fitzgerald's 1925 novel *The Great Gatsby*. The lavish parties thrown by the book's main character, millionaire Jay Gatsby, at his mansion in the Hamptons, Long Island, were awash in champagne. Oddly enough, Fitzgerald actually wrote most of the novel while living in France, but Gatsby represented a world Fitzgerald had lived. He called 1924 "the summer of a thousand parties."

In the wake of all the wealth and glamour, French producers moved quickly to exploit the luxury status of champagne. They were, for their time, marketing revolutionaries. Before television and even billboards, street posters were the primary channel of public advertising, filling the streets of Paris and other major cities in the 1880s. By the 1920s, dramatically colorful *affiches* were affixed to storefronts and lamp posts across Paris, advertising everything modern and luxurious—exotic travel, hotels, automobiles, railroads, cigarettes, perfumes, drinks, and furs. It was a graphically competitive business so artists and agencies tried to outdo each other with bold new designs. Champagne producers were at the head of the pack. To drink champagne was to be alive, joyful, beautiful, sexy, chic, and sophisticated, damn the cost.

Marketing went beyond graphics. Champagne houses brought actresses and celebrities to tour the vineyards and cellars and paid them to use their skills to associate the wine with everything that was sophisticated, French, and patriotic—the product sponsorships we know so well today. The rich and famous sang Champagne's contribution to the war, even the champagne's health benefits, just as French kings had done from Reims and

Versailles centuries earlier. The government, realistic as ever, helped out by promoting studies purporting to show that people in wine regions lived longer than their sober counterparts.

It worked. In 1926 some 37 million bottles of Champagne were sold around the world. That number eclipsed every record the region had set so far, save for 1909. Moreover, those 1926 bottles actually contained of "real" champagne, a product now officially certified by the French government. The world seemed to be in love with champagne. *Bon vivants* were drinking millions of toasts, and the profits of the great Champagne houses were golden.

THE PARTY ENDS WITH A CRASH

To many, it seemed the post-war exuberance would go on forever. But speculation and paper profits were running miles ahead of economic basics. By 1927, steel production ominously declined as new investment and construction dropped off. Car sales slowed. Consumer debt grew. There was a perceptible chill in the air. Demand for damn-the-cost products like champagne dried up almost overnight, and the year saw French champagne sales plummet by 40 percent.

In early 1929, the New York Stock Exchange experienced mini-crashes as worried analysts warned of defaults and excessive speculation. On September 20, the London Stock Exchange was rocked when a top investor was charged with fraud and forgery. Then, on October 24, the NYSE dropped by 11 percent at the opening bell. Although the market recovered almost fully by day's end and continued to rally the following day, the weekend primed a panic selloff of stocks. That Monday, the NYSE dropped by 13 percent. Fear fed fears and on Black Tuesday, October 29, the exchange nosedived by another 12 percent.

In retrospect, the stock markets in Europe and America had become speculative bubbles that burst when they no longer came near to representing underlying economic realities. Besides the craze of individual speculation, that eternal hope for easy money, the tectonic plates of international finance were strained to breaking. England and France, impoverished by the long war, had borrowed heavily from American financial groups. With those loans hanging over their economies, the British and French had demanded nearly impossible war reparations from Germany. That country's economy, devastated by hyperinflation and political turmoil, was on the point of collapsing. Accusations flew back and forth as governments and financial insiders tried to work out solutions. Nations blamed each other, raised punishing protective tariffs, and trade wars followed.

Once the stock markets crashed, grape prices and wine sales cratered. In Champagne, the great wine houses, strapped for cash, could hardly afford to pay their cellar teams, let alone those working in sales, exports, or marketing. Hours and wages were cut. Grape growers, who could no longer get either agricultural credit from banks and wine producers or cash from harvest sales, were driven to the wall. A whole delicately priced industry, dependent as it was on consumption in faraway markets, moved towards collapse.

By 1931, most producers were not even bothering to buy grapes; there was simply no market for champagne. Of course, the sun shone. Grapes grew and were harvested in the ensuing years, but they could only be sold in profitless off-markets as little more than cheap booze. Desperate

Champagne Bollinger.

growers formed their own cooperatives to make cut-rate wine and sell it under village names. The 1933 repeal of prohibition in the United States had little impact on Champagne. French producers had long ago figured out how to skirt US law, but the global depression continued to depress wine sales.

A BRIEF RECOVERY

By 1935, many were turning to radical politics, certain they were witnessing the collapse of both capitalism and liberal democracy. But in the face of widespread social unrest and lack of effective political initiatives, there were glimmers of recovery. In the streets, most people believed there *had* to be an economic turn, eventually. Despite the distant thunder of war in Asia, the unpredictable resurgence of German militarism, and the growing threat of a totalitarian Russian state, life—human life—went on. There was always something to celebrate.

BOOZE BEYOND THE BUBBLES

Many producers in Champagne make small amounts of still wine and other alcoholic beverages. These offerings are rare—and generally expensive. But they show that there's more to champagne than bubbles.

Coteaux Champenois is an AOC designation for still wines from Champagne. These can come from any of the seven grapes that are allowed in the region, but Pinot Noir and Chardonnay are the two most popular. Because of Champagne's cool climate, most Coteaux Champenois comes from the warmest villages, some of which can be named on the wine label. One can find still reds from Bouzy, Aÿ, Sillery, Cumieres, and Vertus. One can find still whites from Chouilly and Mesnil. Rosé is allowed, but it's extremely rare.

Rosé des Riceys is an AOC designation for still rosé from in and around Riceys, a village in the Aube. Made from whole bunches of Pinot Noir, these wines are typically vinified "semi-carbonically," where most juice ferments while still inside the grape. This technique, which is typically associated with Beaujolais Nouveau, imparts bright, fruity flavors to wine. Very few producers make Rosé des Riceys and it isn't produced every year. The appellation is also notable because producers there qualify for three AOCs: Champagne, Coteaux Champenois, and Rosé des Riceys.

Marc de Champagne is a brandy produced by distilling the seeds, skins, and stalks that are left after grapes are pressed. Aged in oak, Marc de Champagne typically has a rich, amber color.

Fine de la Marne is a high quality brandy produced by distilling leftover wine and wine lees. Like Marc de Champagne, Fine de la Marne is aged in oak, but it's more delicate and more floral.

Ratafia de Champagne is a blend of brandy and unfermented grape juice, typically from later pressings.

The Champenois did not lose hope or rip out their ancient vines. The houses, with their old names and older traditions, kept trying to keep champagne alive. Their search for new ways to move champagne led them to the old Benedictine monk, Dom Pérignon.

In Champagne, that dim historical figure had been all but forgotten. In fact, the few records of his life had been mostly lost when his Abbey was destroyed during the French revolution. In the late 19th century, though, he was resurrected by Champagne's Grandes Marques, who realized that Dom Pérignon could help with their marketing efforts. Indeed, at the 1889 world fair, the Grandes Marques handed out illustrated pamphlets—perfect souvenirs for tourists—describing Pérignon as the "father" of sparkling wine.

Photo by Luisa Bonachea.

In 1921, Mercier, a large Champagne producer in Épernay, created a special *cuvée* they decided to brand as *Dom Pérignon*. It sat in Mercier cellars until 1927, when the company brought it out and presented both the wine and the brand to Moët on the occasion of a marriage between the two families. In 1930, Moët appointed an enterprising marketer, Robert-Jean de Vogüé, as its president. Taking inventory of Moët's assets, he realized that, since so little was really known about Dom Pérignon, he could re-invent the crusty old monk to market the 1921 wine as a "prestige" cuvée. De Vogüé's colleagues bought into the plan, and they launched Dom Pérignon as a luxury brand for export markets. The first shipments arrived in London in 1935, where the wine was an instant success. It became a smash hit in New York a few months later.

Growers and producers also began thinking differently about the wine itself. In 1935, Pierre Philipponnat, who had settled in the Mareuil-sur-Aÿ region of Champagne with his brother in 1910, acquired a steep, hillside vineyard called "Clos des Goisses." Like Eugène-Aimé Salon, Philipponnat believed that the greatest Champagne would not come from a traditional blend of grapes, but embody the output of a single superb vineyard. So he created Champagne's first single-vineyard offering—Clos des Goisses. It was a bold and successful move to emphasize a specific terroir. Connoisseurs can debate forever over the advantages of blend versus single-vineyard champagne, but Philipponnat essentially created a new way to position champagne.

WHAT IS TERROIR?

As early as the 14th century, Cistercian monks in Burgundy recognized that different vineyards—and even different plots of land in the same vineyards—produced different wines.

What explains these differences? Terroir, the French term without an English equivalent that is used to capture all the influences—climate, soil, elevation, and more—that shape a wine's final expression. Today, those who obsess over terroir believe that great

Philipponat's most famous single vineyard champagne comes from the Clos des Goisses.

wines have an obligation to translate time and place, clearly expressing the characteristics of their vintage and the soils and climate in which they're grown.

With most champagne, though, terroir is purposefully undetectable. Big champagne houses blend wines from different vintages and different vineyards to deliver a consistent experience to consumers each year. This isn't a bad thing; there's much to be said for consistent elegance.

But today, Champagne is in the midst of a renaissance thanks to terroir. Grower-producers across the region—small vignerons who grow their own grapes and make their own wines—are eschewing consistency in favor of singularity. These growers only account for a small percentage of sales, but they're revolutionizing champagne.

Meanwhile, the French government was refining its earlier geographic initiatives relating to control of French wine production. In July of 1935, the French Ministry of Agriculture created the *Institut National des Appellations d'Origine*, a powerful regulatory body tasked with formally defining the boundaries of each winegrowing appellation and setting rules for quality and consistency in wine production. Thanks to this body, the first *appellation d'origine contrôlée*—or AOC— laws took effect in 1936 and were implemented in Champagne, Bordeaux, and Burgundy before the end of 1937. The new rules and oversight, especially when combined with more scientific approaches in vineyards and cellars, helped ensure that consumers across the world could expect a consistent product when purchasing wine bearing an official French AOC label.

Unfortunately, improvements in production and labeling were the least of France's worries. The enmity between France and Germany was white hot— exacerbated by the Treaty of Versailles that ended the war. While the French built a supposedly impenetrable system of fortifications known as the Maginot Line along its German border, Germany secretly strengthened its navy, air force, and armored units. Adolf Hitler came to power in 1933 on a platform of renouncing the terms of Versailles and making Germany a great power again. He demanded that all *Reichsdeutsche*—German-speaking inhabitants of adjacent countries—have the right to be part of the new Germany. In March of 1938, Germany annexed Austria through a forced and fixed referendum. Czechoslovakia was split up and occupied shortly thereafter.

In 1939, Germany and the Soviet Union—for the moment allies— simultaneously invaded Poland. England and France declared war on Germany to support Poland. World War II had started in Europe.

GERMANY OCCUPIES CHAMPAGNE

German military planners once more knew they faced two powerful enemies—France in the west and Russia in the east. Hitler decided to first turn west and knock France out of the war. On May 10, 1940, with the transmission of the code word "Danzig," German troops swept into Holland and Belgium, completely bypassing the Maginot line by taking the poorly defended northern path into the heartland of France. Formations of 2,500 warplanes bombed cities and airfields in Belgium, Holland, France, and Luxembourg. About 40 percent of those planes flew into northeastern France. In Champagne, bombs rained down on Reims, Épernay, and Chalons-sur-Marne—and German panzer tanks and troops followed.

The German *Blitzkrieg* used a concentrated spearhead of fast tanks and motorized infantry to break through weak points into the enemy's rear, surrounding and destroying enemy units before they could even be formed up. It was highly effective against armies trained to re-fight the

last World War. Champagne fell almost immediately. The Dutch surrendered after just five days; the Belgians after 18. The French defense lasted only six weeks. Soon after the British force was evacuated from Dunkirk, Germans occupied Paris and forced a humiliating armistice on France.

The German occupation was bitterness itself to the French. But in those early days, they had virtually no alternative but to accommodate. German troops loved finding cellars of wine and spent the first few weeks trekking from one to the other, looting and drinking. In just two months, about 2 million bottles vanished.

The victorious Nazis intended to exploit French wine production for the needs of the Reich. In each winegrowing region a German *Weinführer* was appointed to control operations and prevent sabotage.

In Champagne, residents were at first hopeful that their Weinführer, Otto Klaebisch, would be reasonable. Born in Cognac, Klaebisch had actually spent his entire career in the wine and spirits industry, even working as a sales agent in Germany for a number of champagne houses just before the war. For Klaebisch, however, power tasted better than champagne. Within days of his arrival, he ordered the president of Veuve Clicquot, Bertrand de Vogüé, out of the imposing Clicquot château so that he could set up residence there.

In the summer of 1940, Klaebisch ordered that producers must not only supply upwards of 350,000 bottles per week for Nazi Germany and its troops but furnish champagne to German-controlled restaurants across Europe. Only leftovers could be offered to the French. Producers resisted as best they could, hiding bottles, diluting wines with water, and using dirty corks and bottles to sour the wine. But such moves were risky, as Klaebisch and his colleagues spot-checked everything.

As the war went on, Klaebisch's demands increased as he bought favors or passed along demands from his superiors; by 1941, he pushed this forced production to as much as 500,000 bottles per week. Cellar stocks were dwindling too quickly to maintain the consistency that the Germans expected—and there weren't enough hours in the day to produce enough new wine.

In April 1941, Robert-Jean de Vogüé, still serving as president of Moët, teamed up with M. Maurice Doyard, a leading vineyard owner, to create the *Comité Interprofessional du Vin de Champagne*, or CIVC. By presenting a united front to Klaebisch, the men hoped to return some level of sanity to wine production. But the collective bargaining efforts between CIVC and Klaebisch left neither satisfied.

Champagne also was becoming a center of the armed French Resistance. Secret drops of weapons and supplies from England were easily hidden in the region's vast network of limestone cellars. The house of Moët was deeply involved. In addition to negotiating with the Germans as head of the CIVC, Robert-Jean de Vogüé was in fact leading the political arm of the Resistance.

De Vogüé figured out that large champagne shipments to unusual destinations—like Romania and Egypt—portended military offensives. Nazi leaders liked to reward troops by breaking out the champagne after battlefield victories. Resistance operators collected and passed on this information to British intelligence. But this operation was exposed at the end of 1943.

Photo by Luisa Bonachea.

The war memorial in front of the Hôtel de Ville in Épernay. Photo by Luisa Bonachea.

On November 24, de Vogüé was called to Klaebisch's office to discuss the recent harvest. There he was arrested. Brought before a military tribunal, he was sentenced to death.

Champenoise admired de Vogüé, and since the Germans needed locals to produce wine, the workers made the risky decision to strike and stop production. Ultimately, although the death sentence was suspended, de Vogüé remained in prison and Moët was taken over by the Germans. Workers were forced to return to their jobs.

THE RING CLOSES

On December 7, 1941, Japan attacked the American naval base at Pearl Harbor. America declared war. Four days later, Germany and Italy declared war on the United States.

Americans had seen which way the wind was blowing, and the American military was somewhat better prepared than it had been in 1917. Using its huge industrial base, the United States quickly built the largest and best supplied military force the world had ever seen, despite having to fight on widely separated fronts.

With growing American support, the British were eventually able to push the Germans and Italians out of North Africa in the spring of 1943.

A stash of bottles at Champagne Bollinger. Photo by Luisa Bonachea.

As the Russian front was turned after Stalingrad, the Allies were fighting their way through Sicily and into southern Italy. By September of 1943, the Allies had forced Mussolini from power and achieved victory in this southern front.

Preparations were already underway for an invasion of France. On June 6, 1944, the Allies staged the largest air, land, and sea operation in history. More than 160,000 troops landed along a 50-mile stretch of coastline in Normandy. In the first 24 hours, the Allies had pushed back German counterattacks and gained a sustainable beachhead on mainland Europe.

Thereafter, the Allied advance was swift, pushing through France and Belgium and reaching Champagne in July 1944. A few months later, General Dwight D. Eisenhower, supreme commander of the allied forces in Europe, set up a command center in a small schoolhouse in Reims as multiple Allied armies were hammering their way across the Rhine and the Russians closed in from the east.

On May 7, 1945 at 2:41 a.m., the chief of staff for Germany's armed forces, Alfred Jodl, signed Germany's unconditional surrender at that schoolhouse. After Jodl and his staff departed, Eisenhower and his colleagues celebrated with a bottle of Champagne. The next morning, Eisenhower ordered six cases of Pommery's 1934 cuvée so his whole command staff could toast the end of the war in Europe.

DON'T POP THE CORK!

Popping a champagne cork grabs everyone's attention. But it wastes bubbles. And it's dangerous; flying corks can travel up to fifty miles per hour!

Here's how to open champagne:

1. Remove the foil covering. (Most bottles have a tab to pull.)
2. Loosen the cage with six counterclockwise twists, but don't remove it. Once the cage is loosened, be sure to keep one hand holding both the cork and the cage. At this point, the bottle is a loaded weapon.
3. Holding the bottle at an upward-facing angle of about 45 degrees, slowly rotate the base while tightly holding the cage and cork.
4. While keeping downward pressure on the cork, begin twisting it, gently, in the opposite direction of the bottle as it starts to loosen. The cork should come out with a soft sigh.

Chapter Five:

Approaching the Second Millennium

In the fall of 1945, Champagne exported 50,000 cases of wine to England. This shipment, the first to reach France's northern neighbor in more than five years, arrived just in time to celebrate Christmas and ring in the New Year.

Across Europe, prospects for champagne in the post-war years were dismal. The enormous costs of World War II led to severe post-war austerity. Meanwhile, the Iron Curtain's cold war cast its chill over Europe. There seemed to be a real threat of renewed war. In France, Italy, and England left-leaning governments were swept into power. Would there ever again be demand for expensive champagnes?

Champagne's vineyards were in terrible shape. Few had been replanted—or really tended to at all—during the war. Cellars were almost bare after the German "purchase" of about 75 million bottles at cut-rate prices. As a result, producers were short on the reserve wines they needed to blend their products.

However, the destruction of the war did not affect the quality of the grapes harvested during those years. The 1941, 1942, and 1943 vintages were heralded as among the best ever. But where to sell them? With Europe depressed, champagne marketers turned their attention to America. Prohibition was long gone, so the Champenois hoped the Yanks' 16 million returning soldiers would celebrate with champagne . . . and bring a broader taste for the bubbly to the world's new economic powerhouse.

THE REBIRTH OF CONSPICUOUS CONSUMPTION

But Europe did recover, and faster than expected. By 1950 champagne sales were clearly on the rebound. That year, the region sold 32.5 million bottles of wine—a number that matched or exceeded virtually every previous record. Four years later, world sales reached 44 million bottles—a new record. Despite the collapse of colonial empires, brushfire proxy-wars, and the ever-present threat of atomic cataclysm, economies took off. Prosperity returned with a pop and a whoosh to Champagne.

Sophisticated advertising drove sales. Top brands like Moët & Chandon, Veuve Clicquot, and Piper-Heidsieck all recognized and exploited the potential of both old and new media to get their product into the minds of consumers. And it wasn't only the producers, the *Comité Interprofessional du Vin de Champagne*—the trade association of all Champagne's growers and producers established during World War II—invested large sums to solidify and expand champagne's status as a necessary luxury.

The organization—in the tradition of European mercantilism—also sought to shape the product and control supply, competition, and price. Like an agricultural OPEC, CIVC assigned harvest limits to make sure the marketplace had just enough champagne to match demand, but not the excess that could undermine pricing structures. Outsiders and unapproved competitors were excluded when the organization convinced lawmakers in Paris to mandate that all exports from Champagne came with a certificate of origin. By 1949, producers who didn't meet the CIVC's standards were refused certificates and thus were barred from exporting.

CIVC also took to the courts to limit use of the champagne name both inside and, more importantly, outside France. In 1958, the trade group worked with 12 of Champagne's top producers to file a criminal lawsuit against a British company, Costa Brava, which was selling sparkling wine from Spain as "Spanish champagne." While alliance lost the criminal case, the effort generated tremendous publicity. And in a subsequent civil suit against Costa Brava, Champagne won. The quality and price targets of champagne were preserved at a time when international law was just beginning to take up the complex issue of producer "rights" for globally marketed products.

Champagne soon found another source of supplemental revenue—wine tourism. Visitors flocked to view Champagne's vineyards and production houses. Many were local, driving in from Belgium, Switzerland, Germany, and cities in France. But thanks to commercial air travel—and Champagne's

The Moet & Chandon Gift Shop.

proximity to Paris—many tourists traveling to France from far-off destinations added Champagne to their itineraries. In 1965, Reims and Épernay welcomed about 50,000 visitors to their cellars.

The economies of America, Europe, and now the Pacific were creating a remarkable prosperity supplying their own peoples, and increasingly the rest of the world, not only with products but tools to produce wealth. There were many, many winners in this post-war revolution, and new money meant that the pleasures of conspicuous consumption, once limited to social and financial elites, now spread to millions of successful "average Joes." National brands used targeting advertising strategies to push image and aspiration as aggressively as product benefits. Sex-and-status proved effective for positioning high-end luxury goods where price itself established value. Marilyn Monroe, the top-billed actress of the 1950s, claimed she bathed in champagne, just as Cora Pearl, the flamboyant courtesan of the Belle Époque, had done ninety years earlier.

In both Hollywood films and emerging television shows, champagne was flaunted as an easily recognizable symbol of status and sophistication. Whenever James Bond, Ian Fleming's super spy, slipped his arm around the waist of one of his lovelies at the end of a film, there was sure to be a bottle of Bollinger or Dom Pérignon close at hand to complete the effect.

Among the many established and emerging champagne brands, there was now a race to become king of the status mountain. Names like Bollinger sought to mimic the success of Moët & Chandon's Dom Pérignon by releasing their own prestige cuvées. Bollinger released a top-price "R.D." in the early 1960s, as did Taittinger with its "Comtes de Champagne." These wines, in contrast to regular cuvées, were always from a specific vintage.

WHAT IS A PRESTIGE CUVÉE?

A "prestige cuvée"—often called a *tête de cuvée*—is a producer's top wine. Typically from a single vintage and coming from meticulously selected sites, barrels, and/or grapes, these wines almost always spend five years or more on the lees. Most come in fancy bottles with fancy packaging and fancy prices, too.

In addition to Moët & Chandon's Dom Pérignon, some well-known examples include Pol Roger's Sir Winston Churchill, Louis Roederer's Cristal, and Taittinger's Comtes de Champagne.

Champagne cooperatives, which vinified their members' grapes and sold under a cooperative label or directly to *négociants*, became a force in during this period. While there were just 52 cooperatives in 1950, there were 120 by 1965. The cooperatives had little impact on export sales, which continued to be remained dominated by a few big brands. But they gained a foothold in the domestic market.

Through these years, champagne sales rose steadily—and sometimes spectacularly. In 1961, the region broke the 50-million bottle mark for the first time—and that number would double in less than a decade. As the industry expanded, it also underwent considerable consolidation. Moët & Chandon, for example, acquired Ruinart in 1962 and Mercier in 1970.

In America, consumers were slow to warm up to wine; they preferred hard liquor and beer. In the 1950s and 1960s, the United States only purchased about 5 percent of Champagne's annual production, a number that had barely moved since before Prohibition. By the end of the 1960s, intense advertising, a new national mood, and the spread of wealth opened up the American market.

In 1970, Champagne sales broke the 100-million bottle barrier.

AS CONSUMPTION GROWS, VINEYARDS DECLINE

To supply explosively expanding demand, grape production had to be increased. In 1966 the CIVC allowed 9,000 new acres to be put under vine over the next five years. In 1971, 11,000 more acres were added. Most of

these new vineyards were laid out in ignored parts of the Marne Valley and long-neglected areas like the Aube.

Scientific breakthroughs also helped. In 1939, a Swiss chemist discovered the insecticidal qualities of DDT. During the war years, the chemical was quickly deployed to control malaria and typhus among troops and civilians. After

Vineyards in the Aube.

the war, many of the companies that produced DDT and other chemicals for the Allies turned their attention to agriculture, developing pesticides, herbicides, and chemical fertilizers. The risks that these chemicals posed to humans and the environment weren't yet known, but their effectiveness in improving crop yields was obvious. So, like farmers across the world, Champagne's winegrowers embraced these new products.

For instance, the vegetation that grew around and under the vines was known to have many positive effects, sheltering beneficial insects and enhancing soils. But undergrowth also competed with vines for water and as a result could decrease grape yields. Herbicides helped growers eliminate this competing vegetation. Pesticides also targeted insects that spread grapevine diseases. Since growers were paid by the ton, they had every incentive to deploy chemicals to maximize output. These aggressive control measures were part of a new chemical age. By 1952, there were nearly 10,000 different pesticides registered in the United States alone.

It wasn't just chemicals changing the region's soils. Champagne's traditional compost—the nutrient-rich, organic fertilizer comprised principally of food scraps—also changed dramatically after the war. In the early 20th century, Champagne had already become a kind of garbage dump for Paris. As the city's population grew, residents created far more trash. So a deal was struck with

Differences in farming practices in the Vallée de la Marne.

Champagne's winegrowers. So long as the growers covered transportation costs, Paris would provide a virtually unlimited supply of compost.

The deal benefitted both sides and for several decades, the incoming trash made for perfect fertilizer—after all, virtually all waste would have been organic, comprised of fruit and vegetable waste, meal leftovers, human waste, and perhaps wood and cloth. However, after World War II, the content of Paris's trash began to change. There was more steel and cast iron, and for the first time, plastics. Champagne's vineyards were contaminated with inorganic rubbish that adversely affected the quality of the soils. Moreover, the damage was not immediately recognized so the dumping process continued far longer than it should have. And soil pollution was very difficult to reverse.

BOOMS, BUSTS, AND BELLBOTTOMS

In 1973 global sales of champagne hit a record 125 million bottles. But between January 1973 and December 1974, stock prices plummeted and the West's advanced economies suffered one of the worst downturns in modern history. Markets dropped more than 40 percent.

Simultaneously, in reaction to America's involvement in the Yom

Kippur War, the members of the Organization of the Petroleum Exporting Countries, plus Egypt and Syria, imposed a large-scale oil embargo. Between October 1973 and March 1974, the price of oil quadrupled.

Champagne has always been a luxury product and exposed to shifts in global economic weather. Its sales are, in fact, an economic indicator of sorts. Turns can be quick—and devastating. As the oil freeze descended on Europe in 1974, champagne exports to the United Kingdom and Italy dropped by roughly 65 percent. But rebounds can also be astonishingly rapid. By 1976, Champagne almost regained almost all its lost ground, selling 115 million bottles worldwide.

Photo by Luisa Bonachea.

Beyond price and prosperity, sales of champagne also had become increasingly linked to what might be called cultural weather. After all, the market is not an economic abstraction; it is real people drinking wine in specific places at specific times. The human atmosphere of wine consumption is hugely important. That atmosphere is shaped by perception and advertising, and by the obvious fact that drinking champagne is exhilarating—and intoxicating.

So perhaps it's no surprise that champagne sales, especially in the United States, took off with the rise of disco and club culture. That culture was inspired by New York City's gay underground dance scene. And at discotheques across America, patrons embraced champagne as a kind of fountain of youth, a sparkling euphoric for nights of dancing and drinking. Those drinks were typically hard liquor cocktails mixed with champagne, since a spritz of champagne lowered a drink's alcohol percentage and thereby helped revelers to keep dancing the night away.

The consumption of liquor of all kinds surged in the United States in the mid-1970s. While roughly 60 percent of American adults said they drank alcohol in the 1950's and 1960s, the percentage of adult drinkers shot up to 71 in 1978. It was a global trend. That year, 185 million bottles of champagne were sold across the world.

Sales, however, were tied to the economic roller coaster and soon plunged again. The Iranian Revolution of 1979 spooked the global energy market, spawning widespread panic at gas stations. In 1980 Iran and Iraq went to war with each other. The price of crude oil surged, triggering yet another global recession. The world's major economies were also experiencing stagflation—a period of rapid inflation, stagnant economic growth, and high unemployment.

Drop in purchasing power affected worldwide demand for champagne, but sales didn't crater. In 1982, 146 million bottles were sold, a 21 percent drop from the all-time high. Clearly, consumers were still making room for champagne; they just had less money to splurge on "the good stuff."

HUSTLE AND FLASH

Despite setbacks, global economies were in fact expanding—and on the verge of a whole new wave of growth made possible by advances in technology and the personal computer revolution. The idealized "simple life" of the 1960s and 1970s had run its course, and by the mid-1980s, a new breed of young

professionals with high earning potential were coming back to the glitz and glamour of cities in search of social and job opportunities. *Newsweek*, the popular American magazine, declared 1984 "The Year of the Yuppie." Instead of army jackets, boots, jeans and tie-dyes, the new fashion was designer clothing, flashy watches, fast cars, and, well, champagne.

Champagne, of course, was an obvious affordable luxury. In the 1950s and 1960s, it had still been classy, insider drink with not a little snob appeal. In the new world of the 1980s, champagne became the wave-the-money-around symbol of achievable success for just about anyone. It was status you could buy.

At first it was the drink of choice for fashionable urban sophisticates. But champagne producers quickly recognized the potential of a broader market and shaped their advertising accordingly. As a *New York Times* report from the era explained, "slick promotional campaigns featuring long-legged blondes and golden bubbles were created to lift champagne sales. No longer, champagne executives decreed, would their prestigious drink be restricted to what the French called the happy few."

You no longer had to be sophisticated to look sophisticated. Champagne became the show-me-your-money drink at now-legal strip clubs in big cities like New York and Los Angeles. Such establishments barely existed until the 1970s, but with the rise of *Playboy* magazine and society's loosening sexual mores, they became ubiquitous in the 1980s and 1990s. Such clubs offered high-end, private "champagne rooms"—and charged extravagantly for flutes of bubbly. Even today, these clubs have a huge impact on champagne sales. In 2015, America's 3,500 strip clubs had revenues of more than $2.5 billion— and about 40 percent of that cash was spent on alcohol. It's an odd fact that

FORGET THE FLUTE AND TOSS THE COUPE

Today's geekiest wine enthusiasts have cleared their cupboards of flutes. These days, they're drinking champagne out of regular white wine glasses.

The flute gained popularity around 50 years ago as the coupe—the sherbet-style glass folklore claims was molded from Marie Antoinette's left breast—fell out of favor. But like the coupe, it's a terrible vessel for enjoying champagne.

Contrary to popular wisdom, Marie Antoinette's delicious anatomy didn't inspire the coupe. Historians now trace the glass to 17ᵗʰ-century England, long before she became queen of France. They believe the coupe was invented to ease service at large parties, as it held more than regular wine glasses, or simply to take advantage of champagne's rising popularity by offering consumers something new.

While coupes are fun—they can be stacked in layers to build champagne towers and are perfect for recreating scenes from *The Great Gatsby*—they're designed poorly. Like martini glasses, coupes are prone to slosh over. They're top-heavy, so one inevitably holds the bowl, thus warming champagne too swiftly. Most importantly, coupes too quickly dissipate champagne's bouquet and effervescence.

The flute is just as bad. It was designed purely for aesthetics; although the glass's slender walls preserve and accentuate champagne's bubbles, the elongated shape does nothing for champagne's unique aromas. When champagne was more or less a luxury, this hardly mattered. But the flute developed cachet as a status symbol since it was virtually synonymous with champagne.

No one in the Champagne region uses flutes. In cellars, white wine glasses are the rule. Most restaurants prefer tulip-shaped stems—while slim at the base, these glasses gradually open to a wide bowl that then narrows slightly towards the top. Some destinations utilize wide-bottomed red wine glasses, especially for rosé and older vintage champagne. Fuller wine glasses help unlock more aromas, allowing development of the bouquet, better for actually smelling the wine. Plus, need it be said, larger rims make drinking—and drinking more—a lot easier.

Flutes are fine for celebratory toasts with trivial sparkling wines and they work well with festive, bubbly cocktails like mimosas and French 75s. Manhattans, daiquiris, and many other cocktails are best served in coupes. With real Champagne, though, skip both. Serious wines deserve serious glasses.

Americans today spend more money in strip clubs than on theater, opera, ballet, jazz concerts, and classical music concerts combined.

In the 1980s, the champagne message surged into mass-culture media of television, films, music and sports positioned as an easy symbol of success and aspirational wealth. *Lifestyles of the Rich and Famous*, the first television show to glorify the wealthy, was launched in 1984. At the end of every show, the host, Robin Leach, wished his viewers "champagne wishes and caviar dreams." Early rappers Dr. Jeckyll & Mr. Hyde took champagne to the streets with their 1985 song, "Champagne of Rap." For this new flash class, the more outrageous—and expensive— the better. In the Beastie Boys' 1986 debut album, the name Moët came up in two songs. The Boys could bathe in champagne just as well as Marilyn Monroe. Football stars waved around foaming bottles after victories.

Between 1983 and 1986, America fell in love with champagne—US imports of champagne increased by more than 50 percent over that three-year period. But the United States wasn't the only country to acquire the taste. In the mid-1980s, champagne saw huge gains in new European markets like the Netherlands and Spain, and new Asian markets like Singapore, Hong Kong, Japan, and Australia.

WHY DO ATHLETES CELEBRATE WITH CHAMPAGNE?

Champagne has been a celebratory beverage since Clovis, the first king of what would become France, was crowned in 496.

By 1882, champagne was the beverage of choice to "open a railway, launch a vessel, inaugurate a public edifice, start a newspaper, entertain a distinguished foreigner . . . [and] celebrate an anniversary," as a British journalist noted.

Spraying champagne became *de rigueur* for victorious athletes in 1967. That year, at *24 Heures du Mans*, the world's oldest sports car race, the victors, Dan Gurney and A. J. Foyt, ascended the winner's podium with a bottle of Moët & Chandon. Looking down at the crowd, Gurney saw the owners of his team, Carroll Shelby and Henry Ford II, standing alongside several journalists. For fun, he shook the bottle and sprayed the crowd. Images of Gurney's victory celebration swept the world and a new tradition was born.

Grape production, obviously, needed to expand once again for the region to meet demand. In 1980 the CIVC implemented yet another planting program to put an additional 12,500 acres under vine over the decade. By 1989, Champagne had a total of 67,000 acres of vineyards in production, and those acres were cultivated with the most advanced agricultural technology money could buy.

On October 19, 1987, another economic debacle staggered markets—and shortly thereafter, champagne sales. Stock markets around the world crashed. By October's end, the leading stock indices of Hong Kong, Australia, Spain, the United Kingdom, the United States, and Canada had dropped between 22 and 45 percent. New Zealand's market was down by 60 percent.

The village of Oger and its Côte des Blancs vineyards.

The ups and downs continued. Markets recovered over the next two years. Indeed, Japan's consumption of champagne doubled between 1987 and 1989. Two hundred forty-nine million bottles of champagne were sold across the world in 1989, surpassing all previous records. Then the savings and loan industry collapsed, resulting in a five-year global recession. For the Champenois, this was "weather" of a different sort that they had experienced now for centuries across their vineyards.

AS ECONOMY SINKS, ALTERNATIVES SPARKLE

The swings in demand worried producers and growers alike. There was always the fear that the taste for champagne might be just a fad—a fad that could one day be discarded completely and permanently. Recessions were dangerous. Moreover, Champagne's run of successes was attracting competition.

As sales spiked in the 1980s, sales of alternative sparkling wines from other parts of the world began tapping into Champagne's market share. In 1975, for example,

Photo by Luisa Bonachea.

one in four bottles of sparkling wine sold across the world came from Champagne. By 1985, that proportion had dropped to one in eight.

In the United States, champagne producers attempted to counter the threat by taking the champagne brand into new territory. They could produce more "champagne" and cultivate the large part of the market that was not going for premium pricing. In 1973, Moët et Chandon established the first French sparkling wine house in the United States with the launch of Domaine Chandon in Napa Valley. Champagne Louis Roederer quickly followed, purchasing a 580-acre estate in Anderson Valley in 1982. The next year, G. H. Mumm produced its first vintage at Mumm Napa. And in 1987, Claude Taittinger purchased a 138-acre parcel in Napa Valley to launch a counterpart for his family's Champagne house.

The competition was not sitting still. In the United States and across the world, sales of cava, the Spanish sparkler, surged. While Americans consumed 81 million bottles of cava in 1979, they drank 142 million in 1989.

Bargain bin sparklers—many of which were eminently drinkable—also gained traction as giant wine companies responded to consumption trends. In the United States, E. & J. Gallo expanded the footprint of André, the budget sparkler it introduced in 1966. Australia's largest wine producer began exporting its sparkler to Asia and Europe.

As the market for champagne-like wines expanded, Champagne also lost market share because, despite its high prices, it had never really marketed beyond the bubbles. At restaurants and on retail shelves, the 1980s were a golden era for champagne. The region's top producers released one extraordinary prestige cuvée after another. Consider Dom Pérignon. Always a vintage champagne, it's typically released eight years after harvest. And between 1970 and 1982, Moët & Chandon found that eight vintages warranted release. Few regular consumers cared, though, as only serious oenophiles knew that the best champagnes could be as diverse—and spectacular—as the finest offerings from Bordeaux and Burgundy. The region had spent millions convincing consumers that champagne was a mere symbol of sophistication rather than a "real" wine. Indeed, people did develop a taste for crisp sparkling wines, but they also found they could replace expensive sparkling symbols with other good bubblies.

For a while in the 1990s, the Champenois doubled down on premium-status positioning. Big houses poured millions into marketing and introduced fancier wines with fancier labels to convince consumers that only champagne offered a first-class ticket to the good life. The results were mixed. Champagne sales sank to 214 million bottles in 1992, a number that was certainly high, but dropping as a percentage of the global market.

IT'S ALL ABOUT THE BENJAMINS

By 1993, the economy was once again advancing, and global consumption of champagne picked up. Clever marketing produced an unusual marriage with an emerging music genre: hip-hop.

In the early days of hip-hop, champagne was aspirational—a symbol of attainable wealth. Consider

the mentions of Moët in "Represent," a song on the 1994 debut album from Nas, an artist who would go on to sell more than 25 million records. In the song, Nas describes himself as a "Moët drinking, marijuana smoking street dweller who's always on the corner."

Such lyrics echoed the aspirational message champagne marketing had long presented to the world. Sure, the super rich could afford private jets and luxury yachts—but they drank champagne. So if you could afford champagne, too, you had also made it.

Songwriters had to be new, different, outrageous, upside down. As the champagne trope became a kind of status cliché, it morphed into a caricature of conspicuous consumption. Consider "Big Poppa," the first top-10 hit from Notorious B.I.G., one of the most influential rappers in history. Throughout the music video, scantily clad women sip flutes of champagne. But their men are drinking expensive champagne straight out of the bottle.

The flash status of drinking straight out of the bottle soon became tied to what is known as "bottle service"—the sale of a whole bottle of champagne or liquor at a club, typically with a reserved table for the patron's party. In the United States, bottle service traces its origins to Tunnel, a New York City hotspot that attracted hip-hop's biggest stars. In 1993, the club began selling full bottles of champagne to patrons eager to flaunt their wealth—and too impatient to order individual drinks. The concept quickly expanded to other major cities.

Rappers influenced the club scene and clubbers influenced the rap scene. In the mid-90s, both groups were obsessively chasing flamboyance and ostentation. In his 1998 hit "Hard Knock Life (Ghetto Anthem)," rap megastar Jay Z rhymed about sipping Cristal, the prestige cuvée from Louis Roederer which costs about five times more than its entry-level offering. Music videos were soon filled with enough Cristal and Dom Pérignon to drown James Bond. These were the champagnes for those who could indeed afford private planes and luxury yachts. But the sudden omnipresence of champagne helped catalyze greater consumption of sparkling wine at every price.

As the millennium approached, Champagne hit one sales record after another. In 1996, the region broke the 250-million bottle barrier. In 1999, it left all predictions behind as 327 million bottles were shipped out from Champagne's cellars.

MILLENNIUM CRASH

The Nasdaq, America's tech-heavy stock exchange, peaked on March 10, 2000. Over the previous five years, investors across the world had become obsessed with companies beginning with an "e-" or ending with a ".com." But business realities like cash flow and profits—and the lack thereof—eventually caught up with these companies. The air left the bubble.

Accelerated by the September 11, 2001 terrorist attacks in New York, the Nasdaq bottomed out in October 2002, having lost 78 percent of its value. The New York Stock Exchange eventually lost 56 percent.

Champagne consumption declined, too. The world's most successful rap artists might have been able to keep drinking it, but the champagne buzz seemed to be wearing off.

New times. New opportunities. Back in Champagne, the big houses and their marketers were not idle. A revolution was well underway, with growers—and even some producers—working to upend 250 years of tradition.

Grower producers such as Ulysse Collin have made an impact on the global wine market.

Chapter Six:
The Grower Revolution

ST-GROIS FRERES.
TONNELLERIES
CHMAIN CÔTE D
FRANCE

The global economic recovery that began in 2002 lasted six years. It was a heady period. Easy credit fueled consumer spending and real estate development all around the world. Champagne sales soared.

In New York City, sharp dealers on Wall Street were pulling down millions using new, highly leveraged financial instruments that allowed them to make bigger bets and bag windfalls. Their money changed the city. Restaurants with names like Cru, Veritas, and Montrachet opened with extraordinarily deep wine cellars to cater to the splashy tastes of the newly wealthy.

In New York, London, and Hong Kong, wine auction markets exploded as boom times brought in thousands of new collectors. International houses like Sotheby's and Christie's—and wine-focused outlets like Acker Merrall & Condit and Hart Davis Hart—seemed to hit new records each week on the crest of fierce bidding wars. Those who were new to collecting wine—but eager to spend—soon discovered that, besides better known vintages of Bordeaux and Burgundy, serious oenophiles collected wines from the northern Rhône, Piedmont, and Champagne. The most sought-after wines sold for phenomenal prices.

In nightclubs frequented by rappers and hip-hop stars, expensive champagnes once more became part of the good life, although Jay-Z and other celebrities abandoned Cristal after Louis Roederer's president, Frédéric Rouzaud, spoke dismissively of his new devotees. The replacement? Armand de Brignac, a luxury champagne from Cattier that was intentionally designed for the high-flying club scene. "It all began as a kind of joke in early 2000," explained Jacques Cattier, the patriarch of his eponymous champagne house, in 2014. "We wanted to make an entirely superlative champagne—the most beautiful, the most expensive, and the best." Cattier's "Ace of Spades" was certainly over the top with its metallic gold bottle and outlandishly gaudy label.

In 2007, a record 339 million bottles of champagne were sold worldwide. But it was not to last. The US real estate bubble burst, based as it was on easy money fiscal policies and massively overextended government backing of home ownership. Mortgage-backed securities went bottom up. Many Americans found they now owed more on their mortgages than their homes were worth in the market. The real assets of banks and investment houses, the core of their borrowing power, plummeted and a number of banks went under or were forced to merge with stronger partners.

The collapse of the sophisticated but flawed derivatives market reverberated through the US economy and quickly spread to markets around the world. Champagne sales plunged. Consumption—the driver of prosperity—slumped badly. Credit was available but businesses had no incentive to expand. Even the so-called recovery, which finally began in 2010, was unusually slow. Major government stimulus programs had little effect, and runaway government debt itself became increasingly problematic both in the US and in overextended economies in Europe.

During the recession, many consumers felt they had been swindled. In the United States, populist sentiments raged against Wall Street and government policymakers. Many—especially the young—blamed big, distant corporations and embraced what they saw as more trustworthy, local, and natural alternatives. Those who could afford to pay higher prices bought more "authentic" goods.

Anotine Coutier gets ready to tend to his family's vineyard in Ambonnay.

Of course, many entrepreneurs rushed to oblige. Farm-to-table restaurants replaced chain eateries. Locally produced craft beers pulled market share from the old, big name breweries. Big liquor brands started losing out to small-batch spirits. Major corporations quietly launched boutique brands.

Some wine enthusiasts became passionate ambassadors for "natural" wines, turning away from the big houses they saw as contaminated with advertising, farm technology, and chemicals. They rejected established wholesale agents and outlets and turned directly to small, family-owned producers who farmed organically and rejected chemical additives. Natural wine enthusiasts sought out—and helped promote—unusual grapes from unusual places. Even within traditional regions, though, there were plenty of wines that had not been discovered, much less promoted with the financial muscle used by the big names. These new wines came in below the radar and became the talk of the

WHAT IS "NATURAL" WINE?

"Nothing added, nothing taken away." These five words are the mantra of natural wine enthusiasts.

In the early 1980s, Marcel Lapierre, a vigneron in Beaujolais, began calling for a return to pre-industrial winemaking techniques. Inspired by the teachings of Jules Chauvet, a local winemaker and chemist, Lapierre refused to use chemical fertilizers, herbicides, and pesticides in his vineyards. In his cellar, he sorted grapes by hand, relied on indigenous yeasts, refused to spike the alcohol content of his wine by *chaptalizing*, or adding sugar, and minimized the use of sulfur dioxide.

Several French vignerons soon copied Lapierre's behavior. They called their offerings *vin naturel* and inspired a movement. By the mid-1980s, Paris had a handful of wine bars that exclusively promoted offerings from vignerons who intervened minimally in the cellar. By the dawn of the new millennium, this movement had crossed the Atlantic.

Today, the wine world is full of ambassadors for natural wine. While there's no formal set of standards for natural wine producers to follow, most adhere to the following set of rough rules:

Vincent Laval of Champagne George Laval, a celebrated "natural" winemaker.

- Grapes are grown organically or biodynamically.
- Grapes are harvested by hand.
- Fermentation relies on indigenous yeasts.
- Acidification, chaptalization, and other cellar manipulations are rejected.
- The use of sulfur dioxide is limited.

town amongst a whole new generation of wine aficionados who frequented trendy wine bars and fashionable wine shops in Paris and New York. Their tastes, avoiding the monopoly checkpoints of established wine magazines and periodicals, were disseminated on social media channels like Facebook, Twitter, and Instagram.

These new connoisseurs began treating champagne as a *wine*, rather than as just a status symbol. Once that fundamental discovery had been made—a discovery that went against the basic direction of traditional champagne marketing—these newcomers found a whole new world. And in small

steps, they began the slow task of making other consumers aware that there was a lot more to appreciate in champagne than just the pop and whoosh of a freshly uncorked bottle.

THE SEEDS OF A REVOLUTION

Since its earliest days, Champagne has employed a unique production model. Unlike most wine regions, where small estates produce wine from their own grapes, Champagne is dominated by large merchants who buy grapes from many small growers and sell the resulting wines under their own names.

This model has always created perverse incentives. Since producers almost always purchase grapes by weight, growers are incentivized to maximize yields, even if yield comes at the expense of soil conservation and grape quality. This helps explain why chemical fertilizers, herbicides, and pesticides were applied so liberally in the second half of the 20th century. Even today, though the region has mostly moved away from large-scale chemical applications, Champagne's water tables remain heavily polluted. Disregard for soil health also explains why some vineyard owners maintained that Paris's trash worked as compost through the 1980s and 1990s, ignoring the plastic bags and other inorganics that littered their land. It wasn't until 1997 that the all-powerful CIVC finally forbade the disposal of urban trash in Champagne's vineyards.

Champagne's biggest producers were also incentivized to prioritize volume and margins over quality. After all, the region's marketing mavens had decided, long ago, that maximum profits could be achieved by convincing consumers that Champagne offered the world's most sophisticated—and accordingly, premium priced—celebratory beverage. With entry-level, non-vintage champagne, the goal for most was consistency—to create a blend that delivered the same taste year in and year out. For producers and consumers alike, champagne was more a symbol than a wine. The glory of nuance that wine drinkers had come to expect in wines from Burgundy or Bordeaux were not on the Champagne marketing map. Broadly speaking, big houses only cared about nuance when crafting their prestige cuvées.

Many producers have apprenticed in the cellars of Champagne Jacques Selosse.

That is not to say that Champagne did not have *vignerons* with higher ambitions, winegrowers who believed that champagne could be a wine of terroir. They knew the region's greatest offerings would translate time and place, clearly expressing the characteristics of its vintage and the soils and climate in which it has been grown. For these growers, champagne—like wines from elsewhere in France—had intrinsic qualities way beyond the whoosh.

In the 1980s, these exceptional winemakers began planting the seeds of a revolution.

Consider Pierre Cheval-Gatinois. In 1980, Pierre and his wife Marie took over their family's 17-acre Grand Cru vineyard in the Vallée de Marne, where their ancestors had grown grapes since 1696. The family had always made some of its own wine, but sold most of its grapes to nearby *grande marques* like Bollinger. When Pierre took over, he began bottling more of his own wine, selling fewer grapes each year. Today, the estate is run by Pierre's son Louis. While he still sells about half his grapes, he produces 36,000 bottles annually for the global marketplace.

Cheval-Gatinois began scaling back on outward-bound grape sales as a financial hedge. "It's better not to put all your eggs in one basket," Pierre told a *New York Times* reporter in 1989. He no doubt was also enticed by surging demand—and thus surging prices—for champagne. Other entrepreneurial growers made similar moves in the mid-1980s.

The competition upset the region's largest producers. As Patrick Baseden, sales director at Veuve Clicquot, told that same *New York Times* reporter in 1989, "The growers who produce champagne are not making the highest and best use of the industry's raw material."

Fighting words, to be sure. And in 1990, growers and producers couldn't settle on

The next generation at Champagne Gatinois: Louis Cheal-Gatinois, son of the late Pierre Cheval-Gatinois.

a fixed price for grapes as mandated by the *Échelle des Crus*. As a result, the prestigious CIVC was forced to abandon universal price controls and go to free-market pricing.

Most producers continued to pay by weight, though, maintaining their one-size-fits-all focus on the village where the grapes were grown. Totals seemed to count more than the quality and uniqueness of the grapes. In 1992, famously, two young growers—Pierre Larmandier and Jérôme Prévost—came out against tradition and urged large producers to begin paying for grapes based on quality. When their proposal was dismissed out of hand, the two were inspired to begin producing their own wines. Today, Larmandier and Prévost are two of Champagne's top grower-producers.

A LONG HISTORY OF ARTISANAL WINE

Pascal Agrapart of Champagne Agrapart et Fils.

The emergence of new grower-producers in the 1980s didn't do much to impact the global marketplace; big traditional names continued to dominate exports. Throughout the 1980s and 1990s, Champagne's established *négociants* produced 70 percent of the world's champagne but accounted for more than 95 percent of sales outside

France. Within France, consumers had long been knowledgeable about the region's artisanal offerings.

For generations, it was common for Champagne's growers to make small amounts of wine for their own consumption. Consider Chartogne-Taillet, now one of the world's most popular grower-producers. The Chartogne family first purchased land in Champagne in the 1870s—and has likely been producing wine since around that time. Or look at Gaston Chiquet, which has been growing grapes in Champagne since the 1740s and producing its own wines since 1919.

Alexander Chartogne.

In the latter half of the 20th century, a group of these growers decided to make their best wines available to the broader public. Such a move was possible because there was a new and growing group of passionate, knowledgeable wine drinkers. The region's small but elite growers saw an opportunity. They believed the champagne flowing from grandes marques like Veuve Clicquot and Moët paled in comparison to their own wines, and it was time to give serious wine drinkers access to what they and their families had been making and enjoying themselves for generations.

They came together to form the *Club de Viticulteurs Champenois*, an exclusive group of the region's small growers devoted to producing high quality wines. Even today, the "Special Club" champagnes these producers offer are made to demanding specifications. For instance, bottles can only come from each grower's best years and must pass the group's rigorous tasting process. These standards remain so exacting that just 29 growers have earned entry into the club, which today is known as the *Club Trésors*.

The existence of these connoisseur champagnes, derived from old-vine grapes and made to the highest standards of quality, first came to the attention of an American wine importer in the 1980s. It was a discovery long overdue, since these families that had tended the land in Champagne for decades—and in some cases, centuries—and produced products completely outside the dazzle of "commercial" champagne.

HOW TO BUY CHAMPAGNE

If you walk into a good wine shop and watch the savviest consumers, you'll see them flipping bottles over to check the import label. In the United States, these shoppers know that they can rely on importers like Kermit Lynch, Terry Theise, Louis/Dressner, and others to bring in top champagne. In the United Kingdom, they're looking for importers like Vine Trail. These consumers are looking for champagne from grower-producers—small vignerons who grow their own grapes and make their own wine.

Identifying grower champagne is easy. On the label, just look for a numerical code prefixed by two letters. If those two letters are "RM," it's a récoltant-manipulant, or grower-producer. If those two letters are "NM," it's a *négociant-manipulant*, or merchant-producer. Big houses like Moët & Chandon, Veuve Clicquot, and G. H. Mumm will carry the NM moniker.

Some widely available grower champagnes worth finding:
- Pierre Peters
- Chartogne-Taillet
- Pierre Gimonnet
- Paul Bara
- J. Lassalle
- Vilmart & Cie

AMERICA CHANGES THE GLOBAL MARKETPLACE

That such growers remained relatively anonymous for so long is understandable. Most of the region's nearly 20,000 growers own fewer than five acres, and of those, only about 4,500 can be said to make wine. Even then, only about 2,000 actually produce wine themselves. The rest send their grapes to local cooperatives where "their" champagne is made for them.

Moreover, small growers producing basically for local or private consumption just don't have the name recognition enjoyed by high-end brands like Pol Roger. They didn't have advertising agencies—an expensive undertaking—pushing their wines in markets outside the region. It's no wonder that big producers who for decades invested millions saw their names continue to monopolize the global champagne market.

There is something obviously and instinctively appealing about buying from a small grower. Plus, many represent a good value, as they don't have high marketing expenses or bureaucratic overhead. But small farming doesn't always result in superior output. Some crops, even though worked by a great winemaker, are better off in blends. Exceptional grapes are easily ruined by an inexperienced winemaker.

Champagne's biggest producers, many of which have more than 200 years of experience, strive to deliver a consistent experience to consumers each year. And the current offerings from many of them are better than ever before.

Some favorites include:

- Louis Roederer
- Jacquesson
- Pol Roger
- Ruinart
- Taittinger
- Bollinger

Purchasing champagne can be intimidating. Top shops and restaurants have dozens of choices. All are pricey, but not all are delicious. So don't ever hesitate to ask for advice. Most merchants and sommeliers are keen to help patrons find the perfect wine, regardless of the price. They are also interested in introducing new finds that will impress their customers.

Of course, once consumers know that some of the world's finest champagnes don't come from the big names, it becomes a huge adventure to start trying out small grower wines that truly reflect the villages and vineyards in which the grapes actually ripen.

Photo by Luisa Bonachea.

The story of this change in tastes is a fascinating one. More than three decades ago, a writer and musician named Kermit Lynch started to recognize small growers. And in the process, he showed Americans that there was more to champagne than just the name on the bottle.

With a $5,000 loan from his girlfriend, Kermit Lynch launched an eponymous wine shop in 1972. Soon after opening in Albany, California, Lynch became a distributor and importer as well, relocating to Berkeley in the early 1980s.

Today, Lynch is credited with initiating an American wine revolution by educating consumers about the virtues of traditional wines—artisanal outputs, produced with minimal intervention, that express a sense of place. With his 1988 book *Adventures on the Wine Route*, he established himself as one of the nation's premiere wine experts, and almost single-handedly changed the way American wine lovers experience wine. Lynch's taste was so highly regarded, in fact, that his "stamp of approval" for Italian and French wines became an unimpeachable sign of excellence among American wine drinkers. Even today, if a wine is in Lynch's portfolio, you can be sure that is interesting and well-made.

Importer Kermit Lynch. Photo by Judy Dater.

It's hardly surprising, then, that Lynch played an outsized role in overturning clichés about champagne.

In 1981, Lynch made history by introducing a true grower champagne to the United States. The wine came from J. Lassalle, a family-owned estate in Chigny-Les-Roses, a small village on the Montagne de Reims. Established in 1942, J. Lassalle had long been recognized among locals and European connoisseurs for its rigorous standards of quality as well as the subtlety and elegance of its wines.

Chantal Decelle-Lassalle of Champagne J. Lassalle.

Before long, Lynch added another grower—Paul Bara—offering to his portfolio. A native of Bouzy in Montagne de Reims, Bara is still considered by many as the town's greatest producer.

Lynch's portfolio was still chiefly recognized for his selection of red wines from France and Italy. But almost as a byproduct of bringing both of these wines to the United States, he gave Americans their first taste of the possibilities of grower champagne.

One of the oenophiles who tasted those wines was importer Terry Theise, who was quickly gaining a reputation for introducing German and Austrian wines to Americans. While working as a salesman for Washington, DC-based wholesaler in the mid-1980s, he

Chantale Bara of Champagne Paul Bara.

convinced his employers to send him to Germany. The trip, he promised, would help double the company's sales of German wines, which he believed had been misunderstood and wrongly ignored by the American market. Keep in mind that, at this time, most Americans didn't know Riesling from wrestling.

It was during this trip that Theise wrote the first of what would become an annual set of catalogues on German and Austrian wines. His colorfully written essays on local wines came out at first as photocopied pamphlets. In time, however, they became an institution among wine drinkers, establishing not only Theise's own reputation, but making the wines he specialized in— small-production, focused wines of terroir—accessible to an American audience.

His interest in champagne came years later. In 1996, Theise traveled to France in search of champagne for his personal cellar. He met with dozens of producers, and what he found surprised him. Although one wouldn't know it from the studiously consistent offerings churned out each year after year by the big houses, champagne,

Importer Terry Theise. Photo by Anna Stöcher.

he realized, could be as unique and reflective of place, weather, and year as any wine from Burgundy or the Mosel. By the end of his journey, he was determined to add champagne to his import portfolio.

By this time, Theise had become respected as a passionate and persuasive evangelist for great wine. As he had done with German and Austrian wines, he was soon producing an annual catalogue for champagne, extoling the value and virtue of the grower champagnes he encountered. "You should drink 'farmer fizz' if you'd rather buy champagne from a farmer than a factory" became a kind of motto.

If Lynch gets credit for bringing these wines to America, it was Theise who made clear to serious wine drinkers that grower champagne warranted not just appreciation, but religious devotion. A consummate salesman, he praised these wines with an enthusiasm and charisma that made many Americans stand up and take notice.

It wasn't long before oenophiles across America began developing a taste for grower champagne. Other top American wine importers,

READING A CHAMPAGNE LABEL

Champagne producers pack a lot of information onto their labels.

There are exceptions to the region's official rules, but generally speaking, producers must include the brand name, the alcohol content, the bottle's volume, the words "France" and "Champagne," the town of production, and the level of sweetness. The official producer type is also listed, identifiable by two letters immediately before a numerical code. The codes are as follows:

NM: This designation, which stands for *négociant-manipulant*, or merchant-producer, is reserved for those who buy more than 6 percent of their fruit. Big houses like Moët & Chandon and Veuve Clicquot carry this moniker, but so do many much smaller houses. Indeed, one top grower-producer, Emmanuel Lassaigne, recently registered as a *négociant* in order to supplement his production with some fruit from his neighbors.

CM: This designation, which stands for *cooperative-manipulant*, is reserved for cooperatives where many growers join together to share resources and produce wine under a single brand. The best-known CM is Nicolas Feuillate, which is actually comprised of 82 cooperatives sourcing from about 5,000 vineyards. Most cooperatives are much smaller.

RM: This designation, which stands for *récoltant-manipulant*, or grower-producer, is reserved for those who rely on estate fruit for 95 percent or more of their production. Colloquially, these are called "grower champagnes."

SR: This designation, which stands for *société de récoltants*, or union of growers, is reserved for those who pool resources to make wine under one or several labels. Pascal Doquet, one of the top grower-producers in the Côte des Blancs, offers an example. Doquet began working at his parents' estate in 1982 and took over the property in 1995. When his parents retired, they divided their land among their children. Doquet, who had established his own brand, was thus drawing grapes from various siblings. Since the land wasn't all his, he registered as an SR.

MA: This designation, which stands for *marque d'acheteur*, or buyer's brand, is reserved for those that sell champagne as their own even though they didn't produce it themselves. Kirkland Signature, the champagne sold by Costco, is an example. In the United Kingdom, Tesco's champagne offers another example.

RC: This designation stands for *récoltant-coopérateur*, or grower-cooperator. This classification is used when a cooperative handles the winemaking for an individual grower who sells the resulting wine under his own brand.

ND: This designation, which stands for *négociant-distributeur*, or merchant-distributor, is reserved for wine merchants that purchase finished champagne to label and distribute as their own. An obscure classification, these wines should almost always be avoided.

like Joe Dressner and Doug Polaner, were soon seeking out previously obscure champagnes for their own portfolios. The fascination with grower champagne quickly spread. In Britain, importer Nick Brookes, the founder of Vine Trail, introduced a number of top growers to the market. In Asia, too, growers gained attention.

After decades of being relegated to wedding toasts, New Year's parties, and blowout celebrations, champagne was finally being recognized for what it was: a wine capable of great quality, nuance, and depth. A new wine world was discovered by wine enthusiasts, experienced and aspiring alike. This world had been flourishing for centuries in Champagne itself, but went virtually unnoticed abroad.

THE TERROIRIST TRIUMPH

Lynch and Theise might have brought grower wine to the attention of wine

Anselme Selosse.

drinkers outside France. But they merely found and publicized something that was waiting to be discovered. When it comes to understanding the evolution of how small growers produce champagne—and the ways in which they continue to push boundaries and deliver surprising experiences—the story would be incomplete without mention of Anselme Selosse.

Although raised in Champagne, by the time Selosse took over his father's estate in 1974, his winemaking philosophy was more than a little foreign. He had spent much of his early winemaking career in Burgundy, where he was inspired by the legendary chardonnay *vignerons* at Domaine Coche-Dury, Domaine Leflaive, and Domaine des Comtes Lafon. This experience, together with a brief detour to Spain to work in Rioja, left Selosse with a deep appreciation for the myriad ways in which wines reflect the land from which their grapes originate.

These were, of course, the days before terroir became an industry cliché. In Champagne, consistency was still king. The goal of most producers, large and small alike, was the creation of blends that delivered a consistent experience year after year. By turning his attention to the land, Selosse represented a break from tradition—innovations that resulted in some of the most distinctive wines ever made in Champagne.

This focus on the land underlays Selosse's obsession with identifying the most natural way of doing things. A dedication to nature might seem obvious for anyone living in a wine region, but in Champagne, the historic separation between grape growers and winemakers prevented this mentality from taking root.

Selosse's Les Carrelles vineyard, in the background, lies adjacent to a chalk wall in Le Mesnil-sur-Oger.

Selosse took paths that turned away from tradition. He relied on indigenous yeasts to start fermentation. This was common in Burgundy but quite unusual in Champagne. He refused to add sugar to his wines prior to fermentation, even though many producers in the region rely on this tactic—called *chaptalization*—to spike alcohol content. And he worked to avoid sulfur and other additives that might compromise the unique character of his grapes.

To be sure, Selosse gave due respect to many old ways of doing things. This is most evident in his creation of a solera system—a process most commonly used for storing and ageing sherry—that enabled him to produce a blend that removed vintage variation. His use of such a system is both a nod to tradition and a revolutionary innovation.

Selosse's solera also reinforces the fact that champagne is as much about process as it is terroir. While many of today's top growers advertise their hands-off approach to production, it's impossible to remove the human element entirely. Vignerons must make decisions about catalyzing secondary fermentation, the time and frequency of disgorgement, and whether or not to sweeten their wines. Like port, sherry, and many other classic wines, champagne depends on human intervention.

It's difficult to understate the significance of Selosse's approach. More than anyone else, he helped demonstrate that terroir wines from Champagne are in the same league with some of the greatest wines in the world.

The Selosse solera.

Before Selosse, reds and whites were known as wines with depth and variation. But when it came to champagne, only prestige cuvées from big producers were worthy of adulation. Not anymore.

Today, Selosse's wines are some of the most sought-after—and expensive—on the market. The demand is so great, in fact, that in 2013, burglars orchestrated a sophisticated robbery of his cellar, making off with some 300 cases worth about $350,000. And his wines remain incredibly hard to come by. In fact, up until 2007 when the California-based Rare Wine Company began importing his wines, it was nearly impossible to find a bottle anywhere in the United States.

Selosse has also changed the way growers old and young ply their trade. Inspired by Selosse, a new generation of small producers have emerged who are taking his painstaking techniques to levels that might seem excessive even by Selosse's standards. This is evident in the proliferation of single-vintage, single-vineyard, single variety wines with little or no *dosage*, such as those from Jérôme Prévost, Cedric Bouchard, and Ulysse Collin. Serious oenophiles are obsessed with these offerings. Bouchard noted, in 2013, that if it weren't for Selosse, many of today's growers might have never gained the confidence to make their own wine.

Of course, single expression champagnes had been tried before.

TO SWEETEN OR NOT?

Many of today's hottest growers bottle their wines without adding any sweetness. These zero-dosage offerings represent less than 1.5 percent of all champagne sold, but many trendsetting sommeliers and retailers have become obsessed with such wines. The vignerons they adore no doubt believe that by leaving their wines alone, they're offering more transparent expressions of terroir.

There's much to be said for this philosophy. After all, the essence of every great champagne is found in the *vin clair*, or the still wine that's created before secondary fermentation. If bubbles are an accessory, as many top vignerons contend, then surely a dollop of sweetness added just before final corking is, well, dishonest.

Hogwash. Great grapes in the hands of a great winemaker don't necessarily need anything added. But plenty of champagne is too acidic to enjoy without any added dosage. Furthermore, there's ample evidence to suggest that, like Riesling, champagne ages more gracefully when it's at least a little bit sweet.

As with all wines, it comes down to balance. Neither the acid nor sweetness should stick out. Wines with *and* without dosage can honestly reflect terroir and provide enjoyment.

At the turn of the 20th century, Eugène-Aimé Salon sought to prove that the best champagne would be singular, coming from a single village, a single grape variety, and a single vintage. In 1935, Philipponnat took this concept one step further by making a vintage-declared wine from his Clos des Goisses vineyard.

View from atop the Clos des Goisses.

Krug's barrel room. Photo by Luisa Bonachea.

Other producers had followed. The Cattiers, who have been vineyard owners since 1763—and are best known today for producing Jay Z's favorite cuvée, Armand de Brignac—started producing a single-parcel, yet multi-vintage wine in 1951. Krug began producing a single-vineyard, single-vintage *blanc de blancs* in 1979 and a single-vineyard, single-vintage *blanc de noirs* in 1995. But until quite recently, such wines were anomalies.

Today, the new crop of single-expression champagnes flow from a philosophy of wine—and life—that can be traced back directly to Selosse. They are not only derived from a new respect for the earth, they stand as some of the most distinctive champagnes ever created. A new and exciting future for Champagne and the champagnes that come from its vineyards begins with the Selosse concept of terroir.

The Selosse effect is not limited to small family farms. Even established growers have begun to embrace singularity. Didier Gimonnet, a chardonnay master whose family has been making wines in the region since the 1930s, produced a trio of Special Club offerings in 2012 intended to showcase the distinct terroirs of his top parcels.

Selosse's vision is taking Champagne in a new direction—one that simultaneously reflects the region's rich history, while unlocking possibilities that traditional houses had never considered.

A RISING TIDE

The surging popularity of grower champagne has been extraordinary. In 1997, when Theise started bringing champagne to the United States, there were just 33 grower-producers in the US market. By the end of 2015, there were almost 300.

This is not to say that the big names don't continue to dominate America's champagne market—Veuve Clicquot and Moët & Chandon together account for 60 percent of US sales—but premium grower champagnes are gaining a small but increasing market share. In 1998, just 163,000 bottles of grower champagne were shipped to the United States, accounting for 1.3 percent of the market. By 2014, that number had jumped to 955,000, accounting for more than 5 percent of US champagne sales. Every American import company now wants a grower— or several—in its portfolio.

Pierre Larmandier of Champagne Larmandier-Bernier.

The marketing problem is to make consumers aware of their new options when they research a wine online, or pick a bottle off a store shelf. And, as ever, pricing strategies are critical, especially since all true champagne leaves the gate as a high-end, premium priced product.

Given decent economic weather, the market for grower champagne will undoubtedly continue to rise as the word gets out, and Americans slowly develop a nose for choosing wine. Champagne's growers typically are tied to long-term supply contracts with large houses. In view of the success of the new small-scale wines, many growers—especially young ones—are expected to move to independent production as their contracts expire. There is plenty of risk—and plenty of work—in changing Champagne's traditional market, but surging demand and associated profits may make the transition a little easier.

No doubt the big names will find clever ways to get in the terroir-driven business, too.

Making wine in small, boutique wineries is tricky, especially in startups. There is much to learn. It's no surprise that simply "farming small" doesn't always result in superior output. Where skills and dedication are already at hand, some new offerings

Tending to vines in Ambonnay.

The press at Champagne Marie Courtin.

can be fantastic. But others, for whatever reason, are just middling, or worse. Vineyards produce an astonishing spectrum of grapes. Good, bad, indifferent. Some crops, even though worked by a great winemaker, are better off in blends. Exceptional grapes are easily ruined by an inexperienced winemaker. But as the concept advances across Champagne, there is little doubt that the base of knowledge will increase, and overall quality will rise.

Already, the rising popularity of growers—and their commitment to nature—has had an impact across the board in Champagne. Soil conservation is just one example. While many vineyards remain polluted with trash and the chemicals used for decades, Champagne's soils, overall, are healthier than they've been in generations. Many younger growers—even the ones who continue to sell grapes, and thus can't taste the results of their efforts—are insisting on more environmentally sound approaches to vineyard management.

Laurent Vauversin, still several years shy of 30, is slowly taking over his father's responsibilities at his family's 8-acre estate in the Grand Cru village of Oger. Vauversin's family has been growing grapes since 1640 and producing wine commercially since 1930. Vauversin's father was an environmental pioneer—he didn't use weed killers or any systemic chemical treatments—and today, the whole property is now certified organic. In the cellar, Vauversin plans to eliminate filtration, industrial yeast, and chemical additives.

"I'm looking for a champagne that awakens the senses," he recently explained, "and I feel that is not found in industrial wines and chemical viticulture."

Laurent Vauversin.

Of course, the overwhelming majority of Champagne's grapes are still purchased by the region's large *négociants*, but even they are beginning to insist on sustainable viticulture practices from their contract growers. It may simply be good business—in both the short and long term—to limit the use of synthetic chemicals, but data shows that the Champagne region is moving to organic farming faster than any other area in France. Pesticide use, for instance, has dropped dramatically.

Négociant Louis Roederer basically grows its own grapes. The firm's 600 acres of vineyards provide enough fruit for nearly 70 percent of its production. And 30 percent of its acreage is already farmed biodynamically—a form of alternative agriculture derived from a series of lectures given in the 1920s by philosopher Rudolf Steiner. The remaining acres almost all now meet strict organic standards.

Jean Herve Chiquet of Jacquesson. Photo by Luisa Bonachea.

Another big producer, Jacquesson, draws about 80 percent of its grapes from its own vineyards. In these holdings—and in the vineyards from which additional fruit is purchased—Jacquesson limits the use of fertilizers and relies mostly on organic treatments for pest control.

In 2015, Philipponnat began offering bonuses to growers who could document sustainable vineyard practices. Roederer and Philipponnat are also two of the few houses that plough some of their vineyards with horses—a nostalgic undertaking, of course, and one they claim is better for both the environment, because of reduced emissions, and the grapes, since tractors compact soil more than horses.

UNDERSTANDING ORGANIC, BIODYNAMIC, AND SUSTAINABLE VITICULTURE

Grape growers across the world face a host of obstacles. Weather events like early-season frosts and late-season rains can seriously damage vines. Pests and grape diseases can wipe out entire crops.

Chemical fertilizers, insecticides, and herbicides were developed in the second half of the 20th century to help growers meet these challenges. But in recent years, worried about the impact of these treatments on human health and the environment, many growers have moved away from chemicals and toward more natural techniques.

The results of different farming practices in Champagne.

These growers often advertise their farming methods as organic, biodynamic, or sustainable. Colloquially, these words are sometimes used interchangeably. But they have very specific meanings.

Organic viticulture prohibits the use of synthetic fertilizers, herbicides, and pesticides. Certain natural preparations, like copper sulfates, are allowed to fight rot and mildew, and most growers plant specific cover crops to attract beneficial insects that feast on grapevine pests. If a vineyard is certified as organic, it is typically inspected once each year. Many winemakers who practice organic viticulture aren't certified. (Note that while many grapes are now grown organically, very few wines are labeled as organic. The reason? In the United States, only wines without added sulfur dioxide can be labeled as organic. Since SO_2 helps prevent spoilage, organic wine is extremely rare.

Biodynamic viticulture is a form of alternative agriculture and winemaking derived from a series of lectures given in 1924 by philosopher Rudolf Steiner. In their vineyards, biodynamic adherents follow the lunar calendar, apply specially prepared composts, and farm organically. In their cellars, biodynamic adherents are prohibited from inoculating their wines with cultured yeast and utilizing any synthetics. The word "biodynamic" is protected under trademark law, so producers that use the word on their wine labels must be certified by Demeter, a nonprofit group.

Sustainable viticulture has no formal definition. Producers that advertise themselves as sustainable typically eschew synthetic fertilizers, herbicides, and pesticides but have the flexibility to use such treatments if needed. Oftentimes, sustainable producers also strive to conserve energy and water and rely on renewable resources when possible.

Today, as you travel across landscape, it's clear that many of the traditional names are adopting the mentality of the new generation—and certainly share the same commitment to soil and vine conservation and transparency.

There are also new dynamics as new players—with new ideas—enter the

Horses in the vineyards of Champagne Georges Laval. Photo courtesy of Champagne Georges Laval.

business. As *négociants* act more like growers, some growers are actually becoming *négociants*. In 2013, two of Champagne's most exciting young

TRANSPARENCY AND DISGORGEMENT DATES

Consumers everywhere are beginning to value sourcing and demand transparency. Logic dictates that if consumers are going to seek out cage-free eggs and free-range chicken, they'll also seek out wine from vintners who are thoughtful and transparent about production.

Champagne is responding. An increasing number of producers have started providing more detailed information about their wines, like the base vintages of non-vintage cuvées, the breakdown of grape varieties, the dosage, and the disgorgement date.

This is a welcome change. Big houses may wax poetic about the art of blending and contend that year after year, they offer consumers a consistent experience. But with non-vintage offerings at most houses, 85 to 90 percent of the base wine comes from a single vintage—and this makes a huge impact on the quality of the resulting wine.

The interaction between a sparkling wine and the dead yeast that sits inside the bottle prior to disgorgement also has a huge impact on aroma and flavor. Even if the underlying wines are identical, bottles disgorged at different times taste different. At big houses, especially, most offerings— whether non-vintage or vintage—will have several different disgorgement dates, mostly because the longer a wine sits on its lees, the fresher it will typically taste.

On the back label of its non-vintage offerings, Krug now provides a code which, when entered online or via a mobile app, offers detailed information about base wines, harvest conditions for those wines, the disgorgement date, and more. Taittinger offers something similar.

Philipponnat lists all this information and more on the back of each bottle, sharing the disgorgement date, the variety breakdown, details on barrel maturation, and dosage.

These producers aren't alone. Small growers, especially, are packing their labels with similar details. But the movement hasn't been without controversy.

Champagne's two biggest houses, Moët & Chandon and Veuve Clicquot, refuse to offer much of anything on their labels.

Ruinart, one of Champagne's most historic houses, has spoken out against publishing disgorgement dates on non-vintage champagne. The company believes that such information could be misinterpreted by consumers who don't understand what "disgorgement" means. While this may be true, the consumers who can't define disgorgement surely won't pay attention to a back label. Plus, producers could always offer such information through a code, like Krug's, that can only be unlocked with some effort.

producers, Raphaël and Vincent Bérêche—who took charge of their family's 24-acre estate in 2004—launched a *négociant* business to produce champagne from purchased grapes. Similarly, Emmanuel Lassaigne, a rising star who took over his family's 12-acre vineyard and cellar in 1999, recently registered as a *négociant*. He now supplements his production with about 2.5 acres worth of fruit from neighboring vineyards where he has total control.

INFINITE DISCOVERIES

For a region that has been making wine for 1500 years, it's remarkable just how much has changed, and how much change is yet to come.

In just the last decade alone, grower champagne has change from a local wine consumed by growers themselves to one of the wine world's most in-demand products. Whereas champagne was, until very recently, respected for its consistency, champagne conversations now revolve around the almost infinite depth and variation of terroir.

FUTURE EXPANSION OF CHAMPAGNE

Champagne production continues to grow steadily. But the viticultural boundaries of the region haven't grown since they were legally defined in 1927.

The INAO began exploring ways to expand the region in 2003, and in 2008, it approved a plan to bring vineyards from 40 additional villages to Champagne. Possible vineyard sites are still being reviewed by French officials, though, so plantings likely won't begin until 2019 at the earliest.

Aurélien Suenen took charge of his family estate in 2009. Photo by Luisa Bonachea.

But the competing visions of champagne can coexist and even complement each other. There are those like Gimonnet, who continue to perfect classic blending techniques, and those like Selosse, who blends to unearth new reflections of the land beneath the grapes. And there are big *négociants* like Louis Roederer that are making some of the most compelling mass-market wines in the world. All are working to reveal champagne as a living, breathing, always changing wine of terroir.

And while Champagne's complex, surprising history continues to play out, serious wine drinkers everywhere are, for the first time, paying attention.

Hand labeling bottles at Champagne R.H. Coutier. Photo by Luisa Bonachea.

On January 12, 2007, one of the greatest violin players in the world set himself up as an unknown "busker" in a Washington, DC, metro station. Wearing jeans, a long-sleeved T-shirt, and a baseball cap, 39-year-old Joshua Bell pulled out his instrument—handcrafted by Antonio Stradivari in 1713 and purchased in 2003 for nearly $4 million—and proceeded to play six classical songs for rush-hour commuters.

The setting of Bell's 43-minute performance was of course unusual for a man who had been a child prodigy on the violin. By the time he was 14, young Joshua was performing as a soloist for the Philadelphia Orchestra. At 17, he made his first appearance at Carnegie Hall. He has performed three times as a guest soloist for the New York Philharmonic and currently serves as the music director of the Academy of St Martin in the Fields, arguably the world's most celebrated chamber orchestra.

More than 1,000 commuters came within earshot of Bell that morning, witnessing a world-class performance of some of the most demanding violin music ever composed, played on one of the finest instruments ever crafted. Yet among the mass of hurried metro riders, Bell went almost entirely unnoticed.

Commuters were in the presence of genius. They just didn't realize it.

What has any of this to do with Champagne? Quite a bit.

Even today, giant corporate producers like Moët & Chandon and Veuve Clicquot continue to dominate shelves and sales. Yet some of the world's finest champagnes are being produced by a small, unassuming group of growers ignored by the millions of consumers who continue to just buy what they know. When it comes to champagne, we're surrounded by Joshua-Bell brilliance. We just need to pay attention.

Of course, once it's apparent people don't have to get in line at Lincoln Center to hear great music, maybe we'll start noticing the genius in the metro station. Like Joshua Bell, the best champagne—virtuoso champagne—is right before our eyes, "hiding in plain sight." We just need to stop, listen, and savor the bubbly.

Part Two:
Digging Deeper in Champagne

Section One:
The Grande Marques

Photo by Luisa Bonachea

Champagne is France's northernmost winegrowing region.

Consequently, it's a relatively harsh climate. The average annual temperature is just 52 degrees; vines would struggle to ripen if that number were any lower. Even at the height of summer, Champagne is typically cool and damp after the sun goes down. The days are often overcast, too. On average, the region receives just 1,650 hours of sunshine each year. Burgundy, by contrast, sees more than 1,900 hours of sunshine annually; Bordeaux more than 2,050.

Rainfall, fortunately, is ideal. With the North Sea and English Channel to its northwest and the vast expanse of continental Europe to its east and south, Champagne sees steady but moderate precipitation all year round. But frost, hail, and extreme cold are a constant threat. Spring frosts can destroy new buds and interfere with flowering and fruit set; late-summer hailstorms can wipe out crops, and deep winter cold snaps can damage vines.

This rugged environment helps define Champagne. Thanks to the region's cool temperatures and cloudy skies, even slight variations in where and how vineyards are planted have a huge impact on grape maturation. Across the region, grapes ripen slowly, allowing concentration of flavor without reducing freshness.

Champagne's vinous identity also derives from its deep chalk soils. About 70 million years ago, the sea made at least 15 incursions and retreats into northeast France. About 40 million years later, massive earthquakes raised much of the region, breaking up the accumulated chalk and packing it with marine elements and an assortment of minerals.

Today, Champagne's 84,000 acres of vines are divided into four major winegrowing areas: Montagne de Reims; Vallée de la Marne; Côte des Blancs; and the Aube. In every area save the Aube, most vineyards sit on primeval sea deposits of chalk. In some vineyards, this chalk—part of the same great basin that forms the famed white cliffs of Dover—extends to a depth of 1,000 feet.

For growers, chalk offers benefits. The bright white color reflects sunlight, helping warm the vines during the day. Chalk is porous enough to prevent vines from being waterlogged during heavy rain, yet it can absorb up to 40 percent of its volume in water, producing a natural reservoir for dry spells.

Champagne producers certainly recognize that wines are influenced by climate, soil, elevation, and the very air. But historically, microenvironments were not well reflected in the champagne produced, since most champagnes were *blends*. Indeed, geography only mattered as an economic instrument; the region's 320 villages included 17 Grands Crus and 44 Premiers Crus under the *échelle des crus* pricing system. The big house blenders would select wines from different vineyards and different vintages to deliver a consistent experience to consumers each year.

This isn't a bad thing; there's much to be said for consistent elegance. But a system of wine production that buries local variations and hides brilliant outputs is certainly unique.

Bordeaux, on the other hand, is almost always approached from a geographical perspective; consumers know the differences between its left and right banks, and savvy drinkers can readily explain what distinguishes different appellations, like Pauillac and Pomerol. Micro-geography is also the defining concept of Burgundy; a scandal would erupt if a *négociant* in Burgundy began treating different vineyards and different vintages—even *Grand Crus*—merely as mixers for a superstar blend.

Terroir matters, of course, and today, endless conversations revolve around the almost infinite depth and variation of Champagne's various villages and vineyards, soils and microclimates. So the next four sections will explore Champagne's major growing areas and profile the top grower-producers within each.

But old ways persist. Whereas blending would be sacrilegious almost everywhere else, it's the way champagnes have been made for centuries. Champagne's *Grande Marques*, those large *négociants* that, broadly speaking, prioritize consistency over terroir, are profiled in this section.

CHAMPAGNE'S MAJOR GROWING REGIONS

Montagne de Reims: Known for rich, powerful, blended champagnes.

Vallée de la Marne: Known for fruity, easy-drinking Pinot Meunier.

Côte des Blancs: Known for elegant, zippy Chardonnay.

The Aube: Known for soft, easy-drinking Pinot Noir.

NOTABLE GRANDES MARQUES

Ayala
Billecart-Salmon
Bollinger
Delamotte / Salon
Deutz
Drappier
Duval-Leroy
Charles Heidsieck
Gosset
Henriot
Jacquesson
Krug

Laurent-Perrier
Moët & Chandon / Dom
   Pérignon
Perrier-Jouet
Philipponnat
Piper-Heidsieck
Pol Roger
Pommery
Louis Roederer
Ruinart
Taittinger
Veuve Clicquot

AYALA (N.M.)

Production: About 800,000 bottles annually.

The Champagne house Ayala has gone through many periods of change since the son of a Colombian diplomat first established it in 1860. Edmond de Ayala was born in Paris and worked at a small champagne producer in Aÿ before marrying and receiving as a dowry the d'Albrecht family's property in Aÿ, as well as vineyards in Aÿ and Mareuil-sur-Aÿ. One of the original Grandes Marques Champagne Houses, Ayala gained a sterling reputation before being destroyed by the Champagne riots in 1911. It was quickly rebuilt, and bought and sold multiple times in the mid-20th Century.

In 2000, the Frey Group purchased the house and former Perrier-Jouët president Thierry Budin took the reins. When the Bollinger family bought the house in 2005, the vineyards remained with Frey, so the house now purchases all of its grapes. Under this new ownership, president and general manager Hervé Augustin sought to reinvent this iconic house yet again.

Caroline Latrive, who had learned the ropes at Ayala since 2006 and boasts a National Oenology Diploma and a master's degree in Champagne oenology, was promoted to cellar master in 2011. In the past few years, Ayala has aimed for a fresher style, gaining new respect and acclaim with moves toward lower dosage and increased use of Chardonnay.

THE WINES

BRUT MAJEUR (NV)
Dosage: Brut
Price: $40

The house's flagship non-vintage wine is generally a blend of 40% Chardonnay, 40% Pinot Noir, and 20% Pinot Meunier. It's aged on its lees for three years.

BRUT NATURE (NV)
Dosage: Brut Nature
Price: $40

The same blend as the Brut Majeur, this wine ages on its lees for four years before being bottled without any dosage.

ROSÉ MAJEUR (NV)
Dosage: Brut
Price: $50

A blend of 50% Chardonnay, 40% Pinot Noir (including 6% still red wine), and 10% Pinot Meunier. It's aged on its lees for three years.

BLANC DE BLANCS (VINTAGE)
Dosage: Brut
Price: $70

This vintage-dated blanc de blancs is sourced from the Côte des Blancs Grand Crus of Chouilly, Avize, and Le Mesnil-sur-Oger. Only made in certain years, the wine is aged six years on the lees.

ROSÉ N°8 (N.V.)
Dosage: Brut
Price: $55

Made from Premier Crus and Grand Crus in the Montagne de Reims, this wine is composed of Chardonnay from Rilly-la-Montagne and Pinot Noir from Verzy, Aÿ, and Verzenay (including 5% still red wine). The N°8 refers to the eight years the wine spends on the lees.

PERLE D'AYALA (VINTAGE)
Dosage: Brut
Price: $115

The house's prestige cuvée is a blend of 80% Chardonnay and 20% Pinot Noir, sourced entirely from Grand Crus. During the second fermentation, the wines are sealed under cork (as opposed to crown cap) for eight years.

Ayala
2 Boulevard du Nord
51160 Aÿ
www.champagne-ayala.fr
Tel: (33) 3 26 55 15 44
contact@champagne-ayala.fr
Visits by appointment only.

BILLECART-SALMON (N.M.)

Production: About 1.7 million bottles annually.

This famous champagne house was launched in 1818, when Nicolas François Billecart and Elisabeth Salmon were married. The family's vineyard holdings were married then as well, and François decided to leave his law practice and take over the family wine estate.

Almost 200 years later, Billecart-Salmon stands as the oldest continuously family-owned and operated house in Champagne. Seventh-generation brothers François and Antoine Roland-Billecart currently manage the house.

Billecart-Salmon owns about 37 acres of vineyards in Aÿ, 27 of which are in the Vallée de la Marne in Damery, Aÿ, and Mareuil-sur-Aÿ. The remaining 10 acres are in the Côte des Blancs Grand Crus of Chouilly, Avize, and Le Mesnil-sur-Oger. Billecart-Salmon also leases about 125 acres of vineyards. Together, fruit from estate and leased vineyards provide for about 40 percent of its needs; the rest is purchased.

One of the distinctive aspects of Billecart-Salmon is its philosophy that an early harvest yields more elegant and delicate champagnes. Another is its unique practice of double-cold settling, which they have used since 1952. This process helps to eliminate wild yeasts and heavy elements without using enzymes or filtering.

THE WINES

RESERVE (NV)
Dosage: Brut
Price: $60

A blend of three vintages, this wine is comprised of 40% Pinot Meunier, 30% Pinot Noir, and 30% Chardonnay. It ages for three years prior to disgorgement.

ROSÉ (NV)
Dosage: Brut
Price: $90

First introduced in 1954, Billecart-Salmon was one of the first houses to offer a rosé. A rosé d'assemblage, just under 10 percent of the cuvée is comprised of still Pinot Noir from Mareuil. The blend is about 20% Pinot Meunier, 30% Pinot Noir, and 50% Chardonnay.

BLANC DE BLANCS GRAND CRU (NV)
Dosage: Brut
Price: $110

First produced in 1997, this blanc de blancs is sourced from the five Grand Crus of the Côte des Blancs: Avize, Chouilly, Cramant, Oger, and Mesnil-sur-Oger. It ages for four years prior to disgorgement.

SOUS BOIS (NV)
Dosage: Brut
Price: $80

Launched in 2009, this wine is a blend of 40% Chardonnay, 30% Pinot Noir, and 30% Meunier. Each variety is fermented and aged separately in neutral barriques before spending about five years on its lees.

EXTRA BRUT (NV)
Dosage: Extra Brut
Price: $65

A blend of 40% Pinot Meunier, 30% Pinot Noir, and 30% Chardonnay, this wine is made with 40% reserve wine and ages for four years prior to disgorgement.

Cuvée Nicolas Francois Billecart (Vintage)

Dosage: Brut

Price: $190

Created in 1964 as a tribute to Billecart-Salmon's co-founder, this vintage wine is a blend of 60% Pinot Noir and 40% Chardonnay. The wine is partially vinified in barriques, and the wine ages for about ten years prior to disgorgement.

Cuvée Elisabeth Salmon Rosé (Vintage)

Dosage: Brut

Price: $200

Created in 1988 as a tribute to co-founder Elisabeth Salmon, this rosé d'assemblage is comprised of equal parts Chardonnay and Pinot Noir. About 8 percent of the cuvée is still Pinot Noir from Mareuil-sur-Aÿ. It ages for about ten years prior to disgorgement.

Vintage (Vintage)

Dosage: Extra Brut

Price: $250

About 70% Mareuil-sur-Aÿ Pinot Noir and 30% Côte de Blancs Chardonnay, about 10% of this wine is vinified and aged in oak barrels. It ages for about eight years prior to disgorgement.

Le Clos Saint-Hilaire (Vintage)

Dosage: Brut

Price: $450

Sourced entirely from Clos Saint-Hilare, a walled, 2.5-acre vineyard in Mareuil-sur-Aÿ planted to Pinot Noir in 1964. The fruit from this site was originally intended to create still red wine for rosé. Today, it's farmed biodynamically and plowed with horses. It is vinified entirely in oak barrels, ages for about eight years prior to disgorgement, and receives no dosage. It debuted with the 1995 vintage.

Champagne Billecart-Salmon

40 Rue Carnot

51160 Mareuil-sur-Aÿ

www.champagne-billecart.fr

Tel: (+33) 3 26 52 60 22

billecart@champagne-billecart.fr

Visits by appointment only.

BOLLINGER (N.M.)

Production: About 2.5 million bottles annually.

Bollinger dates back to 1829, when Jacques Bollinger and Paul Renaudin founded Renaudin-Bollinger & Cie, a name that remained on labels until the 1960s. Jacques passed away in 1884, so his sons, Joseph and Georges, took over the business. That same year Queen Victoria granted the house a Royal Warrant, enabling it to provide champagne to the royal court.

Georges' son Jacques took over in 1918, and five years later, he married Emily Law de Lauriston Bourbers, better known as "Lily."

After Jacques died in 1941, Lily Bollinger took over the business and promptly began working to expand its size and influence. She purchased more vineyards across Champagne and traveled the world to promote her brand, gaining notoriety for many memorable sayings, such as "I drink [champagne] when I'm happy and when I'm sad. Sometimes I drink it when I'm alone. When I have company I consider it obligatory. I trifle with it if I'm not hungry and drink it when I am. Otherwise, I never touch it— unless I'm thirsty."

Upon her retirement in 1971, Bollinger's nephews, Claude d'Hautefeuille and Christian Bizot, took charge. Both are credited with developing the brand internationally and improving quality even further.

Today, the estate is supervised by Ghislain de Montgolfier, the great-great-grandson of Jacques Bollinger. Jérôme Philipon serves as managing director with Gilles Descôtes working as viticulturalist and winemaker.

Bollinger owns over 405 acres, which provide fruit for about two-thirds of its needs. Its holding include about 240 acres of Grand and Premier Cru Pinot Noir in the Montage de Reims, 94 acres of Grand and Premier Cru Chardonnay in the Côte des Blancs, and 74 acres in the Marne, the majority of which is planted to Pinot Meunier.

All Bollinger's champagnes, which are dominated by Pinot Noir, are vinified in oak. Notably, the house owns more than 3,000 barriques, with an average age of 50 years. Bollinger stores its reserve wines in magnums, which are typically aged for five to fifteen years before being used in blends.

Bollinger is also well known for its relationship with James Bond. This started on paper, in Ian Fleming's 1956 novel, *Diamonds are Forever*, but promptly leapt onscreen. Bollinger has been featured as Bond's champagne of choice in nearly every Bond film dating back to 1973.

THE WINES

SPECIAL CUVÉE (NV)
Dosage: Brut
Price: $60

This wine is a blend of 60% Pinot Noir, 25% Chardonnay, and 15% Pinot Meunier, of which over 85% are sourced from Grand and Premier Crus. About 10% of each year's release is comprised of reserve wines.

ROSÉ (NV)
Dosage: Brut
Price: $80

First released in 2007, Bollinger's rosé is a blend of 62% Pinot Noir, 24% Chardonnay, and 14% Pinot Meunier. A rosé d'assemblage, about 5 percent of the blend is comprised of still Pinot Noir from Verzenay.

La Grande Année (Vintage)

Dosage: Brut
Price: $125

Only produced in exceptional years, this wine is a blend of 70% Pinot Noir, mainly from Aÿ and Verzenay, and 30% Chardonnay from Avize, Chouilly, and Mesnil-sur-Oger. It spends five years on its lees under cork rather than the traditional crown cap.

La Grande Année Rosé (Vintage)

Dosage: Brut
Price: $200

Very similar to La Grande Année, this rosé d'assemblage includes still Pinot Noir from La Côte aux Enfants, a vineyard in Aÿ.

R.D. (Vintage)

Dosage: Extra Brut
Price: $250

R.D. stands for "recently disgorged"— and this wine is effectively the same as Grande Année, but with more time in bottle on its lees. Madame Bollinger was the driving force behind this cuvée, which was established in 1967.

Vielles Vignes Françaises (Vintage)

Dosage: Brut Nature
Price: $850

This zero-dosage champagne is made with Pinot Noir from two parcels of ungrafted vines in Aÿ: Chaudes Terres and Clos St-Jacques. First produced in 1969, this wine is aged for over 10 years in the bottle prior to disgorgement. Although "Vieille Vignes" is translated as "old vines," this wine is named for how the vines are trained, not the age of the rootstock. The oldest vines used in this cuvée are around 50 years old and they are replanted regularly.

Bollinger
16 Rue Jules Lobet
51160 Aÿ
www.champagne-bollinger.com
Tel: (33) 3 26 53 33 66
contact@champagne-bollinger.fr
Visits by appointment only.

DELAMOTTE / SALON (N.M.)

Production: About 700,000 bottles annually.

Delamotte is one of the oldest houses in Champagne, dating back to 1760, when François Delamotte founded the winery in Reims. But as the house focused more and more on Chardonnay grown in the chalky soils of the Côte des Blancs, François's son Alexandre resettled in Le Mesnil-sur-Oger. The house changed hands repeatedly over the next 200 years, at one point coming under the control of the Lanson family. In 1988, the firm was sold to the Laurent-Perrier group, the same entity that bought Salon (Delamotte's next-door neighbor) a few months later.

Aimé Salon founded Salon in Le Mesnil in 1911, and his first vintage was 1905, although the first vintage to be sold commercially was the 1921. He built his brand entirely on his stunning and singular blanc de blancs. When he died in 1943, his nephew took over the house.

Delamotte and Salon are now sister wineries that share headquarters in Le Mesnil, and both houses are controlled by Didier Depond. *Chef de cave* Michel Fauconnet took on the role of winemaker in 2004.

During the years Salon is not produced, the grapes from Salon's contracted growers are usually blended into Delamotte's non-vintage Brut or blanc de blancs. Delamotte owns just 15 acres of vineyards in Le Mesnil, Oger, and Cramant, so the firm sources grapes from a wide array of growers. All Delamotte and Salon wines are made in stainless steel only; no barrels are used. Delamotte wines go through malolactic fermentation, while Salon does not.

THE WINES

DELAMOTTE BRUT (NV)
Dosage: Brut
Price: $40

Generally a blend of 55% Chardonnay, 35% Pinot Noir, and 10% Pinot Meunier, Delamotte's entry-level Brut is aged on the lees for 30 to 36 months and has a dosage of 7 g/l.

BLANC DE BLANCS (NV)
Dosage: Brut
Price: $50

The fruit for this wine comes from the Grand Cru villages of Le Mesnil-sur-Oger, Oger, and Cramant. The wine includes 10% reserve wines and is aged about four years on its lees.

BLANC DE BLANC MILLÉSIMÉ (VINTAGE)
Dosage: Brut
Price: $60

This wine is made from all Grand Cru grapes grown in Le Mesnil, Oger, Avize, and Cramant. This vintage blanc de blancs sees about seven years of aging on the lees.

ROSÉ (NV)
Dosage: Brut
Price: $65

Made from a *saignée* of Pinot Noir, the grapes for Delamotte's rosé hail from the Grand Crus of Ambonnay, Bouzy, and Tours-sur-Marne. The Pinot is blended with about 20% Chardonnay from Le Mesnil-sur-Oger.

SALON CUVÉE S BLANC DE BLANCS (VINTAGE)
Dosage: Brut
Price: $425

One of the most heralded wines in all of Champagne, Salon is always made from 100% Chardonnay grown in the Grand Cru Mesnil-sur-Oger. The grapes come from a 2.5 acre parcel owned by Salon, and from some 20 other smaller parcels originally selected by founder Aimé Salon. The wine is only made in certain years, and 2004 was only the 39th vintage produced since the original release.

Delamotte/Salon
5-7 Rue de la Breche d'Oger
51190 Les Mesnil-sur-Oger
Phone: (+33) 3 26 57 51 65
champagne@salondelamotte.com
www.salondelamotte.com
No visits.

DEUTZ (N.M.)

Production: About 2.2 million bottles annually.

Deutz traces its roots back to 1838 when two wine merchants from Germany, William Deutz and Pierre-Hubert Geldermann, founded a champagne house in Aÿ. The business was passed down to their sons, René Deutz and Alfred Geldermann, who built the reputation of Deutz in foreign markets like England, Germany, and Russia.

By the time their son-in-laws, René Lallier and Charles Van Cassel, took over the company in 1906, Deutz had grown to one of the largest champagne houses, producing 600,000 bottles annually. But the first few decades of the 20th century took a toll on the company. By the time René Lallier's son Jean took over in 1938, production had dropped by more than 80 percent.

Jean worked tirelessly to grow sales, source more fruit, and modernize the winery. In 1972, Jean's son André took over as managing director, and began investing in wineries outside Champagne.

The estate changed hands again when in 1993 the Rouzaud family (which also own Louis Roederer) acquired the house. Deutz is still operated independently.

Today, Deutz sources from just over 600 acres of vines, 100 of which it owns. All wines are vinified in stainless steal, and many parcels are vinified separately. Most wines, but not all, go through malolactic fermentation.

THE WINES

CLASSIC (NV)
Dosage: Brut
Price: $50
Equal parts Chardonnay, Pinot Noir, and Pinot Meunier, this champagne typically includes 20-40 percent reserve wines.

ROSÉ (NV)
Dosage: Brut
Price: $60
A blend of 90% Pinot Noir and 10% Chardonnay, this rosé d'assemblage includes about 8% still Pinot Noir from old vines in Aÿ and Mareuil-sur-Aÿ.

Vintage (Vintage)
Dosage: Brut
Price: $65

Typically 65% Pinot Noir sourced from vineyards in Bouzy, Louvois, Vezernay, and Aÿ, 30% Chardonnay from Le Mesnil and Chouilly, and 5% Pinot Meunier from Pierry and Moussy. This wine ages for at least 3 years on its lees.

Vintage Rosé (Vintage)
Dosage: Brut
Price: $75

A blend of 80% Pinot Noir and 20% Chardonnay, this rosé d'assemblage includes about 8% still Pinot Noir from old vines in Aÿ and Mareuil-sur-Aÿ. It ages for 5 years on its lees.

Blanc de Blancs (Vintage)
Dosage: Brut
Price: $80

A blanc de blancs that typically has a blend of 45% Avize, 35% Le Mesnil-sur-Oger, 10% Villers-Marmery, with the rest split between Oger, Cramant, and Chouilly. It ages for 5 years on its lees.

Cuvée William Deutz (Vintage)
Dosage: Brut
Price: $140

A prestige cuvée first made by William Deutz in 1959, this wine is typically a blend of 60% Pinot Noir, 30% Chardonnay, and 10% Pinot Meunier. It ages for 5 years on its lees.

Amour de Deutz (Vintage)
Dosage: Brut
Price: $130

First introduced with the 1993 vintage, this blanc de blancs is sourced from the Grand Crus of Avize, Mesnil-sur-Oger, and Villers-Marmery. It ages for 7 years on its lees.

Amour de Deutz Rosé (Vintage)
Dosage: Brut
Price: $130

This wine is typically a blend of 55% Pinot Noir, sourced from the Grand Crus Aÿ, Verzenay, and Bouzy, and 45% Chardonnay, sourced from the Grand Crus of Avize, Chouilly, and Villers-Marmery. This rosé d'assemblage includes about 8% still Pinot Noir from old vines in Aÿ and Mareuil-sur-Aÿ. It ages for 7 years on its lees.

Champagne Deutz
16 rue Jeanson
51160 Aÿ
www.champagne-deutz.com
Tel: (+33) 3 26 56 94 00
france@champagne-deutz.com
No visits.

DRAPPIER (N.M.)

Production: About 1.5 million bottles annually.

This house traces its roots back to 1808, when Michel Drappier settled in Urville, where Cistercian monks had settled in the 12th century. Initially, the Drappier family sold its grapes to major champagne houses such as Piper-Heidsieck and Moët & Chandon, but by the early 20th century the family was producing and bottling its own champagne.

It was around this time, at the beginning of the 1930s, that Michel's grandson Georges Collot was the first to plant Pinot Noir in the Aube, a region that was widely planted with Gamay at the time.

Since 1979, Michel Drappier, who represents the seventh generation of the family, has been in charge of the domaine.

Drappier owns over 135 acres of vineyards in Urville and three of the communes in the Bar-sur-Aubois. It leases an additional 100 acres and also purchases some fruit. About 70 percent of its vineyards are planted with Pinot Noir. Drappier also cultivates Chardonnay and Pinot Meunier, which together make up 15 percent, as well as forgotten varieties such as Arbane, Petit Meslier, and Pinot Blanc. A strong focus is placed on organic and sustainable viticulture, as well as minimal use of sulfur in its wines.

The house's cellars are among the oldest and most extensive in Europe, dating back to 1152 when Saint Bernard, Cistercian monk and founder of Clairvaux Abbey, had them built. The Drappier family, whose house is in close proximity to these cellars, purchased them after World War II.

THE WINES

CARTE D'OR (NV)
Dosage: Brut
Price: $50

Launched in 1952, this cuvée is a blend of 75% Pinot Noir, 15% Chardonnay, and 10% Pinot Meunier. A small amount (5%) of the wines age in barrels for one year.

BLANC DE BLANCS SIGNATURE (NV)
Dosage: Brut
Price: $55

A blend of 95% Chardonnay and 5% Pinot Blanc, this wine spends 2-3 years on its lees before disgorgement.

BRUT NATURE (NV)
Dosage: Brut Nature
Price: $55

This 100% Pinot Noir ages on its lees for at least 30 months prior to disgorgement, where it's finished without dosage.

BRUT ROSÉ (NV)
Dosage: Brut
Price: $55

A saignée of Pinot Noir that receives its color from a 3-day maceration, this wine ages on its lees for 24-36 months prior to disgorgement.

Brut Nature Rosé (NV)

Dosage: Brut Nature

Price: $60

A saignée of Pinot Noir that receives its color from a 3-day maceration, this wine ages on its lees for 24-36 months prior to disgorgement, where it's finished without dosage.

Quattuor (NV)

Dosage: Brut

Price: $90

Equal parts chardonnay Arbanne, Petit Meslier, and Pinot Blanc, this wine is vinified entirely in steel to preserve freshness. The wine ages for three years prior to disgorgement.

Millésime Exception (Vintage)

Dosage: Brut

Price: $65

A blend of 65% Pinot Noir and 35% Chardonnay, about half this vintage champagne is vinified in neutral barrique, where it ages for a year. The wine ages on its lees for at least five years prior to disgorgement.

Charles de Gaulle (Vintage)

Dosage: Brut

Price: $75

A blend of 80% Pinot Noir and 20% Chardonnay, this vintage champagne ages *sur latte* for three years prior to disgorgement.

Grande Sendrée (Vintage)

Dosage: Brut

Price: $125

Sourced from a single vineyard planted more than 75 years ago, this champagne is a blend of 55% Pinot Noir and 45% Chardonnay. One-third of the wines are aged in oak barrels for 9 months, and they undergo natural malolactic. It spends more than 6 years on its lees before disgorgement.

Grande Sendrée Rosé (Vintage)

Dosage: Brut

Price: $125

Sourced from the same vineyard as the Grande Sendrée, this saignée of Pinot Noir (with about 5-10% Chardonnay) receives its color from a 3-day maceration. It ages for more than 6 years on its lees before disgorgement.

Champagne Drappier
Rue des Vignes
10200 Urville
www.champagne-drappier.com
Tel: (33) 3 25 27 40 15
info@champagne-drappier.com
Visits by appointment only.

DUVAL-LEROY (N.M.)

Production: About 4.5 million bottles annually.

The house of Duval-Leroy was founded in 1859 when Jules Duval, a vigneron from Vertus, and Edouard Leroy, a wine merchant from Villers-Franqueux, formed a business partnership.

To finalize their arrangement, the men arranged a wedding between Jules's son, Henri, and Edouard's daughter, Louise Eugénie. Their son, Raymond Duval-Leroy, would run the domaine for more than half the 20th century.

The domaine is still family owned, run today by Carol Duval-Leroy. Carol took over operations in 1991 after her husband, Jean Charles, died at just 39. Today, she leads the house with her three sons, Julien, Charles, and Louis.

Carol is one of the leading female voices in Champagne and has worked to expand and modernize the family business. She works closely with the *chef de cave*, Sandrine Logette-Jardin, who became the first woman to hold such a position in Champagne region when appointed in 2006.

Duval-Leroy owns about 490 acres of vineyards, which fulfill about a quarter of its needs. About 35 percent of its vineyards are in Premier Crus and Grand Crus, with holdings in Oger, Le Mesnil sur Oger, Avize, Ambonnay, Bouzy, and Verzennay. Many of the vineyards are devoted to Chardonnay, which is also the dominant grape in many of the cuvées.

The house farms sustainably and was also one of the first Champagne *négociants* to produce a cuvée entirely from organically grown grapes.

THE WINES

RESERVE (NV)
Dosage: Brut
Price: $45

Typically 60% Pinot Noir, 30% Pinot Meunier, and 10% Chardonnay, this wine is sourced from 15 different villages and contains about 30% reserve wine. It ages for three years on its lees before disgorgement.

PREMIER CRU (NV)
Dosage: Brut
Price: $65

A blend of 70% Chardonnay and 30% Pinot Noir, which are sourced from 80% premier and 20% Grand Crus, this wine spends three years on its lees before disgorgement.

ROSÉ PRESTIGE (NV)
Dosage: Brut
Price: $75

A saignée of Pinot Noir (with about 10% Chardonnay), this wine ages for three years on its lees before disgorgement.

BLANC DE BLANCS GRAND CRU (VINTAGE)
Dosage: Brut
Price: $90

Sourced from Grand Cru vineyards in the Côte des Blancs, this 100% Chardonnay ages for six years before disgorgement.

FEMME DE CHAMPAGNE (VINTAGE)
Dosage: Brut
Price: $200

The Chardonnay in this champagne, which comprises 95% of the blend, is sourced entirely from five vineyards: Mont-Aigu in Chouilly, Chapelle in Avize, Terre de Noël in Oger, and Chetillon and Aillerand in Le Mesnil sur Oger. All parcels are vinified separately in barrique. This wine ages for ten years on its lees before disgorgement.

Duval-Leroy

69, avenue de Bammental

51130 Vertus

www.duval-leroy.com

Tel: (33) 3 26 52 10 75

champagne@duval-leroy.com

Visits by appointment only.

CHARLES HEIDSIECK (N.M.)

Production: About 2 million bottles annually.

The Heidsieck name became prominent in Champagne in 1785, when Florens-Louis Heidsieck founded Heidsieck & Co. Three of his nephews would follow in his footsteps and work in the champagne industry: Christian Heidsieck, founder of what is now Piper-Heidsieck; Henri-Louis Walbaum, founder of what is now known as Heidsieck Co. & Monopole; and Charles-Henri Heidsieck, who assisted his uncle with marketing.

Charles-Henri's son, Charles Heidsieck, founded his own house in 1851 at the age of 29. Charles is known for being the first champagne merchant to travel to the United States in 1852, where he earned the nickname "Champagne Charlie."

In 1867, Charles purchased *crayères*, hand-dug, labyrinth-like chalk cellars built by the Romans in the 2nd century, to mature his champagnes. The 2000-year-old *crayères* are now a World Heritage site, and wines are still aged there today.

Charles Heidsieck has changed hands several times since then—first under the Henriot group, then Rémy Cointreau, who brought the Charles and Piper-Heidsieck houses back under one umbrella. The house is now owned by the French luxury firm, Société Européenne de Participations Industrielles. Charles Heidsieck and Piper-Heidsieck continue to maintain a close relationship, as well as shared winemaking facilities, though each operates as a separate company.

Today, Cyril Brun directs the cellar at Charles Heidsieck. The house shares about 160 acres of vines with Piper-Heidsieck, so relies on purchased fruit for the majority of its production.

THE WINES

BRUT RÉSERVE (NV)

Dosage: Brut

Price: $60

The key wine of the house, this champagne is a blend of 40% Pinot Noir, 40% Chardonnay, and 20% Pinot Meunier sourced from 60 selected villages. A total of 40% reserve wines are used in the blend, which have an average age of 10 years. It ages in the bottle for a minimum of 3 years before disgorgement.

ROSÉ RÉSERVE (NV)

Dosage: Brut

Price: $75

First released in 2008, about 7 percent of this rosé d'assemblage is comprised of still red wine. A blend of 40% Pinot Noir, 35% Chardonnay, and 25% Pinot Meunier, this wine ages in the bottle for a minimum of 3 years before disgorgement.

VINTAGE (VINTAGE)

Dosage: Brut

Price: $90

Sourced from Grand Cru and Premier Cru sites in Vertus, Oger, Avize, Cremant, Vidney, Mailly, and Ambonnay, this vintage champagne is a blend of 60% Pinot Noir and 40% Chardonnay. It ages in the bottle for 8 years before disgorgement.

VINTAGE ROSÉ (VINTAGE)

Dosage: Brut

Price: $100

This rosé is a blend of about 65% Pinot Noir sourced from Avenay, Louvois, Tauxières, Ambonnay, and Aÿ, and 35% Chardonnay sourced from Oger, Mesnil-sur-Oger, Cramant, and Vertus. A rosé d'assemblage, Pinot Noir from Bouzy, Ambonnay, Verzenay, Hautvillers, and Les Riceys is used to produce the still red wine that makes up about 8% of the blend. It ages in the bottle for 8 years before disgorgement.

BLANC DES MILLÉNAIRES (VINTAGE)

Dosage: Brut

Price: $200

A blanc de blancs sourced from Cramant, Le Mesnil, Oger, Avize, and Vertus. It ages in the bottle for 15 years before disgorgement.

Charles Heidsieck

12 Allée du Vignoble

51100 Reims

www.charlesheidsieck.com

Tel: (33) 3 26 84 43 00

charles@champagnes-ph-ch.com

Visits by appointment only.

GOSSET (N.M.)

Production: About 1.2 million bottles annually.

Gosset is one of the oldest companies, of any kind, in the world. In 1584, Pierre Gosset began making still red wine from his vineyard in Aÿ. When the region's wines started sparkling in the 18th century, the family shifted its focus to champagne.

The house stayed in the family for a remarkable 16 generations until the Renaud-Cointreau group, owners of the Cognac house Pierre Frapin, purchased it in 1994. *Chef de cave* Jean-Pierre Mareigner, who joined Gosset in 1983, continued to make the wines through the transition and still works for the house.

Gosset has only 2.5 acres of vineyards, so purchases most of the grapes it needs. The *négociant* sources from the same 45 villages each year—and mostly from the same growers—and vinifies the haul from each village separately. Malolactic is mostly blocked.

THE WINES

EXCELLENCE (NV)
Dosage: Brut
Price: $40

Sourced from vineyards in Aÿ, Chigny-les-Roses, Courmas, Cumières, Avize, Cuis, and Trépail, this wine is a blend of 45% Pinot Noir, 36% Chardonnay, and 19% Pinot Noir. This is the only Gosset wine that undergoes malolactic fermentation. It spends 30 months on its lees prior to disgorgement.

GRANDE RÉSERVE (NV)
Dosage: Brut
Price: $60

Sourced from Aÿ, Bouzy, Ambonnay, Le Mesnil-sur-Oger, and Villers-Marmery, this wine is a blend of 43% Chardonnay, 42% Pinot Noir, and 15% Pinot Meunier. It spends three years on its lees prior to disgorgement.

GRAND BLANC DE BLANCS (NV)
Dosage: Brut
Price: $80

First created in 2011, this blanc de blancs is sourced from vineyards in Avize, Chouilly, Cramant, Villers-Marmery, and Trépail. A 100% Chardonnay, it spends three years on its lees prior to disgorgement.

GRAND ROSÉ (NV)
Dosage: Brut
Price: $80

A blend of 58% Chardonnay and 42% Pinot Noir, this rosé is almost a vintage wine, with a very little amount of reserve wine added. Grapes are sourced from Avize, Chouilly, Villers-Marmery, Ambonnay, Verzenay, and Bouzy. The color comes from still Pinot Noir from Bouzy and Ambonnay, which comprises 9% of the cuvée. It ages for three years prior to disgorgement.

GRAND MILLÉSIME (VINTAGE)
Dosage: Brut
Price: $90

This vintage wine is a blend of 56% Pinot Noir sourced from Ambonnay, Avenay, Aÿ-Champagne, Chignyles-Roses, and Louvois, and 44% Chardonnay sourced from Avize, Cramant, Le Mesnil-sur-Oger, Trépail, and Vertus. It ages for eight years prior to disgorgement.

CELEBRIS (VINTAGE)
Dosage: Extra Brut
Price: $165

First produced in 1995, the Celebris cuvée is a blend of 52% Chardonnay and 48% Pinot Noir sourced from Aÿ, Bouzy, Verzy, Chouilly, and Cramant. It spends 10 years on its lees prior to disgorgement.

CELEBRIS ROSÉ (VINTAGE)
Dosage: Extra Brut
Price: $155

A blend of 59% Chardonnay and 41% Pinot Noir sourced from Avize, Chouilly, Cramant, Vertus, Aÿ-Champagne, and Bouzy. The color comes from still Pinot Noir from Bouzy and Ambonnay, which comprises 8% of the cuvée. It ages for six years prior to disgorgement.

PETITE DOUCEUR ROSÉ (NV)
Dosage: Extra Dry
Price: $80

The latest Gosset champagne, this wine is a blend of 60% Chardonnay and 40% Pinot Noir sourced from Bouzy, Ambonnay, Cumières, Avize, and Le Mesnil-sur-Oger. The color comes from still Pinot Noir from Bouzy and Ambonnay, which comprises 7% of the cuvée. It receives a dosage of 17g/L and ages for 3 years prior to disgorgement.

Gosset
1-3, rue Malakoff
51200 Épernay
info@champagne-gosset.com
Tel: (33) 3 26 56 99 56
www.champagne-gosset.com
No visits.

HENRIOT (N.M.)

Production: About 1.3 million bottles annually.

The Henriots settled in Champagne in 1640. That year, the family left Lorraine to work in Reims's bustling textile industry. As merchants, wine brokerage came naturally. So little by little, the family began acquiring vineyards.

About 150 years later, Nicolas Henriot—who owned many vineyard parcels and one of Champagne's top hotels—married Apolline Godinot, who owned vineyards in the Montagne de Reims.

When Nicolas died in 1808, Apolline founded a champagne house under the name "Veuve Henriot Aîné." Her wines were an immediate hit, becoming the favored champagne among royals in the Netherlands, Austria, and Hungary. The Henriot estate has been family owned and operated ever since.

In 1880, the Henriots further expanded their holdings when Paul Henriot married Marie Marguet, whose dowry was vineyard parcels in the Côte des Blancs. Today, seventh-generation descendent Thomas Henriot heads the house.

Henriot's 87 acres of vines—spread across the Vallée de la Marne, the Montagne de Reims, and the Côte des Blancs—fulfill about 20 percent of its needs. For the rest, Henriot relies on growers with whom it has long-term contracts.

In its cellars, Henriot vinifies all its parcels separately in stainless steel tanks. The house ages its wines longer than most; even its entry-level cuvées spend three years *sur latte*, and the wines typically rest in Henriot's cellars for nine months or more after disgorgement.

The Wines

Souverain (NV)
Dosage: Brut
Price: $45

This non-vintage blend is made up of 40% Chardonnay sourced mostly from the Côte des Blancs, and 60% Pinot Noir sourced mostly from the Montagne de Reims. It has 20% reserve wines added, and ages *sur latte* for about three years before riddling and disgorgement.

Blanc de Blancs (NV)
Dosage: Brut
Price: $60

Sourced mainly from the Côte des Blancs, this blanc de blancs includes about 30% reserve wine and ages *sur latte* for about four years.

Rosé (NV)
Dosage: Brut
Price: $60

Equal parts Chardonnay (mostly from the Côte des Blancs) and Pinot Noir (mostly from the Montagne de Reims), about 10% of this rosé d'assemblage is composed of still Pinot Noir from Mareuil-sur-Aÿ. It includes about 25% reserve wine. This ages *sur latte* for about three years.

Millésimé (Vintage)
Dosage: Brut
Price: $90

Equal parts Chardonnay and Pinot Noir, grapes for this wine are sourced from 15 villages, including the Grand Crus of Mailly, Verzy, Verzenay in the Montagne de Reims and Mesnil-sur-Oger, Avize, Chouilly in the Côte des Blancs. This ages for about six years before disgorgement.

Cuvée des Enchanteleurs (Vintage)
Dosage: Brut
Price: $200

Equal parts Chardonnay and Pinot Noir, grapes for this wine are sourced entirely from Grand Crus. The Chardonnay comes from Mesnil-sur-Oger, Avize, Chouilly in the Côte des Blancs, while the Pinot Noir comes from Mailly, Verzy, and Verzenay in the Montagne de Reims. This ages for 12 years before disgorgement.

Cuve 38
Dosage: Extra Brut
Price: $700 (Magnum Only)

In 1990, Henriot began building a perpetual blend composed entirely of Grand Cru Chardonnay. Outstanding wine has been added to the tank every year since, and in 2009, 1,000 magnums were drawn out. Those magnums are then aged five years before disgorgement, and then rested for another 12 months in the Henriot cellars. The first magnums were released in 2015, and another 1,000 magnums will be released each year.

Henriot
81 Rue Coquebert
51100 Reims
www.champagne-henriot.com
Tel: (33) 3 26 89 53 00
contact@champagne-henriot.com
Visits by appointment only.

JACQUESSON (N.M.)

Laurent and Jean Hervé Chiquet of Champagne Jacquesson.

Production: About 350,000 bottles annually.

As bubbles swept the world in the early 19th century, Jacquesson became one of the most popular champagne houses.

Founded in 1798 by Memmie Jacquesson, the renown of the house grew in the wars after the French Revolution as rumors spread that it was Napoléon Bonaparte's favorite. By 1867, Jacquesson's annual sales crossed the 1 million bottles mark.

The house then went into a long and steep decline, though, after Adolphe Jacquesson died in 1875.

Jacquesson's descendants had little interest in the family business, so ownership regularly changed hands.

In 1974, Jacquesson was purchased Jean Chiquet. He quickly revived the estate. Since 1988, brothers Jean-Hervé and Laurent Chiquet have run Jacquesson.

Jacquesson's 77 acres of vines are split between the Vallée de la Marne, where parcels are owned in Aÿ, Grand Cru, and Dizy and Hautvillers, both Premiers Crus; and in the Côte des Blancs, where parcels are owned in Avize and Oiry. These vineyards fulfill 80 percent of Jacquesson's needs. The rest of its fruit is purchased from growers in these same villages, where the Chiquet brothers manage the vineyards.

In the vineyards, the brothers farm mostly organically—they eschew fertilizers, pesticides, and herbicides—although they aren't certified. Their vineyards are regularly plowed and filled with grass, too.

In the cellar, the brothers vinify their wines in neutral barriques, regularly stirring the lees. They store reserve wines in demi-muids. They never chaptalize.

Without question, Jacquesson has reemerged as one of the finest houses in Champagne.

THE WINES

CUVÉE 700 (NV)
Dosage: Brut
Price: $65

In 2000, Jacquesson named its main cuvée "728." (In the estate's ancient cellar book, which began in 1898 with Cuvée n° 1, this was the 728th wine ever produced.) A blend that is generally composed of 60% Chardonnay, 20% Pinot Meunier, and 20% Pinot Noir, reserve wine generally takes up about one-third of the final blend. By giving each cuvée a unique number, the brothers are demonstrating that each vintage offers a different identity. This wine ages for 4 years before release.

CUVÉE 700 DÉGORGEMENT TARDIF (NV)
Dosage: Brut
Price: $80

Otherwise identical to the regular 700 series, this wine ages for nine years before release.

MILLESIME (VINTAGE)
Dosage: Brut
Price: $140

About equal parts Chardonnay and Pinot Noir, the vintage blend is typically 35% Avize Chardonnay, 15% Chouilly Chardonnay, 35% Dizy Pinot Noir, and 15% Aÿ Pinot Noir, although the percentages (and vineyard sources) change with each release. This wine ages on its lees for about 7 years before release.

DIZY CORNE BAUTRAY (VINTAGE)
Dosage: Brut
Price: $215

Sourced from a 2.5-acre parcel of Chardonnay in Dizy planted in 1960, this blanc de blancs ages on its lees for 8.5 years.

DIZY TERRES ROUGES (VINTAGE)
Dosage: Brut
Price: $175

Sourced from a 3.3-acre parcel of Pinot Noir in Dizy planted in 1993, this blanc de noirs is aged on its lees for 3.5 years.

AVIZE CHAMP CAÏN (VINTAGE)
Dosage: Brut
Price: $200

Sourced from a 3-acre parcel in Avize planted in 1962, this blanc de blancs ages on its lees for 8.5 years.

AŸ VAUZELLE TERME (VINTAGE)
Dosage: Brut
Price: $350

Sourced from a 0.75-acre parcel in Aÿ planted in 1980, this blanc de noirs ages on its lees for 8.5 years.

Jacquesson
68 Rue du Colonel Fabien
51530 Dizy
www. champagnejacquesson.com
Tel: (33) 3 26 55 68 11
info@champagnejacquesson.com
Visits by appointment only.

KRUG (N.M.)

Cellar Master Eric Lebel and House Director Olivier Krug.
Photos by Champagne Krug.

Production: About 600,000 bottles annually.

The story of Krug begins with Johan Joseph Krug, a German immigrant who arrived alone in Reims in the early 19th century. In 1834, Krug began working at Jacquesson as an accountant, rising to second-in-command within a decade. In 1843, unsatisfied with his employer's wines, he decided to create his own champagne house.

It quickly gained a reputation as one of the region's best. It maintains that reputation today.

Krug owns about 50 acres of vines, split fairly evenly between the Côte des Blancs and Montagne de Reims. These vineyards provide fruit for about 30 percent of its needs. The rest of its fruit comes through long-term contracts with growers and cooperatives. Since 1929, for example, Krug has continuously sourced Pinot Meunier from the cooperative in Leuvrigny, a village in the Vallée de la Marne.

Each and every parcel of fruit that Krug brings in is fermented separately in neutral, 205-liter oak barrels. Malolactic fermentation is neither suppressed nor provoked. Once finished, those wines are then utilized for that year's assemblage or transferred to small, stainless-steel vats where they remain until blending.

While Krug is owned by LVMH, the world's largest luxury conglomerate, the Krug family is still involved with the winery. Olivier Krug, a sixth generation family member, directs the house.

THE WINES

GRANDE CUVÉE (NV)

Price: $185

Krug insists on describing its entry level offering as "multi-vintage"—rather than "non-vintage"—because it's a blend of about 120 wines from 10 or more vintages, some going back 15 years or more. Sourced from a variety of vineyards, the wine always includes Pinot Noir, Chardonnay, and Pinot Meunier. After bottling, it's aged for a minimum of six years before release. This wine accounts for 85% of Krug's production.

ROSÉ (NV)

Price: $315

A relative newcomer, Krug Rosé was introduced in 1983. While produced in a similar fashion to the Grand Cuvée, it is a completely unique wine, generally drawing on fewer wines from fewer vintages. The color is derived from still Pinot Noir. After bottling, this wine is also aged for six years or more before release.

VINTAGE

Price: $300

Krug hopes to translate vintage—in its own, signature style—through its vintage wine, which is only produced in the best years. After bottling, this wine sits in Krug's cellars for at least 10 years before release.

COLLECTION (VINTAGE)

Price: $600

Introduced in the early 1980s, offerings from the Krug "Collection" are simply the vintage offerings with 10 or more years of additional aging in the cellar.

CLOS DU MESNIL (VINTAGE)

Price: $900

In 1971, Krug purchased a walled, 4.5-acre Chardonnay vineyard in the heart of Mesnil-sur-Oger that was first planted in 1698. While Krug planned to use the grapes for its Grande Cuvée, the house began producing a vineyard-declared wine in 1979. This single variety, single-vineyard wine is only produced in the best years and sits in Krug's cellars for at least 12 years before release.

CLOS D'AMBONNAY (VINTAGE)

Price: $2,000

In 1994, inspired by Clos du Mesnil, Krug purchased a walled, 1.7-acre Pinot Noir vineyard on the edge of Ambonnay. The house declared its first vintage from the vineyard one year later. This single variety, single-vineyard wine is only produced in the best years and sits in Krug's cellars for at least 12 years before release.

Krug
5 Rue Coquebert
51100 Reims
www.krug.com
Tel: (+33) 3 26 84 44 20
krug@krug.fr
No visits or direct sales.

LAURENT-PERRIER (N.M.)

Production: About 7 million bottles annually.

Laurent-Perrier traces its roots to 1812. That year, Alphonse Pierlot, a bottler and cooper from Chigny-lès-Roses, purchased two vineyards in Tours-sur-Marne and began making champagne.

Pierlot willed the company to his *chef de cave*, Eugène Laurent, who eagerly took charge, running the company with the help of his wife, Mathilde Emilie Perrier.

When Eugène died in 1887, Perrier combined the two family names and decided to expand the business. At first, Perrier succeeded. Notably, she created one of the first zero-dosage champagnes, called "Grand Vin Sans Sucre" in 1889. But the First World War and the Great Depression took a toll on the company. So in 1939, her daughter Eugénie sold the company to Marie-Louise Lanson de Nonancourt of the famous Lanson family. Thanks to the Second World War, though, hard times continued.

In 1949, Nonancourt's son Bernard took control of the house. One of his first decisions was to move to away from wood—and toward stainless steel—in an effort to better capture champagne's freshness. He created a range of new cuvées and developed the style that Laurent-Perrier still embraces. Since 1949, Laurent-Perrier has only had three *chef de caves*.

Today, Laurent-Perrier owns about 370 acres of vineyards, which fulfill about 10 percent of its needs, and the house contracts with over 900 grape growers. The current *chef de cave*, Michel Fauconnet, has spent his entire career at Laurent-Perrier, beginning as a cellar intern in 1973. Bernard de Nonancourt's daughters, Alexandra and Stephanie, direct the estate.

THE WINES

BRUT (NV)
Dosage: Brut
Price: $40

A blend of 50% Chardonnay, 35% Pinot Noir, and 15% Pinot Meunier sourced from over 55 different villages. Contains up to 20% reserve wine. It ages on its lees for 3 years before disgorgement.

ULTRA BRUT (NV)
Dosage: Brut Nature
Price: $60

A blend of 55% Chardonnay and 45% Pinot Noir sourced from about a dozen villages, mostly Premier Crus. It ages *sur latte* for 4 years before disgorgement. It is finished without dosage.

CUVÉE ROSÉ BRUT (NV)
Dosage: Brut
Price: $75

This saignée rosé receives its color from a 2–3 day maceration. Composed entirely of Pinot Noir, the grapes for this rosé are sourced from over a dozen villages, mainly from the Montagne de Reims. It ages *sur latte* for 4 years before disgorgement.

BRUT MILLÉSIMÉ (VINTAGE)
Dosage: Brut
Price: $60

Equal parts Chardonnay and Pinot Noir, this vintage wine is sourced entirely from Grand Crus. The Chardonnay comes from Chouilly, Cramant, Oger, and Le Mesnil-sur-Oger; the Pinot Noir comes from Verzy, Verzenay, Mailly, Louvois, and Bouzy. It ages on its lees for 8 years before disgorgement.

GRAND SIÈCLE BRUT (NV)

Dosage: Brut
Price: $150

This prestige cuvée is comprised of 55% Chardonnay and 45% Pinot Noir, sourced entirely from Grand Crus. The Chardonnay comes from Avize, Chouilly, Cramant, and Le Mesnil-sur-Oger; the Pinot Noirs comes from Ambonnay, Bouzy, Louvois, Mailly, Tours-sur-Marne, and Verzenay. Interestingly, this wine is always a blend of three exceptional vintages. Once blended, the wine ages for 7-8 years before disgorgement.

ALEXANDRA ROSÉ (VINTAGE)

Dosage: Brut
Price: $325

This rosé is only produced in exceptional years; only seven vintages have been released since 1982. Approximately 80% Pinot Noir and 20% Chardonnay, sourced entirely from Grand Crus, this saignée rosé receives its color from a 2-3 day maceration, where the two varieties co-ferment. This wine ages for 7 years before disgorgement.

Laurent-Perrier
32 Avenue de Champagne
51150 Tours-sur-Marne
www.laurent-perrier.com
Tel: (33) 3 26 58 91 22
marketing@laurentperrierus.com
No visits or direct sales.

MOËT & CHANDON / DOM PÉRIGNON (N.M.)

Production: About 35 million bottles annually.

In 1743, Claude Moët, a wine merchant accredited to serve the royal court, launched his own champagne house. He quickly found plenty of thirsty clients in Paris and beyond. Demand for champagne surged during the reign of King Louis XV. It surged afterwards, too, thanks largely to Jean-Rémy Moët, Claude's grandson.

While in his early 20s, Jean-Rémy was tasked with soliciting orders for his family's champagne. One of his clients was the military academy of Brienne-le-Château, where he befriended Napoléon Bonaparte. The two were fast friends, and legend has it that Bonaparte would visit the Moët cellars before each military campaign to pick up champagne for his troops.

This could have very well been a marketing tactic. During his tenure at the estate, Jean-Rémy Moët transformed his grandfather's company into a worldwide luxury brand.

The company was renamed Moët et Chandon in 1833 after Jean-Rémy handed the estate over to his son, Victor, and his son-in-law Pierre-Gabriel Chandon. Under their direction, the company continued to grow and innovate. The company released its first vintage wine in 1842 and introduced today's best-selling champagne, Impérial, in the 1860s.

The company took more leaps forward in the first half of the 20ᵗʰ century under the direction of Robert-Jean de Vogüé, a brilliant marketer.

In the early 1930s, de Vogüé created Champagne's first "prestige" cuvée, Dom Pérignon. The first shipments of the wine arrived in London in 1935, where it was an instant success. It became a smash hit in New York a few months later.

Today, Moët is the largest champagne company, producing more than 30 million bottles annually. Part of the luxury giant LVMH, Moët owns 2,800 acres of vineyards, half of which are in Grand Crus and 25 percent of which are in Premier Crus. These vines don't fulfill all its needs, of course, so the company also sources from producers across the region, purchasing grapes from about 200 of Champagne's villages.

The cellars at Moët are managed by Benoît Gouez, who has been the *chef de cave* since 2005. Gouez reports to Richard Geoffroy, who has been the *chef de cave* for Dom Pérignon since 1990. While the two companies are inexorably linked, the two men try to avoid technical conversations to preserve the independent styles of Moët and Dom Pérignon.

THE WINES

IMPÉRIAL (NV)
Dosage: Brut / Demi Sec
Price: $40

The best-selling champagne in the world, this wine is typically composed of 35% Pinot Noir, 35% Pinot Meunier, and 25% Chardonnay. About 20% of each bottling consists of reserve wines. Aged *sur latte* for 18-24 months before disgorgement. This is released with two different levels of dosage.

ROSÉ IMPÉRIAL (NV)
Dosage: Brut / Demi Sec
Price: $50

Typically composed of 45% Pinot Noir (10% of which is still red wine), 40% Pinot Meunier (10% of which is still red wine), and 15% Chardonnay. About 20% of each bottling consists of reserve wines. Aged *sur latte* for 18-24 months before disgorgement. This is released with two different levels of dosage.

RÉSERVE IMPÉRIAL (NV)
Dosage: Brut
Price: $45

This wine is distinct from Moët's regular Impérial because it has a higher percentage of Pinot Noir and spends more time on its lees. Typically, this wine is half Pinot Noir, and a quarter of both Pinot Meunier and Chardonnay. About 25% of each bottling consists of reserve wines. Aged *sur latte* for about 36 months before disgorgement.

GRAND VINTAGE (VINTAGE)
Dosage: Brut
Price: $60

About 40% Pinot Noir, 40% Pinot Meunier, and 20% Chardonnay, this wine ages on its lees for seven years before disgorgement.

GRAND VINTAGE ROSÉ (VINTAGE)
Dosage: Brut
Price: $65

About 45% Pinot Noir, of which half is still red wine, 31% Chardonnay, and 24% Pinot Meunier, this wine ages on its lees for seven years before disgorgement.

DOM PÉRIGNON (VINTAGE)
Dosage: Brut
Price: $165

The world's most famous prestige cuvée, Dom Pérignon is sourced entirely from a core group of vineyards in nine villages, eight of which are Grand Crus. About 60% of the blend is Chardonnay, sourced from the Grand Crus of Chouilly, Cramant, Avize, Le Mesnil-sur-Oger. The remaining 40% is Pinot Noir, sourced from the Grand Crus of Aÿ, Bouzy, Mailly, and Verzenay, and the Premier Cru of Hautvillers. The wine ages on its lees for 8-10 years before disgorgement. Note that Dom Pérignon holds a large percentage back for later releases in tranches it calls "plenitudes." The "P2" ages *sur pointe* on its lees for about 15 years and the "P3" for 30-40 years. (These releases used to be called "Oenothèque.")

DOM PÉRIGNON ROSÉ
Dosage: Brut
Price: $300

Sourced from the same vineyards as the regular Dom Pérignon, about 60% of this wine is Pinot Noir, of which almost half is still red wine. The remaining 40% is Chardonnay. This wine also has the same lees aging as the regular Dom Pérignon.

Moët & Chandon
20 Avenue de Champagne
51200 Épernay
www.moet.com
www.domperignon.com
Tel: (33) 3 26 51 20 20
visites@moet.fr
Tours and tastings available.

PERRIER-JOUËT (N.M.)

Production: About 3 million bottles annually.

The story of this house begins in 1810, when the Épernay-based cork supplier Pierre Nicolas Perrier married Adèle Jouët, the daughter of a Calvados producer. Perrier's family owned vineyards in Dizy, Chouilly, AÐ, so in 1811, the newlyweds founded Perrier-Jouët to begin producing champagne. They purchased the building where the company is still headquartered in 1813.

Adèle focused on vineyards and winemaking; Pierre Nicolas focused on sales and marketing. Shipments to Great Britain began in 1815 and to the United States in 1837.

Their son Charles took over after Pierre Nicolas's death in 1854, having already played a role in Champagne's history by introducing the first brut champagne six years earlier. (A British wine merchant had fallen in love with

Perrier-Jouët's vin clair in 1846, so asked the champagne house to send him some wine without dosage. It was criticized as too "brute" by the merchant's customers, so most was returned to Épernay.) Charles would later go on to introduce the estate's first vintage-dated champagne, a much more successful effort.

With no children of his own, Charles passed the house down to his nephew Henri Gallice in 1874. The Gallice family sold the house to Champagne Mumm in 1959, and since 2005 it has been under the Pernod Ricard umbrella of brands.

In 1969, Perrier-Jouët released its first "Belle Époque" cuvée, just in time to celebrate Duke Ellington's 70th birthday in Paris. Based on a design created by Art Nouveau artist Emile Gallé, the bottles were intricately decorated with white anemones, an iconic design that still appears on the cuvée today. (Note that this cuvée was called "Fleur de Champagne" in the United States until the release of the 2004 vintage.)

Perrier-Jouët owns over 160 acres of vineyards, with more than half in the Grand Crus of Cramant and Avize. Other sizeable holdings are in Aÿ and Mailly. The company's vineyards fulfill about one-third of its needs.

The Wines

Grand (NV)
Dosage: Brut
Price: $45

A blend of 40% Pinot Noir, 40% Pinot Meunier, and 20% Chardonnay sourced from over 35 villages. Between 10 and 20 percent of reserve wines are added to the blend, and it ages *sur latte* for 3 years before riddling and disgorgement.

Blason Rosé (NV)
Dosage: Brut
Price: $75

Perrier-Jouët produced its first non-vintage rosé in 1956. It is a blend of 50% Pinot Noir, 25% Pinot Meunier, and 25% Chardonnay. It ages for 3 years .

Belle Epoque Fleur de Champagne (Vintage)
Dosage: Brut
Price: $150

Typically a blend of 50% Chardonnay from Cramant, Avize and Chouilly;

45% Pinot Noir from Mailly, Verzy and Aÿ; and 5% Pinot Meunier from Dizy. It ages on its lees for over 6 years.

Belle Epoque Fleur de Champagne Rosé (Vintage)
Dosage: Brut
Price: $300

Typically identical to the composition of the traditional Belle Epoque, with still Pinot Noir from Ambonnay and Aÿ blended into the cuvée. This champagne, too, ages on its lees for over 6 years.

Belle Epoque Fleur de Champagne Blanc de Blanc (Vintage)
Dosage: Brut
Price: $325

Sourced entirely from two parcels in Cramant: Bourons Leroy and Bourons du Midi. This blanc de blancs ages on its lees for over 6 years.

Perrier-Jouët
28 Avenue de Champagne
51200 Épernay
www.perrier-jouet.com
Tel: (33) 3 26 53 38 10
contact@perrier-jouet.com
Visits by appointment.

PHILIPPONNAT (N.M.)

Production: About 600,000 bottles annually.

Even in this deeply historic region, the Philipponnat family history is impressive. Apvril le Philipponnat owned vines near Aÿ since the early 1500s, and the family of merchants and winegrowers supplied Louis XIV's court.

Pierre Philipponnat established the current house in 1910. Bruno Paillard purchased the house in the mid-1990s, and still owns it today. But, sixteen generations since Apvril le Philipponnat, Charles Philipponnat carries the torch and manages the family house.

The company owns more than 40 acres of vines in Aÿ, Mareuil-sur-Aÿ, and Avenay. The jewel of the house is Clos des Goisses, a 13.5-acre, walled vineyard planted on a very steep, south-facing slope in soil of pure chalk. From this site, which Pierre Philipponnat purchased in the 1930s, the house crafts a vintage-dated, single-vineyard cuvée designed to demonstrate the unique and profound character of the site.

The company finished its new winery in Mareuil-sur-Aÿ in 2004, and now its press and cellars are all close together. *Chef de cave* Thierry Garnier vinifies the wine in tank and barrels, allows varying levels of malolactic fermentation, and generally employs a low dosage.

THE WINES

ROYALE RÉSERVE (NV)
Dosage: Brut
Price: $45

A blend of the three staple varieties, this entry-level cuvée has recently seen more Pinot Noir (about 60-70% of the blend) and less Pinot Meunier. Some of the blend is aged an extra year and finished without dosage.

ROYALE RÉSERVE ROSÉ (NV)
Dosage: Brut
Price: $55

A blend of 75% Pinot Noir, 20% Chardonnay, and 5% Pinot Meunier from Grand and Premier Cru villages. About 8% of the Pinot Noir is blended in as still red wine.

GRAND BLANC (VINTAGE)
Dosage: Extra Brut
Price: $60

This blanc de blancs comes from mostly Côte des Blancs vineyards, but sometimes includes grapes from younger vines in the house's Clos des Goisses vineyard and other villages.

BLANC DE NOIRS (VINTAGE)
Dosage: Extra Brut
Price: $60

The Pinot Noir for this blend comes from the Montagne de Reims and estate vineyards in Mareuil-sur-Aÿ. It's aged five to seven years on the lees.

CUVÉE 1522 (VINTAGE)
Dosage: Extra Brut
Price: $80

This wine debuted in 1996 as a non-vintage blend, but the house changed it to a vintage-dated wine in 2000. The fruit is sourced from the estate's best vineyards, including Pinot Noir from the Le Léon parcel in Aÿ. The wine also includes Chardonnay from Cramant and Le Mesnil-sur-Oger.

CUVÉE 1522 ROSÉ (VINTAGE)
Dosage: Extra Brut
Price: $95

The rosé takes the 1522 and adds about 8% still Pinot Noir from estate vines in Mareuil-sur-Aÿ. The name of these wines refers to the year a Philipponnat first planted vines in Champagne.

CLOS DES GOISSES (VINTAGE)
Dosage: Extra Brut
Price: $170

This walled, 13.5-acre vineyard in Mareuil-sur-Aÿ is home to Philipponnat's most coveted wine. It's a blend of Pinot Noir with some 30-40% Chardonnay, about half of which is fermented in oak barrels. This vintage, low dosage wine does not go through malolactic fermentation, and it's considered one of the purest expressions of terroir.

LE LÉON (VINTAGE)
Dosage: Extra Brut
Price: $125

Debuting in the 2006 vintage, this single-plot wine is made of 100% Pinot Noir, about half of which is fermented in cask.

MAREUIL-SUR-AŸ (VINTAGE)
Dosage: Extra Brut
Price: $125

This 100% Pinot Noir comes from several sites planted in clay soils of Mareuil-sur-Aÿ. Like Le Léon, this wine debuted in 2006 and is made in very small quantities.

Philipponnat
13 Rue du Pont
51160 Mareuil sur Aÿ
www.philipponnat.com
Tel: (+33) 3 26 56 93 00
info@philipponnat.com
No visits.

PIPER-HEIDSIECK (N.M.)

Production: About 5.5 million bottles annually.

The first Heidsieck champagne company was organized in 1785 by Florens-Louis Heidsieck. When he died in 1828, his nephew Christian continued the Heidsieck house, which gained renown as official supplier to royalty like Hapsburg princes and imperial courts of the Chinese emperor. Another nephew's descendent started a separate house, Charles Heidsieck, in 1851.

After his death, Christian's widow went on to marry Henri-Guillaume Piper, and in 1845 they started selling champagne as Piper-Heidsieck. The house was controlled by several families as it continued to thrive into the 20th century. During the Nazi occupation, the house's cellars were used to hide weapons to supply the Champagne Resistance.

The two houses, Piper-Heidsieck and Charles Heidsieck, came under the control of the Rémy-Martin firm in the mid-1980s. The two houses functioned as corporate sisters under the P&C Heidsieck umbrella, and they were bought in 2011 by the French company EPI.

Today, the two houses operate closely, sharing winemaking equipment, vineyards, and even base wines. Piper-Heidsieck is managed by Cecile Bonnefond, who previously worked for Veuve Clicquot, and the *chef de cave* is Régis Camus. The wines are fermented in stainless steel and go through full malolactic fermentation.

THE WINES

CUVÉE BRUT (NV)
Dosage: Brut
Price: $40

A Pinot Noir-led wine (with about 30% Pinot Meunier and a small amount of Chardonnay), the house's entry-level non-vintage blend is sourced from more than 100 different crus.

VINTAGE BRUT (VINTAGE)
Dosage: Brut
Price: $65

Pinot Noir leads the way in the house's basic vintage-dated champagne, largely sourced from the Montagne de Reims, and about 40% Chardonnay is blended in. The grapes come from a blend of 7 Premier Crus and 9 Grand Crus. The wine is aged six years on its lees.

Cuvée Sublime (NV)

Dosage: Demi-Sec

Price: $45

This higher dosage wine is based on the Cuvée Brut and aged for an additional year.

Rosé Sauvage (NV)

Dosage: Brut

Price: $50

This wine is also based on the Cuvée Brut, but about 20% still Pinot Noir is blended in (which is sourced from villages including Ambonnay and Bouzy).

Rare (Vintage)

Dosage: Brut

Price: $175

This wine debuted in 1985 to mark the original house's bicentennial. Mostly composed of Chardonnay, with about 30% Pinot Noir, the grapes from this prestige cuvée are sourced from 17 crus in the Montagne de Reims. It's aged on its lees for seven years before disgorgement.

Piper-Heidsieck

12 Allée du Vignoble

51100 Reims

www.piper-heidsieck.com

Tel: (+33) 3 26 84 43 00

contact.piperheidsieck@champagnes-ph-ch.com

Tours and tastings available.

POL ROGER (N.M.)

Production: About 1.6 million bottles annually.

Pol Roger founded his eponymous and historic champagne house in 1849 in Épernay. He built a strong reputation for the company, and strong trade ties with Great Britain, until he died in 1899. Disaster struck a year later, when the cellar collapsed, destroying 500 casks and more than 1 million bottles of champagne. Pol Roger's sons, Maurice and Georges, picked up the pieces. Then, of course, came the suffering of two World Wars.

In the 1950s, the business really began to take off under the control of Pol Roger's grandsons, Christian de Billy and Christian Pol-Roger. The long-running trade relationship with Britain helped, although the United States became Pol Roger's biggest export market in the 1990s. Pol Roger's descendants still run the house and *chef de cave* Dominique Petit has been carrying the winemaking torch since 1999.

The company owns more than 220 acres of vineyards in the Vallée de la Marne, Montagne de Reims, and Côte des Blancs. This fulfills slightly more than half of the firm's needs, so the rest of the grapes are purchased from growers.

THE WINES

RÉSERVE (NV)
Dosage: Brut
Price: $50

A blend of Chardonnay, Pinot Noir, and Pinot Meunier from 30 different villages, the blend contains 25% reserve wine and is aged on its lees in the cellar for four years prior to disgorgement.

VINTAGE (VINTAGE)
Dosage: Brut
Price: $70

Usually a blend of 60% Pinot Noir and 40% Chardonnay, this wine comes from fruit grown in 20 different Grand and Premier Cru villages in the Montagne de Reims and Côte de Blancs. The wine is aged eight years on its lees before disgorgement.

ROSÉ (VINTAGE)
Dosage: Brut
Price: $80

Making its debut in 1961, Pol Roger's vintage rosé is made from the base of the Brut Vintage (a 60/40 Pinot Noir/Chardonnay blend). Before secondary fermentation, the wine is blended with 15% still Pinot Noir from the Montagne de Reims. The wine is aged seven years on its lees before disgorgement.

RICH (NV)
Dosage: Demi-Sec
Price: $45

Launched in 2001, this is the same blend as the Brut Réserve but made in a demi-sec style.

PURE (NV)
Dosage: Extra Brut
Price: $55

Launched in 2008, this is technically a non-dosé (Brut Nature) but it's labeled as Extra Brut.

BLANC DE BLANCS (VINTAGE)
Dosage: Brut
Price: $85

This vintage-dated Chardonnay is made from Côte de Blancs Grand Crus Oiry, Chouilly, Cramant, Avize, and Oger. The wine ages seven years on its lees before disgorgement.

SIR WINSTON CHURCHILL (VINTAGE)
Dosage: Brut
Price: $215

One of the most renowned top cuvées, this wine made its debut in 1975. Pol Roger pays homage to Sir Winston Churchill's love for champagne with this blend of Pinot Noir and Chardonnay sourced entirely from Grand Cru vineyards. The wine ages 11 years on its lees before disgorgement.

Pol Roger
1 Rue Winston Churchill
51200 Épernay
www.polroger.com
Tel: (+33) 3 26 59 58 00
polroger@polroger.fr
No visits.

POMMERY (N.M.)

Production: More than 5 million bottles annually.

The roots of what would become Pommery date back to 1836, when Narcisse Greno bought the Dubois Gossart house and produced still red wine. In the 1850s, he joined forces with Alexandre Pommery, who came from a wealthy Reims family that operated in the wool trade and owned large vineyards, and the two of them formed Champagne Pommery & Greno. Mr. Pommery died two years later, and his widow, 39-year-old Louise Pommery, stepped in and reshaped the company, Champagne Pommery, by focusing on producing sparkling wine and making inroads into the booming British market.

Madame Pommery held the reins for 30 years, as she propelled the house's brand and the increased the quality of its wines. When she died in 1890, she left Pommery with more than 700 acres of Grand Cru vineyards. Her daughter Louise, and her husband Prince Guy de Polignac, managed the house after Madame Pommery's death, and de Polignac maintained control until 1979.

Today, Pommery is part of the Épernay-based Vraken company, which, along with its other holdings in Champagne, boasts total production of more than 20 million bottles a year. Thierry Gasco holds the helm as *chef de cave*, and he also oversees the house's vineyard operations.

The house is known for its expansive cellars, which stretch more than ten miles through deep chalk tunnels and connect to more than 100 crayères. In keeping with Madame Pommery's love of champagne and art, the cellars frequently host art exhibitions.

THE WINES

ROYAL (NV)
Dosage: Brut
Price: $40

Equal parts Chardonnay, Pinot Meunier, Pinot Noir sourced from more than 40 different crus. The wine is aged three years on its lees before disgorgement.

ROSÉ (NV)
Dosage: Brut
Price: $55

Equal parts Chardonnay, Pinot Meunier, Pinot Noir, the color comes from still Pinot Noir from Bouzy, which makes up 7% of the blend. The grapes are sourced from more than 40 crus, and the wine is aged on its lees for three years before disgorgement.

MILLÉSIMÉ (VINTAGE)

Dosage: Brut
Price: $65

This vintage-dated wine is composed of 60% Chardonnay and 40% Pinot Noir from Grand Cru villages of the Montagne de Reims. The wine is aged four years on its lees before disgorgement.

APANAGE (NV)

Dosage: Brut
Price: $60

This newer non-vintage prestige cuvée is composed of 40% Chardonnay, 35% Pinot Noir, 25% Pinot Meunier. The wine is aged more than three years on its lees before disgorgement.

APANAGE ROSÉ (NV)

Dosage: Brut
Price: $60

This newer non-vintage prestige cuvée is a rosé d'assemblage composed of 50% Chardonnay, 25% Pinot Noir, 25% Pinot Meunier. The wine is aged more than three years on its lees before disgorgement.

CUVÉE LOUISE (VINTAGE)

Dosage: Brut
Price: $130

A blend of 60% Chardonnay (entirely from Avize and Cramant) and 40% Pinot (entirely from Aÿ), this wine pays homage to Madame Pommery. The wine is aged on its lees for eight years before disgorgement.

Pommery
5 Place du Général Gouraud,
51100 Reims
www.champagnepommery.com
Phone: (+33) 3 26 61 62 56
contact@vrankenpommery.fr
Visits by appointment.

LOUIS ROEDERER (N.M.)

Production: About 3 million bottles annually.

Louis Roederer's eponymous champagne house was founded in 1833, when Roederer took control of the Dubois Père & Fils house, which had been in existence since 1776. Louis Roederer drastically increased the company's business by expanding into the thirsty Russian market. By the 1870s, the Roederer house sold about one out of every ten bottles of champagne, which amounted to a mind-boggling 2.5 million bottles a year. A few years later, Louis Roederer's son, who shared his father's name, launched a private wine for the Tsar of Russia, bottled in crystal—and Cristal was born.

Although the Russian Revolution of 1917 dried up Roederer's prime market, Louis Roederer began to rebound under the control of Camille Olry-Roederer, who began managing the house in 1932. Since then, Roederer has further increased production, and grown to purchase other properties such as

Deutz. Today, Jean-Baptiste Lécaillon, who began working with Roederer in the late 1980s, holds the position of *chef de cave*.

Though registered as a *négociant*, Roederer owns a vast amount of vineyards, which total some 600 acres. All the cuvées, spare the non-vintage Brut Premier, come from estate vines. Roederer is also the largest producer of biodynamic champagne, with more than 150 acres of vines farmed biodynamically. Many of Roederer's other vineyards are farmed organically, and the house uses some horse-drawn plows. Almost all of the parcels are vinified individually, and fermentation takes place in both stainless steel and large oak *foudres*.

THE WINES

BRUT PREMIER (NV)
Dosage: Brut
Price: $45

The only cuvée that contains non-estate grapes, some 30 to 40% if the grapes are purchased from other growers. This is also the only wine that undergoes some malolactic fermentation, and the only cuvée that includes Pinot Meunier (about 20%). The rest of the blend is typically an even split between Chardonnay and Pinot Noir, and the blend includes about 20% reserve wine.

BLANC DE BLANCS (VINTAGE)
Dosage: Brut
Price: $75

Sourced from estate vines in Avize and Le Mesnil, the blend typically contains some Chardonnay from Chouilly or Cramant. Some of the wine is fermented in large foudres and left to age five years on the lees. The finished wine is usually bottled at a lower four atmospheres of pressure.

VINTAGE BRUT (VINTAGE)
Dosage: Brut
Price: $75

Most of the Pinot Noir for this vintage-dated wine hails from Verzenay and Verzy, while some 30% Chardonnay from Grand Cru villages in the Côte des Blancs is blended in. The wine is aged on its lees for four years before disgorgement.

ROSÉ (VINTAGE)
Dosage: Brut
Price: $70

Roederer's vintage rosé is composed of Pinot Noir from Cumières made via the saignée method. To that, the *chef de cave* adds about 30% Côte des Blancs Chardonnay.

CRISTAL (VINTAGE)
Dosage: Brut
Price: $245

This iconic prestige cuvée is usually a 60/40 blend of Pinot Noir and Chardonnay, which is sourced from estate vineyards, including Grand Crus of the Montagne de Reims, the Marne, and the Côte des Blancs. It ages on its lees for five years before disgorgement and is then left in the cellars for almost another year before release.

CRISTAL ROSÉ (VINTAGE)
Dosage: Brut
Price: $515

The Cristal Rosé is made from a saignée of Pinot Noir from estate vineyards in Aÿ. This accounts for about 70% of the wine, while Chardonnay from the Grand Crus of Avize and Le Mesnil-sur-Oger fills out the blend.

Louis Roederer
21 Boulevard Lundy
51100 Reims
www.louis-roederer.com
Tel: (+33) 3 26 40 42 11
contact@louis-roederer.com

RUINART (N.M.)

Production: 2.5 million bottles annually.

In 1729, Nicolas Ruinart established the first champagne house, which came just a year after Louis XV's royal decree that allowed for the shipment of sparkling wine. Ruinart's family was in the business of selling cloth, but Nicolas dedicated himself to producing sparkling wine, making it his sole occupation in 1735. He grew the house's production from 170 bottles in 1730 to 36,000 bottles in 1761.

In 1782 the firm acquired its iconic crayères in Reims, a series of deep chalk tunnels, which are used to store and age Ruinart wines to this day. The house remained controlled by Nicolas's descendants, until Gérard Ruinart de Brimont took control in 1925. He held the reins during the trying times of the Depression and World War II, but then ceded control of the historic house to a relative on his mother's side. In 1963, the Moet & Chandon group purchased Ruinart. Today, Ruinart is another jewel in the crown of LVMH, the luxury mega company that owns Veuve Clicquot, Moet & Chandon, and Krug.

Jean-Marc Gallot is the house's managing director, and Frédéric Panaïotis holds the *chef de cave* position. Ruinart owns some 40 acres of vines, but purchases fruit from all over Champagne. A Chardonnay-focused producer, Ruinart sources from many heralded Crus in the Côte des Blancs, but also purchases Chardonnay from the northern Montagne de Reims and the Massif de St-Thierry.

THE WINES

R DE RUINART (NV)
Dosage: Brut
Price: $50

The basic non-vintage brut from Ruinart has traditionally been a blend of about 60% Pinot Noir and 40% Chardonnay, although recent iterations have seen a small amount of Pinot Meunier.

BLANC DE BLANCS (NV)
Dosage: Brut
Price: $70

This wine debuted in 2001, and it's usually blended from some 20 different villages, including Premier Crus in the Côte des Blancs and Montagne de Reims, and some grapes from the Sézanne. The wine is fermented in stainless steel and undergoes full malolactic fermentation.

ROSÉ (NV)

Dosage: Brut

Price: $70

This rosé contains a high percentage of Chardonnay (up to 45%), while the rest of the blend is Pinot Noir, about 20% of which is still red wine.

DOM RUINART BLANC DE BLANCS (VINTAGE)

Dosage: Brut

Price: $170

Named for Nicolas Ruinart's uncle, Dom Thierry Ruinart, the first vintage of the house's prestige cuvée was the 1959. The wine is composed entirely of Grand Cru Chardonnay, most of which comes from Côte des Blancs (Chouilly, Le Mesnil, Avize), while some 30% comes from the Montagne de Reims. This wine ages on its lees for 10 years or more before disgorgement.

DOM RUINART ROSÉ (VINTAGE)

Dosage: Brut

Price: $265

The Dom Ruinart Rosé is composed of 80% Grand Cru Chardonnay, mostly sourced from the Côte des Blancs, but some fruit comes from the Montagne de Reims villages of Puisieulx and Sillery. The wine is blended with 20% Pinot Noir (from Sillery and Verzenay) made as still red wine. This wine ages on its lees for 10 years or more before disgorgement.

Ruinart

4 Rue des Crayeres

51100 Reims

www.ruinart.com

Tel: (+33) 3 26 77 51 51

reception@ruinart.com

Visits (and crayères tours) by appointment.

TAITTINGER (N.M.)

Production: About 5.5 million bottles annually.

As a champagne house, Taittinger's history dates back to the 1700s. But it wasn't until the 1930s that Pierre Taittinger purchased the company—then known as Forest-Fourneaux—and set it on track to become the big house stalwart it is today. In 1933, the house moved to its current headquarters in Reims, above a series of deep caves that descend some 60 feet into the hard, chalky earth. Taittinger grew under the auspices of brothers François and Claude, who ran the company beginning in 1960. Pierre-Emmanuel Taittinger, Claude's nephew, took over in 2005 and still runs the house.

For a *négociant*, Taittinger owns a large amount of vineyards, totaling some 750 acres. The estate vines (about half Pinot Noir, 35% Chardonnay, and 15% Pinot Meunier) are spread across more than 35 villages. These grapes supply about half of Taittinger's production, while the other half is sourced from a wide variety of independent growers and several cooperatives.

In 2005, Taittinger briefly came under the control of an American investment firm called Starwood Capital. But a year later, Pierre-Emmanuel Taittinger bought back the estate, which is still controlled by the Taittinger family. The *chef de cave* is Loïc Dupont, whose career with Taittinger dates back to 1984. Dupont took over the cellar in 2001 after the retirement of Maurice Morlot.

THE WINES

LA FRANÇAISE (NV)

Dosage: Brut

Price: $45

Tattinger's widely-distributed, entry-level wine is typically a blend of 40% Chardonnay, with the remainder a mix of Pinot Noir and Pinot Meunier, sourced from dozens of different villages. The wine is aged on the lees for about four years.

PRESTIGE ROSÉ (NV)

Dosage: Brut

Price: $60

The Pinot Noir portion of this blend comes from Bouzy and Ambonnay, and Les Riceys. About 15% of the Pinot is made produced as still red, and 30% Chardonnay is blended in. The wine is aged on the lees for about three years.

PRÉLUDE GRANDS CRUS (NV)

Dosage: Brut

Price: $60

The Pinot Noir (which makes up 50% of the blend) is sourced from Mailly, Bouzy, and Ambonnay, while the Chardonnay hails from Avize and Le Mesnil sur Oger. Only the first-press wine is used in the blend. Labeled non-vintage, this wine does can come from a single vintage, but reserve wines are blended in sometimes.

MILLÉSIMÉ (VINTAGE)

Dosage: Brut

Price: $65

The basic vintage wine is an even split between Grand Cru Chardonnay from the Côte de Blancs and Grand Cru Pinot Noir from the Montagne de Reims. The wine is aged on the lees for five years.

FOLIES DE LA MARQUETTERIE (NV)

Dosage: Brut

Price: $55

This single-vineyard wine is a blend of about 55% Pinot Noir and 45% Chardonnay. From estate vines near Château de la Marquetterie in Pierry, some of the wine is fermented in old oak. The wine is aged on the lees for about five years.

NOCTURE (NV)

Dosage: Sec

Price: $55

This Sec is a blend of 40% Chardonnay, 35% Pinot Noir, and 25% Pinot Meunier sourced from about 35 different villages. The wine is aged on the lees for about four years, after which 18 g/l of cane sugar is added to the wine.

NOCTURE ROSÉ (NV)

Dosage: Sec

Price: $65

The rosé Sec is a blend of about 40% Chardonnay, 40% Pinot Noir, and 20% Pinot Meunier from about 30 different sites and multiple vintages.

COMTES DE CHAMPAGNE BLANC DE BLANCS (VINTAGE)

Dosage: Brut

Price: $160

The top of the Taittinger line, this wine first debuted in 1952, and has become a widely respected prestige cuvée. The Chardonnay grapes are grown in the Grand Crus of Avize, Le Mesnil, and Oger. About 5% of the wine spends a few months in new oak barrels. The wine is aged on the lees for about ten years.

COMTES DE CHAMPAGNE ROSÉ (VINTAGE)

Dosage: Brut

Price: $210

The Rosé blends about 70% Pinot Noir from the Montagne de Reims with Chardonnay from the Côte des Blancs, all from Grand Cru villages. About 10% of the Pinot Noir is made as still red wine and blended in. The wine is aged on the lees for about ten years.

Taittinger
9 Place Saint-Nicaise
51100 Reims
www.taittinger.com
Phone: (+33) 3 26 85 45 35
info@taittinger.com
Tours and tastings available.

VEUVE CLICQUOT (N.M.)

Production: About 18 million bottles annually.

With its bright yellow label and dominant marketing presence, Veuve Clicquot is recognized the world over. But this popular brand has been built up over centuries of effort. Reims merchant Philippe Clicquot-Muiron established the house in 1772. François took over from his father some 25 years later and married Barbe Nicole Ponsardin. When Francois died, 27-year-old Barbe Nicole Ponsardin (Madame Clicquot) became the head of the company, which was named Veuve Clicquot Ponsardin in 1810. Madame Clicquot died in 1866, but she is immortalized in the house's prestige cuvée, La Grande Dame.

The company has always focused strongly on export markets, including the United States, which first imported Veuve Clicquot in 1798. Russia was a huge market in the 1800s, receiving some 60% of the company's champagne.

When the 1987 merger of Louis Vuitton and Moët Hennessy, Veuve Clicquot became part of the mega-luxury giant LVMH. Stéphane Baschiera manages the house and the *chef de cave* is Jacques Péters. Today, the company is located in Reims, where it produces all its champagne. The company owns about 1,200 acres of vines, but sources grapes from all over Champagne to fulfill its production needs.

THE WINES

YELLOW LABEL (NV)
Dosage: Brut
Price: $50

One of the most widely distributed and recognizable champagnes, Veuve's yellow label is a worldwide phenomenon. But its creation dates back to the 1900s, when it was first bottled for the British market. The wine is based on about 50% Pinot Noir from more than 50 villages, blended with Chardonnay and about 15% Pinot Meunier.

ROSÉ (NV)
Dosage: Brut
Price: $65

A Pinot Noir-based wine, this rosé also includes Chardonnay and Pinot Meunier. This wine usually includes about 25-35% reserve wine and some still red.

RICH (VINTAGE)
Dosage: Sec
Price: $60

Made of 45% Pinot Noir, 40% Pinot Meunier, and 15% Chardonnay, this contains some 28 g/l sugar, and the house markets the wine as a mixologist's champagne.

DEMI-SEC (NV)
Dosage: Demi-Sec
Price: $55

A blend of 50 different wines, this contains a bit more Pinot Meunier than the non-vintage Yellow Label Brut, and it is dosed to 45 g/l.

VINTAGE (VINTAGE)
Dosage: Brut
Price: $70

The house debuted a vintage-dated champagne in 1810, and Veuve Clicquot's basic vintage wine now comprises Pinot Noir, Pinot Meunier, and Chardonnay from some 20 Premier and Grand Cru villages.

VINTAGE ROSÉ (VINTAGE)
Dosage: Brut
Price: $75

This wine is the product of the Vintage Brut blend mixed with about 10% still red wine from Pinot Noir in Bouzy.

LA GRANDE DAME (VINTAGE)
Dosage: Brut
Price: $150

The house's prestige cuvée debuted in 1972 in honor of the estate's bicentennial. The blend is dominated by Pinot Noir, sourced from all Grand Cru villages (mostly Verzenay), while the Chardonnay hails from Avize, Oger, and Le Mesnil-sur-Oger.

LA GRAND DAME ROSÉ (VINTAGE)
Dosage: Brut
Price: $290

Debuting with the 1988 vintage release, the wine is blended with still red wine from the renowned Clos Colin plot in Bouzy.

Veuve Clicquot
1 Place des Droits de l'Homme
51100 Reims
www.veuve-clicquot.com
Tel: (+33) 3 26 89 53 90
Tours and tastings by appointment.

Section Two:

Montagne de Reims

Sunset over the Montagne de Reims

Champagne's northernmost vineyards lie in the Montagne de Reims, a semicircular growing region that begins southwest of Reims and ends about 18 miles south, just before Épernay.

The best vineyards sit close to the thickly forested mountain (*montagne*) in three sub-regions: **Massif de St. Thierry, Vesle et Ardre**, and **Grande Montagne de Reims.**

The height of the actual mountain isn't very impressive. Its summit—Mont Sinai—is actually more of a plateau and peaks at a bare 928 feet, high enough to have served as an observation post during the First World War. The mountain's moderately steep slopes, though, create ideal growing conditions by combining great drainage with excellent sunlight exposure.

Rain dissipates rapidly down the slopes. But the steep terrain also helps shield the vines against cold winds and spring frosts. The winding ridge also provides shelter from damaging hail storms, and the like.

On the north side of the mountain, the slopes fall away toward the Vesle river valley, which is home to Reims, and the Ardre river valley. On south side, the slopes face the Marne. The dividing ridge line thus also offers a variety of different sunlight exposures. The aspect of a slope—its direction—has a huge impact on grape development; in cool climates like Champagne, southern slopes are preferable as they receive more sunlight. Yet in the Montagne de Reims, counterintuitively, many vineyards are planted along north-facing slopes because the steep terrain effectively drains cool air from the vineyards.

The differences in slope, elevation, and exposure—combined with the effects of the thick

QUICK FACTS

20,500 planted acres
3,944 growers
Pinot Noir: 41%
Pinot Meunier: 34%
Chardonnay: 25%

GRAND CRUS

Ambonnay
Beaumont-sur-Vesle
Bouzy
Louvois
Mailly
Puisieulx
Sillery
Verzenay
Verzy

SUB-REGIONS

Massif de St. Thierry
Vesle et Ardre
Grande Montagne de Reims
Monts de Berru

PREMIER CRUS

Avenal-Val-d'Or
Bezannes
Billy-le-Grand
Chamery
Chigny-les-Roses
Cormontreuil

Continued . . .

forest that borders many vineyards—create a seemingly infinite number of microclimates. Consequently, no single grape dominates the region. About 41 percent is planted to Pinot Noir, 34 percent to Pinot Meunier, and 25 percent to Chardonnay.

The Montagne de Reims is dominated by chalk, of course, combined with small amounts of clay, sand, sandstone, marl, and brown coal. The soils along the slopes are younger and packed with "belemnite" chalk, which, thanks to erosion, is purer, finer-grained, and more porous than the "micraster" chalk that's found closer to the river valleys. Historically, belemnite was thought to be superior. But scientists now know that there's no real physical difference between the two chalks; however belemnite vineyards are thought to be better positioned, and to produce better wines.

The Champenois have long recognized the magic of the Montagne de Reims' slopes. In the 17th century, Champagne's wines were sometimes called *vin de coteaux*— or "wine of the slopes"—thanks largely to these vineyards. Today, the region is home to more Grand Cru villages than any other district in Champagne. In all nine of the Montagne de Reims' Grand Crus, Pinot Noir rules.

The grands crus begin around 8 miles southeast of Reims with **Puisieulx**, **Sillery**, and **Beaumont-sur-Vesle**, three villages that sit on the plain at the foot of the mountain. These villages are

Coulommes-la-Montagne
Ecueil
Jouy-les-Reims
Les Mesneux
Ludes
Montbré
Mouzon-Leroux
Pargny-les-Reims
Rilly-la-Montagne
Sacy
Sermiers
Taissy
Tauxières-Mutry
Trépail
Trois Puits
Vaudemanges
Ville-Dommange
Villiers-Allerand
Villiers-aux-Noeuds
Villiers-Marmery
Vrigny

LEADING PRODUCERS

L. Aubry Fils
Henri Billiot
Francis Boulard
Emmanuel Brochet
Chartogne-Taillet
André Clouet
R. H. Coutier
Paul Dethune
Egly-Ouriet
David Léclapart
Marie-Noelle Ledru
J. Lassalle
Margaine
Jérôme Prévost [La Closerie]
Savart
Vilmart & Cie

considered lesser Grand Crus, as neither the slopes nor soils can match the quality of the mountainside itself.

As one drives up the mountain heading east, vineyards seem to emerge from the forest. Here, one finds the Grand Cru villages of **Mailly**, **Verzenay**, and **Verzy**, which arguably offer the most structured, focused Pinot Noir in Champagne. As the slope of the mountain curves south and west, one encounters **Ambonnay**, **Bouzy**, and **Louvois**. Since these southern villages are warmer, the vineyards produce more extracted, powerful wine. Indeed, many still reds come from these villages, and are either bottled as Coteaux Champenois or simply used to lend color to rosé.

The only other sub-region of the Montagne de Reims, **Monts de Berru**, begins about 4 miles east of Reims. With only around 1,000 acres under vine—most of which is planted to Chardonnay—the region isn't very well-known.

PRODUCERS TO KNOW

Barnaut
André Beaufort
Bourdaire-Gallois
Marc Chauvet
Paul Clouet
Roger Coulon
Huré Frères
Hugues Godmé
Benoit Lahaye
Jean Lallement
Benoit Marguet
Minière F&R
Mouzon-Leroux
Thomas Perseval
Perseval-Farge
Guillaume Sergent
Pehu-Simonnet
SoutiranPloyez-Jacquemart
Pascal Redon
Eric Rodez
Camille Savès

ICONIC WINES OF TERROIR

Emmanuel Brochet: Les Haut Chardonnay
Emmanuel Brochet: Les Hauts Meuniers
Chartogne-Taillet: Les Barres
Egly-Ouriet: Les Vignes de Vrigny
Krug: Clos de Mesnil
Marie-Noëlle Ledru: Cuvée du Goulté
Jerome Prévost: Les Béguines

L. AUBRY FILS (R.M.)

Production: About 120,000 bottles annually.

The Aubry team comprises twin brothers Pierre, who studied enology, and Philippe, who studied biology. The brothers trace their winemaking roots in the region all the way back to 1790, but their distinctive champagnes show a flair for the experimental.

Aubry holds more than 40 acres of estate vineyards, mostly in the Premier Crus of Jouy-les-Reims, Pargny-lès-Reims, Villedommange and Coulommes-la-Montagne, while some wine from other vineyards is sold to *négociants*.

Stainless steel is used for fermentation, although some Chardonnay sees time in barrel. Malolactic fermentation is usually encouraged because by taming the acidity, the Aubrys believe it enables them dose more lightly.

The Aubry brothers are perhaps most well known as champions of Champagne's long-forgotten varieties Arbanne, Petit Meslier, and Pinot Gris, traditional grapes which fell by the wayside as Pinot Noir, Chardonnay, and Pinot Meunier grew in prominence. The Aubrys planted their first Arbanne and Petit Meslier in the late 1980s with the goal of producing a special cuvée in honor of the estate's bicentennial. These lesser-known grapes now appear in several Aubry cuvées.

THE WINES

AUBRY (NV)
Dosage: Brut
Price: $40

This entry-level champagne is a blend of a recent vintage with some reserve wine (which dates back to 1998). The wine has traditionally been based largely on Pinot Meunier, with varying amounts of Chardonnay and Pinot Noir, although more recent blends have included dashes of Arbanne and Petit Meslier as well.

DUALIS (NV)
Dosage: Brut
Price: $110

This non-vintage blend is produced in the Sablé style, with 4 atmospheres of pressure as opposed to the usual 6, which translates to gentler bubbles and a softer mouthfeel. The Chardonnay from Jouy-les-Reims is aged in new oak and the Pinot Noir from Villedommange is aged in old oak.

Rosé (Vintage)

Dosage: Brut

Price: $50

Although not included on the label, Aubry's rosé always comes from a single vintage. About two parts Pinot Noir and one part Chardonnay, the color comes from still Pinot Meunier—sourced from an old-vine parcel in Jouy-lès-Reims—which comprises about 15% of the cuvée.

Aubry de Humbert (Vintage)

Dosage: Brut

Price: $70

This flagship vintage wine is made from equal parts Chardonnay, Pinot Noir, and Pinot Meunier, although recent releases have included a bit of Petit Meslier and Arbanne. Named after the bishop who set the cornerstone at the cathedral of Reims, the grapes come from Jouy-les-Reims and Villedommange.

Ivoire et Ebene (Vintage)

Dosage: Brut

Price: $50

Not a true single vineyard wine, but all the grapes all come from the same limestone and clay soils, resulting in a wide spectrum snapshot of the terroir. The Chardonnay (which makes up 60-70%) hails from a southwest-facing parcel in Jouy-lès-Reims called L'Auditeur, and the Pinot Meunier is sourced from the opposing hillside called Les Bonnes Fontaines. Recent vintages have seen some Pinot Noir added to the mix.

Le Nombre d'Or Campanae Veteres Vites (NV)

Dosage: Extra Brut

Price: $55

Starting in 1994 vintage, the Aubry brothers decided to display all their lesser-known grape varieties (Pinot Gris, Petit Meslier, Arbanne) with this blend. In 1998, this cuvée become a tool to show off all of seven of their grape varieties, so they added Pinot Blanc, Chardonnay, Pinot Noir, and Pinot Meunier to the wine. All of the grapes come from Jouy-lès-Reims and Villedommange.

Le Nombre d'Or Sablé Blanc des Blancs (Vintage)

Dosage: Brut

Price: $70

This wine frequently uses all the white grapes, Arbanne, Petit Meslier, Chardonnay, and Pinot Blanc. The Sablé style is achieved by adding less sugar in the liqueur de tirage, so the secondary fermentation leaves the finished wine with less pressure.

Sablé Rosé Nicolas Francois Aubry (Vintage)

Dosage: Brut

Price: $65

A fascinating wine composed of lightly macerated Pinot Noir, sometimes co-fermented with Pinot Meunier, blended with Chardonnay, Arbanne, Petit Meslier, Pinot Blanc and a small portion of still red wine. With no dosage, and a lower four atmospheres of pressure, this is a unique interpretation of rosé Champagne.

L. Aubry Fils

6 Grande Rue

51390 Jouy-lès-Reims

www.champagne-aubry.com

Tel: (+33) 3 26 49 20 07

info@champagne-aubry.com

No visits or direct sales.

H. BILLIOT & FILS (R.M.)

Production: About 50,000 bottles annually.

In the early 1900s, Louis Billiot tended the family's vines in the village of Ambonnay, located in the Montagne de Reims. After purchasing a press, he began pressing grapes for Mumm and Moët & Chandon, though he set aside some grapes to make his own wine. His grandson, Henri, took control of the family's holdings in Ambonnay and shifted to producing only estate wines. Much of the estate's reputation stems from the work of Henri's son, Serge, who held the winemaking reins from 1954 to 2011. His daughter, Laetitia, now carries on the family tradition.

The estate comprises about 12 acres spread across 18 different parcels in Ambonnay, and almost all of the parcels are in favorable middle-slope locations. Ambonnay is home to mostly Pinot Noir, and H. Billiot's holdings are composed of 75 percent Pinot Noir and 25 percent Chardonnay. The wines are stainless-steel fermented, but the two prestige cuvées see time in old oak. All the estate's wines are produced without malolactic fermentation, fining, or filtration.

THE WINES

RÉSERVE (NV)
Dosage: Brut
Price: $50

Made from the first press, this Pinot Noir-dominated wine is usually a blend from three different vintages, aged three years *sur latte* before riddling and disgorgement.

MILLÉSIME (VINTAGE)
Dosage: Brut
Price: $50

Known for its bold, Pinot Noir-heavy expression, this more structured, vintage wine is produced to show off the age-worthy character of Ambonnay Pinot.

ROSÉ (NV)
Dosage: Brut
Price: $55

Made from all first-press juice, this wine is the product of stricter selection from the same wines that end up in the Brut Réserve. The color comes from still Pinot Noir, which comprises 8% of the cuvée. The final wine is aged two years before disgorgement.

CUVÉE LAETITIA (NV)
Dosage: Brut
Price: $95

Unusual for Ambonnay, this wine is made from mostly Chardonnay, with Pinot taking second chair. The wine is composed of two-thirds base wine, from a recent vintage, and one-third of reserves from a perpetual blend created in 1983.

CUVÉE JULIE (NV)
Dosage: Brut
Price: $80

Serge Billiot first crafted this cuvée in 1999, named after his granddaughter. This wine is generally all made from the same vintage, although a vintage is not indicated on the label. Equal parts Pinot Noir and Chardonnay, this wine is vinified in oak barrels, where it ages for six months. The final wine ages for at least four years before disgorgement.

H. Billiot & Fils
1 Place de la Fontaine
51150 Ambonnay
www.champagnebilliot.fr
Tel: (33) 3 26 57 00 14
hbil@aol.com
Visits by appointment.

FRANCIS BOULARD (N.M.)

Production: About 25,000 bottles annually.

Francis Boulard's family roots in Champagne go back five generations. His grandfather started off with only five acres of vines, so registered as a *négociant-manipulant* in order to expand production. Francis' father, Raymond, planted vines in Massif de St-Thierry, and he eventually grew his holdings to about 25 acres of vines in eight different villages. In 1973, Francis took control of production at the domaine, called Champagne Raymond Boulard.

Boulard wanted to reduce the need for chemicals in the vineyard and sulfur in the wine, so began farming some plots organically. In the early 2000s, he began using biodynamic methods on a small scale, and soon found the wines from those plots were more expressive of the terroir. Boulard became convinced the entire estate should be converted to biodynamic farming, but his brother and sister resisted, so Boulard broke off and started his own company with his daughter Delphine.

Today, Boulard farms just 7 acres of vines, split between 40% Pinot Meunier, 30% Pinot Noir, and 30% Chardonnay. His largest holdings are in the Massif de Saint-Thierry in Cormicy and Cauroy-les-Hermonville, and he has some vines in La Neuville-aux-Larris, Cuchery, and Belval-sous-Châtillon.

Although he is still registered as an N.M., that designation is simply a relic from the Raymond Boulard days. Francis's own vineyards fulfill all his needs.

Boulard uses low amounts of dosage and, in keeping with the tradition of his father, many cuvées are released in both Extra Brut and Brut Nature styles. Boulard relies on indigenous yeasts, utilizes stainless steel and neutral oak, and vinifies all his parcels separately.

THE WINES

CHAMPAGNE MILLESIMÉ (VINTAGE)
Dosage: Extra Brut
Price: $45

This blend of three classic grapes is vinified in neutral oak.

LES MURGIERS (NV)
Dosage: Extra Brut, Brut Nature
Price: $35

A blanc de noirs typically composed of 70% Pinot Meunier and 30% Pinot Noir, all from clay and limestone soils in the Valleé de la Marne. This wine is released with and without dosage.

BLANC DE BLANCS VIELLES VIGNES (NV)
Dosage: Extra Brut, Brut Nature
Price: $40

This wine comes from the sand-limestone terroir of a plot named Le Murtet, in Massif de Saint-Thierry. The average vine is 35 years old. This wine is released with and without dosage.

LES RACHAIS (VINTAGE)
Dosage: Brut Nature
Price: $55

Boulard's second vintage champagne, first released in 2002, comes from 40-year-old Chardonnay vines in a single sand/limestone vineyard. This was the first parcel Boulard turned to when he began experimenting with biodynamics.

GRAND CRU GRAND MONTAGNE (NV)
Dosage: Extra Brut, Brut Nature
Price: $50

This wine comes from the limestone soils of the Grand Cru Montagne de Reims, and the wine consists of Pinot Noir with about 10% Chardonnay. This wine is released with and without dosage.

GRAND CRU MAILLY-CHAMPAGNE (NV)
Dosage: Extra Brut, Brut Nature
Price: $55

This 90% Pinot Noir, 10% Chardonnay blend comes from the Grand Cru Mailly-Champagne, a village on the Montagne de Reims. The wine is vinified in small oak barrels and includes some 30% barrel-aged reserve wine. This wine is released with and without dosage.

PETRAEA (NV)
Dosage: Brut Nature
Price: $65

In 1997, Boulard started a perpetual blend composed of 60% Pinot Noir and equal parts Pinot Meunier and Chardonnay. Every year, after adding the new vintage, he draws out 25% of the reserve for a release.

Francis Boulard
RN 944 Reims-Laon
51220 Cauroy-lès-Hermonville
www.francis-boulard.com
Tel: (+33) 3 26 61 52 77
contact@francis-boulard.com
Visits by appointment.

EMMANUEL BROCHET (R.M.)

Production: About 9,000 bottles annually.

Emmanuel Brochet farms a little more than six acres of vines, all of which are planted in single parcel, the *lieu-dit* Le Mont Benoit. The site is located in the Premier Cru of Villers-aux-Noeuds, just south of Reims. In the 19th Century, this area was home to about 500 acres of vines, but many of the vines were pulled up as the city of Reims expanded, and today the village has only around 60 acres planted.

Brochet's family has owned Le Mont Benoit for generations, but they didn't tend the vines themselves. When a tenant's lease expired in 1997, Emmanuel took charge of the property, producing his own champagne five years later. He has already made quite a reputation for himself.

Emmanuel Brochet.

The oldest vines on Brochet's site, which is planted to about 37 percent Pinot Meunier, 30 percent Chardonnay, and 23 percent Pinot Noir, were planted in 1962. About half the vineyard was replanted in 1986.

In the vineyard, Brochet farms organically and has been certified since 2011. In the cellar, he separates his grapes by variety, vine age, and location, vinifying each lot separately in barrique. Brochet inoculates with a yeast strain cultivated by Fleury. Some wines go through malolactic fermentation, others don't. His wines are lightly dosed with *moût concentré rectifié*—concentrated and rectified grape must—rather than the more traditional *liqueur d'expédition*.

The Wines

Le Mont Benoit (NV)
Dosage: Extra Brut
Price: $55

Brochet's flagship cuvée, this wine is a blend of all three grapes, but the amounts change from year to year. Le Mont Benoit is typically about 80% base wine with 20% reserve wine.

Les Haut Chardonnay (Vintage)
Dosage: Extra Brut
Price: $100

Sourced entirely from Chardonnay planted in 1962, this champagne is made without malolactic fermentation.

Les Hauts Meuniers (Vintage)
Dosage: Extra Brut
Price: $105

First produced in 2008, this Pinot Meunier champagne comes from the highest vines on Brochet's vineyard, which were planted in 1962.

Emmanuel Brochet
7 Impasse Brochet
51500 Villers-aux-Nœuds
Phone: (+33) 3 26 06 99 68
Visits by appointment only.

CHARTOGNE-TAILLET (R.M.)

Production: About 90,000 bottles annually.

Chartogne-Taillet in based just northwest of Reims in Merfy, in Massif de Saint-Thierry's southern slopes. Chartogne-Taillet is this village's sole *récoltant-manipulant*. The estate was born of the marriage between Marie Chartogne and Étienne Taillet, but both families have their own deep histories in Champagne. The Chartogne family traces its Merfy roots back to 1870, while the Taillets possess written winemaking records dating back to the 1700s.

In 2006, Alexandre Chartogne took control of the family's vineyards and cellar from his parents, Philippe and Élisabeth, who had held the reins since 1978. Alexandre worked with Anselm Selosse, who had a strong influence on his winemaking style and methods. Alexandre ferments every one of his parcels separately, mostly in stainless steel but some old barrels and concrete eggs are thrown into the mix. He uses native yeast fermentation and allows malolactic fermentation to occur, or not, on its own.

The estate comprises a little less than 30 acres, divided into 30 parcels, most in Merfy but also in nearby Saint-Thierry. The vineyards are planted to Pinot Noir, Chardonnay, Pinot Meunier, and about 2 percent Arbanne, in soils composed of clay and sandstone over chalk.

THE WINES

CUVÉE SAINTE-ANNE (NV)
Dosage: Brut
Price: $45

Named after Merfy's patron saint, this champagne is a blend of the three classic grapes from a range of soils and sites around the village. It's vinified in stainless steel and bottled without filtration.

LE ROSÉ (NV)
Dosage: Brut
Price: $55

About equal parts Chardonnay and Pinot Noir, and frequently all from a single vintage, this rosé d'assemblage includes about 10% still Pinot Noir from Les Orizeaux, a parcel in Merfy that was planted in the early 1950s.

MILLÉSIME (VINTAGE)
Dosage: Brut
Price: $70

This vintage wine is a blend of 60% Pinot Noir and 40% Chardonnay sourced entirely from the Les Couarres vineyard in Merfy. The vines, planted in rich clay with sand and chalk, average 30 years of age.

HEURTEBISE (VINTAGE)
Dosage: Extra Brut
Price: $70

A single-vineyard blanc de blancs from the south-facing Heurtebises parcel, these Chardonnay vines are, on average, 35 years old and grown in clay and sand over limestone. The wine is fermented in stainless steel and concrete eggs.

LES BARRES (VINTAGE)
Dosage: Extra Brut
Price: $115

This blanc de noirs comes from a parcel of ungrafted Pinot Meunier vines grown in sandy soils, with less limestone than nearby parcels, planted in the 1950s. The wine is fermented in oak barrels.

CUVÉE FIACRE (VINTAGE)
Dosage: Brut
Price: $170

Chartogne-Taillet's tête de cuvée, this wine is usually dominated by Chardonnay, grown in the red sandy soils of Chemin de Reims, and Pinot Noir from older vines grown in Orizeaux. Named for the family's ancestor, Fiacre Taillet, this stainless steel-fermented blend is only released in certain vintages.

Chartogne-Taillet
37 Gr Grande Rue
51220 Merfy
www.chartogne-taillet.com
Phone: (+33) 3 26 03 10 17
chartogne.taillet@wanadoo.fr
Visits by appointment only.

ANDRÉ CLOUET (R.M.)

Production: About 200,000 bottles annually.

Jean-François Clouet has Bouzy in his blood. The current winemaker for the historic André Clouet estate was born into this family with a long history of producing excellent champagne. Acknowledging his luck to be born and raised amid the soils and history of this heralded village, Jean-François still lives in the 17th century home built by his ancestors, who worked as printers for Louis XV's Royal Court at Versailles.

The domaine owns some 20 acres in the Grand Cru villages of Bouzy and Ambonnay, and their parcels are situated in the coveted middle slopes. The Montagne de Reims village of Bouzy is historic Pinot Noir territory, and Clouet is a savvy Pinot Noir specialist. The house produces a full range of champagnes from Pinot Noir grapes, including the well-known tête de cuvée, Cuvée 1911.

Jean-François ferments the wine in stainless steel and some neutral oak barrels, and the wines go through malolactic fermentation. André Clouet's bottles are easily recognizable by their ornate and old-fashioned labels, which seems befitting for descendants of royal printers.

THE WINES

MILLÉSIME (VINTAGE)
Dosage: Brut
Price: $50

Sourced from Bouzy and Ambonnay, Clouet's vintage-dated blanc de noirs is fermented in stainless steel and neutral oak barrels and usually aged four years on the lees.

GRANDE RÉSERVE (NV)
Dosage: Brut
Price: $35

Sourced from Bouzy and Ambonnay, this blanc de noirs is fermented in stainless steel and aged on the lees for six years.

SILVER (N.V.)
Dosage: Brut Nature
Price: $40

A pure and striking expression of Pinot Noir from a single parcel in Bouzy, this wine is finished without dosage. It is fermented and aged in neutral oak barrels.

ROSÉ (N.V.)
Dosage:
Price: $40

About 8% of this rosé d'assemblage is comprised of still Pinot Noir from Bouzy.

CUVÉE 1911 (N.V.)
Dosage: Brut
Price: $75

Clouet's tête de cuvée is sourced from the estate's top ten parcels in Bouzy. Each iteration is limited to 1,911 bottles.

André Clouet
8 Rue Gambetta
51150 Bouzy, France
Tel: (+33) 9 61 45 12 58
jfclouet@yahoo.fr
Visits by appointment.

R. H. COUTIER (R.C.)

Antoine Coutier.

Production: About 50,000 bottles annually.

The Coutier family has been producing champagne since 1901, when the grandfather of René Coutier, the estate's current proprietor, bottled his own wine instead of selling it all off to Charles Heidsieck and others. But the family has been tending vines since before the French Revolution. René has been making wine from his family's vineyards since 1971, and he took control in 1983.

Coutier possesses about 22 acres of vines, all of which are located in the Montagne de Reims Grand

Cru of Ambonnay, with the oldest vines dating back to the 1920s. About 17 of those acres are farmed organically. Coutier continues to sell some of his grapes to big houses like Moët & Chandon, Veuve Clicquot, and Taittinger, but he bottles his own estate wines under the R. H. Coutier label. Since Coutier presses his grapes in the cooperative of Ambonnay, he is registered as an R.C., not R.M.

Ambonnay is renowned for high quality Pinot Noir, but after World War II, René's father became the first to plant Chardonnay in the village. Keeping with that history, Chardonnay accounts for some 30 percent of the house's production. Chardonnay is blended into some wines to balance the power of Ambonnay Pinot Noir, but the estate bottles a blanc de blancs and a blanc de noirs. René also produces very small amounts of still Pinot Noir (Couteaux Champenois) from 30- to 40-year-old vines.

René's son, Antoine, recently returned to the estate after studying winemaking and will take over operations in the coming years.

THE WINES

TRADITION (N.V.)
Dosage: Brut
Price: $45

The Brut Tradition is a blend of about 75% Pinot Noir and 25% Chardonnay. This wine usually sees 100% malolactic fermentation.

BLANC DE BLANCS (N.V.)
Dosage: Brut
Price: $45

One of only a few Ambonnay producers who makes a blanc de blancs, Coutier's grapes comes from the oldest (and first) Chardonnay vines in the village, planted in 1946.

MILLÉSIME (VINTAGE)
Dosage: Brut
Price: $55

Normally a blend of 75% Pinot Noir and 25% Chardonnay, the wine is fermented and aged in stainless steel.

CUVÉE HENRI III (VINTAGE)
Dosage: Brut
Price: $55

This 100% Pinot Noir, first released in 1995, is partly vinified and aged in neutral barrique. It spends four years on its lees before disgorgement. The cuvée is named for the King of France who, in 1578, decreed an annual wine fair in Ambonnay.

R. H. Coutier
7 Rue Henri III
51150 Ambonnay, France
Tel: (+33) 3 26 57 02 55
Visits by appointment.

PAUL DÉTHUNE (R.M.)

Production: About 50,000 bottles annually.

Pierre Déthune carries on a long family tradition of producing estate-grown champagne that dates back to the late 19th century, although the Déthune family has been tending vines in Champagne since the early 1600s. Pierre's father, Paul, however, was the first to leave the family's other commercial crops aside and focus exclusively on estate champagne.

Pierre Déthune, who took over the estate from his father in 1990, now holds some 18 acres, consisting of 30 separate parcels peppered throughout the Grand Cru of Ambonnay. The estate vineyards are planted to 70% Pinot Noir and 30% Chardonnay. A sustainable grower, Déthune doesn't use insecticides, only uses organic fertilizer, and fills all his parcels with cover crops.

Over the past quarter century, Déthune and his wife Sophie have gone to great lengths to modernize the winery, purchasing temperature-controlled vats, installing solar panels for electricity, and investing in a rainwater collection system. Déthune doses with *moût concentré rectifié*—concentrated and rectified grape must—rather than the more traditional *liqueur d'expédition*, as he feels it provides for purer champagne. And he sources a lot of local Champenois oak for his barrels. For a relatively small grower-producer, Déthune produces an impressive range of wines.

THE WINES

GRAND CRU (NV)
Dosage: Brut, Extra Brut
Price: $45

The basic non-vintage is composed of about 70% Pinot Noir and 30% chardonnay. The wine includes a relatively high percentage of reserve wine (30-50%), which comes from a perpetual cuvée that has been in place for 30 years. This wine is released with two different levels of dosage.

ROSÉ (NV)
Dosage: Brut
Price: $45

Made from 80% Pinot Noir blended with 20% Chardonnay, this wine also includes some 30-50% reserve wine. A rosé d'assemblage, it takes its color from a small percentage of still red wine.

MILLÉSIME (VINTAGE)
Dosage: Brut
Price: $80

The basic vintage champagne from Déthune is usually a blend of 60% Chardonnay and 40% Pinot Noir, vinified and aged entirely in barrique.

BLANC DE NOIRS (VINTAGE)
Dosage: Brut
Price: $60

The Pinot Noir for this vintage-dated wine usually comes from Les Crayères, but always from vines that are a minimum of 35 years old. The wine is vinified and aged oak barrels.

BLANC DE BLANCS (VINTAGE)
Dosage: Brut
Price: $55

Something of a rarity in Pinot-dominated Ambonnay, this 100% Chardonnay goes through malolactic fermentation and is vinified and aged in oak.

CUVÉE PRESTIGE (NV)
Dosage: Brut
Price: $60

A 50/50 blend of Pinot Noir and Chardonnay, 70% of the wine comes from the current vintage while 30% is drawn from a perpetual blend started about 30 years ago. The wine is fermented and aged in old large oak barrels.

CUVÉE À L'ANCIENNE (VINTAGE)
Dosage: Brut
Price: $115

Déthune's top wine is equal parts Pinot Noir and Chardonnay, vinified and aged in oak and aged on its lees—under a cork and staple closure—for 7 years. The wine undergoes malolactic fermentation.

Paul Dethune
2 Rue du Moulin
51150 Ambonnay
www.champagne-dethune.fr
Phone:+33 3 26 57 01 88
info@champagne-dethune.com
Visits by appointment.

EGLY-OURIET (R.M.)

Production: About 100,000 bottles annually.

The Egly estate in Ambonnay dates back to 1930, but for many years the family sold most of its grapes, while bottling small amounts for family and friends. Charles Egly began producing estate champagne on a decent scale in the 1970s, but he still sold off most of the estate grapes. When current proprietor Francis Egly took over in 1982, he began bottling all of the estate fruit. He quickly developed a sterling reputation for high-quality champagne.

Egly-Ouriet is focused mainly on Pinot Noir, although some 30 percent of their vines are planted to

Francis Egly.

Chardonnay. The estate comprises about 30 acres, most of which are located in the Grand Cru of Ambonnay. Egly-Ouriet also has holdings in other Montagne de Reims Grand Crus of Bouzy and Verzenay, and a five-acre parcel of Pinot Meunier in the Premier Cru of Vrigny in the Petite Montagne.

Francis picks later than usual, choosing to harvest grapes at 12-13 percent potential alcohol. He relies on indigenous yeasts and ferments many of his wines in barriques, aging them for up to eight months. The small barrels allow him to vinify his parcels individually. With a wide range of wines, Egly-Ouriet is heralded by many champagne lovers as one of the finest.

THE WINES

TRADITION (NV)
Dosage: Brut
Price: $60

A blend of mostly Pinot Noir, with 30% Chardonnay, this contains 50% reserve wine from different vintages. The fruit comes from Ambonnay, Bouzy, and Verzenay.

LES VIGNES DE VRIGNY (NV)
Dosage: Brut
Price: $55

This is a unique champagne made from 100% old vine Pinot Meunier from a parcel in the Premier Cru of Vrigny. The wine is fermented in tanks, includes several vintages of reserve wine, and ages *sur latte* for at least three years prior to riddling and disgorgement.

VIEILLISSEMENT PROLONGÉ (NV)
Dosage: Extra Brut
Price: $80

Vieillissement Prolongé means extended aging, and this wine spends 70 months on its lees. A blend of mostly Pinot Noir and some Chardonnay, the dosage is generally less than 3 g/l.

BLANC DE NOIRS LES CRAYERES (NV)
Dosage: Brut
Price: $125

This wine comes from an intensely chalky single vineyard of Ambonnay Pinot Noir, which was planted in the late 1940s. The wine is fermented entirely in barrique and spends five years on its lees before release. Historically made from a single vintage (though not stated on the label), Egly now blends in reserve wine.

MILLÉSIME VIEILLES VIGNES (VINTAGE)
Dosage: Brut
Price: $125

Egly-Ouriet's only vintage-dated wine, this is a typical house blend of 70/30 Pinot Noir/Chardonnay, but ages on its lees for as long as 10 years. From 40-plus-year-old vines in Ambonnay, this wine is vinified in oak.

Egly-Ouriet
9 Rue de Trepail
51150 Ambonnay
www.egly-ouriet.fr
Phone: (+33) 3 26 57 82 26
contact@egly-ouriet.fr
Visits by appointment only.

Production: About 15,000 bottles annually.

Champagne runs in David Léclapart's blood. His father, grandfather, and great-grandfather made champagne from the family's vines in Trépail, a village on the southeast slopes of the Montagne de Reims, just north of Ambonnay. And after studying agriculture in college, Léclapart began working at Leclerc-Briant, a small, biodynamic producer in Épernay.

But when his father died in 1996, Léclapart would only agree to enter the family business if he could farm biodynamically. His family obliged. In 1998, Léclapart launched his eponymous domaine, which has been certified biodynamic since 2000. Unlike other villages on the slopes of the mountain, Trépail is planted almost entirely to Chardonnay. Indeed, 90 percent of Léclapart's 7.5 acres—which are spread across 22 separate parcels—is Chardonnay.

David Léclapart.

In the cellar, Léclapart relies on indigenous yeast for primary fermentation, rejects chaptalization (although it was performed in 2001 and 2007), bottles without fining or filtration, and minimizes the use of sulfur. All his wines are finished without dosage. Léclapart doesn't utilize reserve wines; all his champagnes are from a single vintage, which appears on the label. All his wines see full malolactic fermentation. Wines that see oak are vinified in neutral barriques purchased from Domaine Leflaive in Burgundy.

THE WINES

L'AMATEUR (VINTAGE)
Dosage: Brut Nature
Price: $100

Sourced from six different Chardonnay parcels in Trépail, this wine is vinified entirely in enamel-coated steel tanks.

L'ARTISTE (VINTAGE)
Dosage: Brut Nature
Price: $150

Sourced from three different plots of old-vine Chardonnay, half this wine is vinified in enamel-coated steel tanks and half in neutral barriques.

L'APÔTRE (VINTAGE)
Dosage: Brut Nature
Price: $200

Sourced from a single vineyard, called La Pierre St-Martin, which was planted in 1946. This blanc de blancs is vinified entirely in barrique.

L'ASTRE (VINTAGE)
Dosage: Brut Nature
Price: $215

Léclapart reserves his four parcels of Pinot Noir—planted in 1957, 1968, 1997, and 2001, respectively—for this blanc de noirs, which is vinified entirely in barrique.

David Léclapart
10 Rue de la Mairie
51380 Trépail
Tel: (+33) 3 26 57 07 01
david.leclapart@wanadoo.fr
No visits or direct sales.

MARIE-NOËLLE LEDRU (R.M.)

Marie-Noëlle Ledru.

Production: About 30,000 bottles annually .

The wines of Marie-Noëlle Ledru are the produce of a true one-woman show.

In 1984, she took the helm of her family's winery, which had been in existence since her father founded it a few decades earlier. Ledru handles every aspect of the operation herself, by hand—from farming and pressing to riddling and disgorging.

In 2010, a family dispute caused her to lose two-thirds of her vineyard land. Today, Ledru tends a little less than five acres in Ambonnay planted to 40-year-old pinot noir and chardonnay vines. She does not use herbicides, insecticides, or any other synthetic chemicals in her vineyards.

Ledru displays a similar respect for nature's way in the winery, which is next to the old stone house where she—and her family before her—have lived for years. She relies on indigenous yeast for primary fermentation, which takes place in stainless steel or enameled steel tanks. She does not filter her wines or use sulfur at disgorgement. Ledru allows her wines to undergo natural malolactic fermentation; intervening to block it would be out of character.

Ledru ages her non-vintage wines on the lees for an average of three years and her vintage wines for five years.

THE WINES

BRUT GRAND CRU (NV)
Dosage: Brut
Price: $65
Ledru's basic cuvée is 85% Pinot Noir and 15% Chardonnay. This wine is dosed at 6 g/l.

EXTRA BRUT GRAND CRU (NV)
Dosage: Brut Nature
Price: $65
The same as Ledru's basic cuvée, but finished without dosage.

BRUT ROSÉ GRAND CRU (NV)
Price: $65

A rosé d'assemblage, 15% of this wine is composed of still Pinot Noir from Ambonnay. The rest consists of Ledru's basic cuvée.

BRUT RESERVE GRAND CRU (VINTAGE)
Dosage: Brut
Price: $75

In exceptional years, Ledru bottles her basic cuvée (a blend of 85% Pinot Noir and 15% Chardonnay) without any reserve wine. This wine is dosed at 6 g/l.

BRUT NATURE GRAND CRU (VINTAGE)
Dosage: Brut Nature
Price: $75

The same as Ledru's vintage "Reserve" cuvée, but aged for longer on its lees and finished without dosage.

CUVÉE DU GOULTÉ (VINTAGE)
Price: $80

Ledru's flagship champagne, the Cuvée du Goulté is a Blanc de Noirs that comes from the best sites on the mid-slope of her vineyards in Ambonnay. The name is a reference to an old Champenois word for the first—or best—juice to run off the press. It's often, but not always, single-vineyard; that depends on the year. The Cuvée du Goulté is also typically vintage, but in some rare cases, Ledru will blend in a bit of reserve wine.

Marie-Noëlle Ledru
5 Place de la Croix
51150 Ambonnay
Tel: (33) 3 26 57 09 26

J. LASSALLE (R.M.)

Production: About 150,000 bottles annually.

Located in the Montagne de Reims village of Chigny-Les-Roses, this estate was founded in 1942 by Jules Lassalle, who developed a reputation for exquisite grower champagne. When Jules died in 1982, his wife, Olga, and daughter, Chantal Decelle-Lassalle, kept the tradition going. Chantal's daughter, Angéline Templier, became the estate winemaker in 2006, keeping true to their motto of *"une femme, un esprit, un style."*

J. Lassalle was the first true grower champagne to enter the US market, when respected wine importer Kermit Lynch brought the estate's wines to America in 1981.

Today, the Lassalle's farm some 40 acres of Pinot Meunier (48 percent), Chardonnay (30 percent), and Pinot Noir (22 percent). The 45 different parcels are spread among the villages of Chigny Les Roses, Ludes, Montbré, Puisieulx, Rilly La Montagne, Sermiers, and Villers Allerand. The average vine is an impressive 50 years old.

Chantal and Angéline still use the same wooden basket press that Jules set in place decades ago, and the parcels are vinified individually. The non-vintage champagnes are usually aged four years, the vintage wines for ten.

THE WINES

CACHET D'OR (NV)

Dosage: Brut

Price: $35

Typically a blend of equal parts Pinot Noir, Pinot Meunier, and Chardonnay, this affordable intro to the Lassalle portfolio is aged 36 months on its lees before disgorgement.

CUVÉE PRÉFÉRENCE (NV)

Dosage: Brut

Price: $45

This wine is typically a blend of 60% Pinot Meunier, 20% Pinot Noir, and 20% Chardonnay, aged four years before disgorgement.

ROSÉ (NV)

Dosage: Brut

Price: $55

Mostly Pinot Noir, this wine also includes about 10% Chardonnay and 5% Pinot Meunier.

CUVÉE ANGÉLINE (VINTAGE)

Dosage: Brut

Price: $70

Only produced in the best years and limited to 6,000 bottles, this is usually a blend of 60% Pinot Noir and 40% Chardonnay. It's aged at least seven years before disgorgement.

ROSÉ CUVÉE SPÉCIALE (NV)

Dosage: Brut

Price: $80

This blend of the Pinot Meunier, Pinot Noir, and Chardonnay grapes spends at least six years on its lees before disgorgement. It's created only for the US market.

SPECIAL CLUB (VINTAGE)

Dosage: Brut

Price: $80

Based on Lassalle's oldest vines and the best parcels, this vintage-dated wine is a blend of 60% Chardonnay and 40% Pinot Noir that goes through malolactic fermentation. It is only produced in certain vintages from the best cuvées.

J. Lassalle

21 Rue du Châtaignier Fourchu

51500 Chigny-les-Roses

www.champagne-jlassalle.com

Phone: (+33) 3 26 03 42 19

contact@jlassalle.com

Visits by appointment.

A. MARGAINE (R.M.)

Production: About 55,000 bottles annually.

In the 1920s, Gaston Margaine bottled still wine grown from estate vineyards, but it wasn't until the 1950s that André Margaine began taking champagne production seriously. The estate expanded throughout the 1970s, and the current proprietor Arnaud Margaine has held the reins since 1989.

Arnaud Margaine.

Margaine's 16 acres of vines are located in the Montagne de Reims Premier Cru of Villers-Marmery, with a small parcel of Pinot Noir in the Grand Cru of Verzy. In an area dominated by Pinot Noir, the village of Villers-Marmery is a haven for Chardonnay, and about 90% of Margaine's vines are planted to Chardonnay, including a clone that is unique to the area. The average vine age is more than 30 years. Margaine recently eliminated the use of all chemical herbicides in his vineyards and is filling his parcels with cover crops.

In the cellar, Margaine takes an open-minded approach, refraining from sticking to specific blending recipes and altering the particular parcels used for his non-vintage and vintage wines. He has moved away from malolactic fermentation in recent years, preferring the freshness of champagne when it's blocked, but some of his wines still go through it. Some 20 percent to 30 percent of the wines see time in neutral barriques, and he takes the rare approach of storing some reserve wines in bottles.

THE WINES

LE BRUT (NV)
Dosage: Brut
Price: $45

The standard non-vintage blend from Margaine, this wine is generally 90% Chardonnay and 10% Pinot Noir. It typically includes a relatively high percentage of reserve wine, sometimes as much as 50%.

ROSÉ (NV)
Dosage: Brut
Price: $50

Typically, this wine is composed of 70% Chardonnay and 30% Pinot Noir. A rosé d'assemblage, about 10% of the cuvée is still Pinot Noir. It is vinified entirely in stainless steel and ages *sur latte* for 24 months before disgorgement.

BLANC DE BLANCS (VINTAGE)

Dosage: Extra Brut
Price: $65

Generally produced without malolactic fermentation, this wine is vinified in about 80% stainless steel and 20% neutral barrique. It spends 5 years on its lees before disgorgement.

SPECIAL CLUB (VINTAGE)

Dosage: Brut
Price: $80

The top of the line for Margaine, this vintage-dated wine debuted in 1978. The grapes come from a chalky, south-facing site called Les Allouettes Saint-Betzs, although some other parcels are blended in from vintage to vintage. All Chardonnay, about 20% is vinified in barrique, the rest in stainless steel. It ages for about 8 years before disgorgement.

A. Margaine

3 Avenue de Champagne

51380 Villers-Marmery, France

Phone: (+33) 3 26 97 92 13

Visits by appointment.

JÉRÔME PRÉVOST [LA CLOSERIE] (R.M.)

Production: About 15,000 bottles annually.

In 1987, Jérôme Prévost inherited a 5.5-acre parcel of vines in Gueux, a village just west of Reims in the Vesle river valley. His grandmother had leased out the vineyard—called "Les Béguines"—to local farmers. But 21-year-old Prévost decided to manage the property on his own and sell the grapes.

Jérôme Prévost.

Prévost quickly recognized the quality of his soil. A mix of lime-rich clay and sand packed with marine fossils—with chalk, of course, buried deep below—it had been planted to Pinot Meunier in the early 1960s. In 1992, Prévost began urging producers in the region to ignore the antiquated *Échelle des Crus* rankings and pay for grapes based on quality. The effort failed, but it no doubt helped inspire Prévost to begin making his own wine.

In 1998, thanks to a friendly push from Anselme Selosse, Prévost launched his own estate, called "La Closerie." In the years since, his wines have gained a dedicated following.

In the vineyard, Prévost farms organically, avoiding synthetic pesticides and herbicides. In the cellar, he relies on indigenous yeasts for primary fermentation, which takes place in neutral barriques and demi-muids, rejects chaptalization, bottles without fining or filtration, and minimizes the use of sulfur. He ages his wines *sur latte* for 18 months prior to riddling and disgorgement and then releases them immediately. His wines are finished without dosage.

Since vintage-dated champagne must age on its lees for three years, Prévost's wines aren't technically vintage offerings. But his wines are always the product of a single year. Fortunately, an easily deciphered code—with "LC" prefacing the vintage year—can be found on the label of each bottle.

Prévost also owns a half-acre parcel of vines directly adjacent to Les Béguines that's co-planted with Chardonnay, Pinot Blanc, Pinot Meunier, and Pinot Noir. Prévost blends this fruit into his production, but might eventually bottle this parcel separately.

THE WINES

LES BÉGUINES (VINTAGE)
Dosage: Brut Nature
Price: $110
    A single-vintage Pinot Meunier from Les Béguines.

FAC-SIMILE (VINTAGE)
Dosage: Brut Nature
Price: $150
    Each year, Prévost makes a miniscule amount of still red wine from a small parcel of Les Béguines that's afflicted with *court-noué*, a disease that stunts flowering and concentrates juice. This still red is blended into the regular Les Béguines production to make Fac-Simile, a rosé. Only about 3,000 bottles of Fac-Simile are produced each year.

La Closerie
2 Rue de la Petite Montagne
51390 Gueux, France
Tel: (+33) 3 26 03 48 60
champagnelacloserie@orange.fr
No visits or direct sales.

SAVART (R.M.)

Production: About 35,000 bottles annually.

In 1947, René Savart purchased a parcel of vines in Ecueil, the small village that marks the start of the Montagne de Reims ridge, and began making wine. His son Daniel took over about 20 years later, boosting production throughout the 1980s by expanding his family's vineyard holdings.

Daniel's son Frédéric hoped to escape the family business and instead play professional soccer. But destiny eventually came calling. So in 1993, he returned home to study at Avize Viti Campus, the local oenology school.

In the vineyard and the cellar, he also began pushing for changes. In 2005, Frédéric officially took charge. By then, he had eliminated the use of synthetic chemicals in all his vineyards.

Today, Savart owns 10 acres of vines. About three quarters of the family's holdings are in Ecueil; the rest are in the adjacent village of Villers-aux-Noeuds. A full 90 percent of Savart's vines are Pinot Noir; just 10 percent are Chardonnay.

In the cellar, Savart has no set formula. Some wines go through malolactic fermentation, others don't. Some wines are vinified and aged in steel, others in old and new demi-muids, others in old and new barriques. Some of Savart's oak barrels come from Burgundy, others from the forest around Ecueil. Every decision depends on the wine and what the vintage demands. For dosage, which is always light, Savart uses *moût concentré rectifié*, or concentrated and rectified grape must, rather than the more traditional *liqueur d'expédition*, as he feels MCR is more neutral.

THE WINES

L'OUVERTURE (NV)
Dosage: Brut
Price: $45
A blanc de noirs vinified in stainless-steel vats. The wine goes through malolactic fermentation. About 70 percent of the cuvée comes from the current vintage, the rest is reserve wine.

L'ACCOMPLIE (NV)
Dosage: Brut
Price: $55
A blend of 70% Pinot Noir and 30% Chardonnay, vinification is split equally between oak and stainless-steel vats. This wine is typically comprised of two vintages. Partial malolactic fermentation is allowed.

BULLE DE ROSÉ (NV)
Dosage: Brut
Price: $60
This rosé d'assemblage is comprised of 82% Pinot Noir, 10% Chardonnay, and 8% still red wine. Half the cuvée comes from the current vintage wine; the rest is reserve wine. About 80% is vinified in stainless-steel vats. Partial malolactic fermentation is allowed.

L'ANNÉE (VINTAGE)
Dosage: Extra Brut
Price: $70
Savart's largest-production vintage offering is produced by co-fermenting 55% Pinot Noir and 45% Chardonnay. It is vinified and aged entirely in oak barrels and malolactic fermentation is arrested.

DAME DE COEUR (VINTAGE)
Dosage: Extra Brut
Price: $110
A single-vineyard blanc de blancs, vinified in demi-muids, sourced from Le Mont des Chrétiens in Ecueil. Malolactic fermentation is arrested.

EXPRESSION (VINTAGE)
Dosage: Brut Nature
Price: $150
A blanc de noirs sourced from parcels with more than 60 years of vine aged in Ecueil. Vinified in barriques.

Savart
1 Chemin de Sacy
51500 Ecueil
www.champagne-savart.com
Tel: (33) 3 26 84 91 60
hello@champagne-savart.com
Visits by appointment.

VILMART & CIE (R.M.)

Production: About 105,000 bottles annually.

Vilmart & Cie traces its roots to 1872. That year, Désiré Vilmart purchased vines in Rilly-la-Montagne. The champagne house was launched 18 years later when he decided to begin making his own wine. Ever since, Vilmart has refused to sell grapes to *négociants*.

Today, the domaine is run by fifth-generation vigneron Laurent Champs, who took over the property from his mother, Nicole Vilmart, and his father René, who was originally a vineyard worker, in 1989.

Since day one, Champs has rejected the use of all synthetic fertilizers, herbicides, pesticides, and insecticides. Vilmart's 27 acres are split over just 12 parcels, so they're relatively sheltered from chemical treatments in nearby vineyards. Most of Vilmart's vines are in Rilly-la-Montagne, but a few plots are in the neighboring commune of Villers-Allerand. Vilmart's vines are 60 percent Chardonnay, 36 percent Pinot Noir, and 4 percent Pinot Meunier.

Champs ferments and ages all his wines in oak, a technique that his parents adopted back when most champagne producers were relying on concrete. Today, Champs mostly uses large foudres for his non-vintage offerings and barriques for his vintage wines. Vilmart's wines do not go through malolactic fermentation.

The Wines

GRANDE RÉSERVE (NV)
Dosage: Brut
Price: $50

Vilmart's basic offering, this blend of 70 percent Pinot Noir and 30 percent Chardonnay is aged for 10 months in large foudres.

GRAND CELLIER (NV)
Dosage: Brut
Price: $70

A blend of 70 percent Chardonnay and 30 percent Pinot Noir from two parcels in Rilly-la-Montagne: Les Hautes Grèves and Les Basses Grèves. Vinified and aged in large foudres before spending about 18 months *sur latte*.

CUVÉE RUBIS (NV)

Dosage: Brut

Price: $100

Historically, this rosé was created by blending in still red wine. In 2010, though, Vilmart began producing this as a *saignée* champagne, so it now receives its color from maceration. A blend of 90 percent Pinot Noir and 10 percent Chardonnay, typically from two vintages, this wine is sourced entirely from parcels in Rilly-la-Montagne. Vinified and aged in large foudres before spending about 18 months *sur latte*.

GRAND CELLIER D'OR (VINTAGE)

Dosage: Brut

Price: $90

A blend of 80 percent Chardonnay and 20 percent Pinot Noir from "Les Blanches Voies Bas," a parcel in Rilly-la-Montagne. This wine spends 10 months in neutral barriques and then about four years on its lees.

GRAND CELLIER RUBIS (VINTAGE)

Dosage: Brut

Price: $150

This vintage rosé is made by creating a *saignée* of Pinot Noir, which comprises about 60 percent of the final blend, and then adding Chardonnay.

COEUR DE CUVÉE (VINTAGE)

Dosage: Brut

Price: $150

Sourced from vines in "Les Blanches Voies Bas," a parcel in Rilly-la-Montagne, that were planted in the early 1950s, this wine is made with the "Coeur"—or heart—of the cuvée, which is the term used for the best part of a harvest's initial pressing. This wine is fermented and aged in 1-3-year-old barriques before spending about 6.5 years on its lees before disgorgement.

Vilmart & Cie

5 Rue des Gravières

www.champagnevilmart.fr

51500 Rilly-la-Montagne

Tel: (33) 3 26 03 40 01

vilmart@champagnevilmart.fr

Visits accepted.

Section Three:
Vallée de la Marne

Vineyards north of the town of Ambonnay.

The Vallée de la Marne comes into Champagne country from the southeast, about three miles south of Bouzy. There, as one heads west towards the Seine and Paris, vineyards cover the steep slopes that line both sides of the famed river and the tinier slopes that line the dozens of small streams that feed into it. The Marne Valley's vineyards, which together form Champagne's largest sub-region, end about 45 miles west of Épernay in the village of Saâcy-sur-Marne.

The valley was created by a geological upheaval which raised the Alps and lowered the Paris basin. It also drove the region's chalk deposits deep underground. The Marne valley's chalk is far further below the surface than in Montagne de Reims and Côtes des Blancs. Its topsoil, while still chalky, is packed with more clay and sand. Most villages sit along the riverbanks with vineyards running up the hillsides. But alluvial deposits also abound. And as one moves further west of Épernay, soil quality—and ratio of chalk—decreases. Indeed, Champagne's westernmost Premier Cru is Cumières, which is just three miles west of Épernay.

Since icy air is easily trapped between the valley's two slopes, the region is especially prone to frost. Consequently, Pinot Meunier dominates—accounting for 61 percent of plantings—since it flowers later and ripens sooner than Pinot Noir and Chardonnay. About 23 percent of the valley is planted to Pinot Noir and 16 percent to Chardonnay.

Pinot Meunier is a workhorse, and the Marne valley has long been a kind of grape factory for Champagne's largest producers. Historically, this variety of grape played third fiddle to Pinot Noir and Chardonnay; it was

QUICK FACTS

29,500 planted acres
5221 growers
Pinot Meunier: 61%
Pinot Noir: 23%
Chardonnay: 16%

SUB-REGIONS

Coteaux Sud d'Épernay
Grande Vallée de la Marne
Condé
Vallée de la Marne Rive Gauche
Vallée de la Marne Rive Droite
Vallée de la Marne Ouest

PREMIERS CRUS

Avenay-Val-d'Or
Bisseuil
Champillon
Cumières
Dizy
Hautvilliers
Mareuil-sur-Aÿ
Mutigny
Pierry

prized for lending fruity aromas and youthful softness to blends, but rarely taken seriously on its own. Today, though, an increasing number of vignerons are proving that Pinot Meunier can be just as distinctive and compelling as Champagne's more famous grapes.

Although Pinot Meunier is the most planted grape, Pinot Noir rules the valley's Grand Crus and Premier Crus, which are sandwiched between Montagne de Reims and the Côte des Blancs in the east.

The first Grand Cru, **Tours-sur-Marne**, is a riverside town with a handful of vineyards on the slopes, away from the alluvial soils. Heading west, one encounters three Premier Crus—Bisseuil, Mareuil-sur-Aÿ, and Mutigny—before encountering **Aÿ**, one of Champagne's top communes. Aÿ's vineyards run east, offering ideal south and southwest sun exposure to the grapes. The Marne Valley's remaining Premier Crus, Champillon, Cumières, Dizy, and Hautvilliers, all lie within four miles of Aÿ. All these villages lie in the sub-region of the **Grande Vallée de la Marne.**

Champagne's next major growing region, the Chardonnay-dominated Côte des Blancs, begins directly across the Marne River from Aÿ, to the southeast of Épernay. To the southwest of Épernay, though, lies a major sub-region of the Vallée de la Marne called the **Coteaux Sud d' Épernay.** This 3,000-acre growing area shares characteristics with both the Vallée de la Marne and Côte des Blancs.

GRAND CRUS

Aÿ
Tours-sur-Marne

LEADING PRODUCERS

Bérèche et Fils
Gaston Chiquet
Gatinois
Geoffroy
Henri Goutorbe
Marc Hébrart
Laherte Freres
Georges Laval
Christophe Mignon
Moussé Fils
R. Pouillon
Tarlant

PRODUCERS TO KNOW

Françoise Bedel
Bourgeois-Diaz
Didier-Ducos
Bruno Gobillard
Grumier
Michel Loriot
Lamiable
Henri Mandois
José Michel
Charles Orban
Franck Pascal
Ruelle Pertois
Jean-Marc Séleque

So as one might expect, Pinot Meunier and Chardonnay are planted about equally, with about 10 percent of the region planted to Pinot Noir. Historically, wine enthusiasts ignored this region. But an increasing number of young vignerons are proving that the terroir of the Coteaux Sud d' Épernay can produce exceptional champagne.

ICONIC WINES OF TERROIR

Bérèche et Fils: Reflet d'Antan
Billecart Salmon: Le Clos Saint-Hilaire
Bollinger: Vielles Vignes Françaises
Georges Laval: Chênes
Georges Laval: Les Hautes-Chèvres
Jacquesson: Aÿ Vauzelle Terme
Krug: Clos d'Ambonnay
Philipponnat: Clos des Goisses
Tarlant: BAM!

BÉRÈCHE ET FILS (N.M.)

Production: About 85,000 bottles annually.

The Bérèche domaine was founded in 1847. Yet it only recently gained global acclaim. In 2004, fifth-generation vigneron Raphael Bérèche took over from his parents, Jean-Pierre and Catherine. He immediately began converting to organic farming, eliminating the use of synthetic chemicals in all the family's vineyards. His brother Vincent joined the family business in 2008 and helped push their efforts into overdrive. Today, all the family's holdings are packed with cover crops and worked by hand. The brothers are also moving toward biodynamics.

Today, Bérêche owns 24 acres of vines spread over 21 parcels. Most of the family's vines are split between three growing areas: the chalky soils of Montagne de Reims in and around Ludes; the sandy in Ormes; and the chalky-clay soils in the western Vallée de la Marne around Mareuil-le-Port. The brothers have smaller parcels on the southeastern slope of the Montagne de Reims in Trépail and south of Mareuil-le-Port in Festigny. In 2012, they acquired a one-third-acre parcel in the Grand Cru village of Mailly. The holdings are split roughly evenly between Chardonnay, Pinot Noir and Pinot Meunier.

In the cellar, the Bérêche brothers vinify and age each parcel separately, relying on indigenous yeast for primary fermentation. They block malolactic in all their wines. Interestingly, their sur lie aging is done under cork—not the standard crown cap—to introduce a small amount of oxygen during lees aging. Every bottle is hand disgorged and dosage is always light.

Note that Bérêche is a *négociant-manipulant*, not a récoltant-manipulant. The brothers changed their status in 2013 to boost production of their basic cuvée (about 15 percent of the wine's fruit now comes from three nearby growers) and to develop a new brand, called "Raphaël et Vincent Bérêche," for a new range of wines. The rest of the lineup remains entirely estate grown.

THE WINES

BRUT RÉSERVE (NV)
Dosage: Brut
Price: $45

About equal parts Chardonnay, Pinot Noir and Pinot Meunier, about 70 percent of this wine is comprised of one recent vintage with the balance coming from reserve wines. Since 2013, about 15 percent of the fruit for this wine has been purchased.

LES BEAUX REGARDS (VINTAGE)
Dosage: Extra Brut
Price: $70

A single-vintage blanc de blancs sourced from just two vineyards. About 70 percent of the cuvée is sourced from a parcel in Ludes planted in 1902; the rest from a vineyard in Mareuil-le-Port planted in 1970.

RIVE GAUCHE (NV)
Dosage: Extra Brut
Price: $85

A blanc de noirs comprised entirely of Pinot Meunier from Les Misy, a vineyard in Port à Binson planted in 1969.

CAMPANIA REMENSIS (NV)
Dosage: Extra Brut
Price: $80

A rosé d'assemblage comprised of 65% Pinot Noir, 30% Chardonnay, and 5% percent still Pinot Noir. All the fruit comes from Ormes.

LE CRAN (VINTAGE)
Dosage: Extra Brut
Price: $100

A single-vintage cuvée, sourced from two vineyards in Ludes, that is equal parts Pinot Noir and Chardonnay. The Chardonnay is sourced from Les Hautes Plantes, which was planted in 1969, while the Pinot Noir is sourced from La Vigne St-Jean, which was planted in 1973.

REFLET D'ANTAN (NV)
Dosage: Extra Brut
Price: $115

Equal parts Chardonnay, Pinot Noir and Pinot Meunier, this wine is drawn from a perpetual blend started in 1985, two-thirds of which is replaced each harvest.

Bérèche et Fils
33 Route de Louvois
51500 Le Craon de Ludes
www.bereche.com
Tel: (33) 3 26 61 13 28
maison@bereche.com
Visits by appointment only.

GASTON CHIQUET (R.M.)

Production: About 220,000 bottles annually.

The story of Gaston Chiquet begins in 1919. That year, brothers Fernand and Gaston Chiquet began making wine from the vines that their family had been tending for nearly 200 years. At first, the wines were bottled and sold as Chiquet Frères. In 1935, though, Gaston separated from his brother to create his own brand

In the 1950s, Gaston and his son Claude expanded their vineyard holdings, purchasing vineyards in the Aÿ and Hautvillers. Today, the estate is in the hands of Claude's two sons Antoine and Nicolas, who farm about 57 acres in Hautvillers, Dizy, Mareuil-sur-Aÿ, and Aÿ. The distribution of grapes planted is 46 percent Chardonnay, 34 percent Pinot Meunier, and 20 percent Pinot Noir, and the average age of the vines is 27 years.

Every parcel is vinified separately and always goes through malolactic fermentation. No wood is used in the cellar.

Antoine Chiquet of Champagne Gaston Chiquet.

Gaston Chiquet farms sustainably, keeping chemical use to an absolute minimum and filling its vineyards with grass as a cover crop. It has been a member of the *Club Trésors de Champagne* since it was first founded in 1971.

THE WINES

TRADITION BRUT (NV)
Dosage: Brut
Price: $50

A blend of 40% Pinot Meunier, 35% Chardonnay, and 25% Pinot Noir, this wine is sourced from vineyards with an average age of 25 years in the villages of Hautvillers, Dizy, and Mareuil-sur-Aÿ. Aged *sur latte* for about three years before disgorgement.

BLANC DE BLANCS D'AŸ BRUT (NV)
Dosage: Brut
Price: $55

Aÿ is Pinot Noir country, so this Chardonnay is extraordinarily unique. The average age of the vines is 25 years, and it is aged *sur latte* for about three years before disgorgement.

CUVÉE DE RESERVE (NV)
Dosage: Brut
Price: $50

Sourced entirely from Hautvillers, Dizy and Mareuil-sur-Aÿ, this wine is a blend of 45% Pinot Meunier, 35% Chardonnay, and 20% Pinot Noir.

ROSÉ BRUT (NV)
Dosage: Brut
Price: $55

Sourced from Hautvillers, Dizy, and Mareuil-sur-Aÿ this rosé is a blend of 40% Pinot Meunier, 30% Pinot Noir, and 30% Chardonnay. The color comes from still Pinot Noir, which comprises 18% of the cuvée.

BLANC DE BLANCS D'AŸ BRUT (VINTAGE)
Dosage: Brut
Price: $150

Sourced from vineyards in Aÿ with an average of 25 years, this 100% Chardonnay ages for 8 years before disgorgement. Only available in magnum.

SPECIAL CLUB MILLESIME BRUT (VINTAGE)
Dosage: Brut
Price: $75

A blend of 70% Chardonnay and 30% Pinot Noir sourced from vineyards with an average age of 35 years in Hautvillers, Dizy, and Mareuil-sur-Aÿ. It ages on its lees for 7 years before disgorgement.

Gaston Chiquet
912 Avenue du Général Leclerc
51530 Dizy
www.gastonchiquet.com
Tel: (+33) 3 26 55 22 02
info@gastonchiquet.com
Open for visits Monday–Friday, and Saturday by appointment.

GATINOIS (R.M.)

Louis Cheval-Gatinois demonstrates hand disgorging in his family's cellar.

Production: About 50,000 bottles annually.

The Gatinois name began appearing on bottles in 1921, when Marie Michel-Le Cacheur, whose family had been tending vines and making wine in Champagne since 1696, married Charles Gatinois.

After the Second World War, the domaine was passed to Emile and Micheline Gatinois, who ran it until 1980. The domaine was then passed to their daughter, Marie, and her husband Pierre. They boosted production and brought global acclaim to the Gatinois wines.

Today, Marie and Pierre's son, Louis Cheval-Gatinois runs the estate. A 12th-generation vigneron, he oversees 17 acres of vines, spread over 27 parcels in the Grand Cru of Aÿ. While the vines are mostly planted to Pinot Noir, there is a small amount of Chardonnay.

Farming is sustainable. In the cellar, all fruit is handled minimally. Cheval-Gatinois relies on indigenous yeast for primary fermentation, which takes place in stainless steal. Natural malolactic fermentation is allowed and wines are finished without fining or filtering. No oak is used to make the champagne and dosage is kept low.

THE WINES

TRADITION GRAND CRU (NV)
Dosage: Brut
Price: $40
Sourced entirely from Aÿ, this wine is a blend of 80% Pinot Noir and 20% Chardonnay. The champagne ages *sur latte* for two years and is disgorged by hand.

RESERVE GRAND CRU (NV)
Dosage: Brut
Price: $40
Sourced entirely from Aÿ, this wine is a blend of 85% Pinot Noir and 15% Chardonnay. The champagne ages on its lees for four years and is disgorged by hand.

ROSÉ GRAND CRU (NV)

Dosage: Brut

Price: $50

Sourced entirely from Aÿ, this rosé d'assemblage contains a touch of still Pinot Noir from Aÿ sourced from 60-year-old vines. It is comprised of about 95% Pinot Noir and 5% Chardonnay. The champagne ages on its lees for three years and is disgorged by hand.

MILLÉSIMÉ GRAND CRU (VINTAGE)

Dosage: Brut

Price: $70

Sourced entirely from Aÿ, this wine is a blend of 85% Pinot Noir and 15% Chardonnay. The champagne ages for four years and is disgorged by hand.

Gatinois
7 Rue Marcel Mailly
51160 Aÿ
www.champagne-gatinois.com
Tel: (+33) 3 26 55 14 26
contact@champagne-gatinois.com
Visits by appointment only.

RENÉ GEOFFROY (R.M.)

Production: About 110,000 bottles annually.

The Geoffroy family can trace its winegrowing roots in Cumières as far back as the 17th century. The majority of their vineyards are still located there, but the winery today resides in Aÿ.

Today, Jean-Baptiste Geoffroy and his father René work 32 acres of vines, 27 of which are located on the slopes of Cumières, with the rest in Damery, Hautvillers, and Fleury-la-Rivière. The vineyards are planted with 42 percent Pinot Noir, 39 percent Pinot Meunier, and 19 percent Chardonnay. The average age of the vines is 20 years old, and the oldest plot dates back to 1926.

In his vineyards, Jean-Baptiste farms sustainably. In the cellars, he relies on gravity to move most juice, thus minimizing human handling. Every parcel is vinified separately in a mix of enameled-steel vats, barriques, demi-muids, and foudres. Jean-Baptiste blocks most malolactic fermentation and doses his wines with *moût concentré rectifié*—concentrated and rectified grape must—rather than the more traditional *liqueur d'expédition*.

Geoffroy's champagnes are red grape dominated cuvées, and the percentages of grapes used for all wines can vary from year to year. Jean-Baptiste sometimes makes both a still Pinot Noir and a still Pinot Meunier, but the wines are rare and depend on the vintage.

The Wines

Expression (NV)

Dosage: Brut

Price: $50

Sourced from Cumières and Hautvillers, this wine is generally a blend of 50% Pinot Meunier, 40% Pinot Noir, and 10% Chardonnay. It's made with 30% of reserve wine partly kept in oak casks, and is aged on its lees for a minimum of two years.

Cuvée Empreinte (Vintage)

Dosage: Brut

Price: $60

A blend of 79% Pinot Noir, 15% Pinot Meunier, and 6% Chardonnay sourced from vines with an average age of 30 years, partially vinified in oak barrels. Generally, this wine ages on its lees for three years.

Cuvée Volupte (Vintage)

Dosage: Brut

Price: $75

Sourced from Geoffroy's oldest vines on the slopes of Cumières, this blend is made up of 80% Chardonnay, 10% Pinot Noir, and 10% Pinot Meunier and vinified in neutral oak. Generally, this wine ages on its lees for three years.

Millesime (Vintage)

Dosage: Extra Brut

Price: $115

A blend of 30% Pinot Noir, 17% Pinot Meunier, and 53% Chardonnay, this wine is vinified in neutral oak and ages on its lees for seven years.

Les Houtrantes Complantés (NV)

Dosage: Brut

Price: $200

This wine is sourced from a old, single-vineyard field blend of all legal Champagne varieties, made from a blend of three different vintages.

Rosé de Saignée Brut (Vintage)

Dosage: Brut

Price: $65

This saignée rosé of Pinot Noir is always made from a single year.

René Geoffroy

4 rue Jeanson

51160 Aÿ

www.champagne-geoffroy.com

Tel: (+33) 3 26 44 32 31

info@champagne-geoffroy.com

Visits by appointment only.

HENRI GOUTORBE (R.M.)

Production: About 180,000 bottles annually.

Shortly after World War I, Emile Goutorbe established a vine nursery while working as the vineyard manager for Perrier-Jouët. The business was profitable enough for Emile to spend some of his earnings on vineyard parcels in Aÿ, and in the late 1940s, his son Henri began producing champagne.

Henri's son René took charge of the estate in 1970, and quickly worked to boost the family's vineyard holdings and upgrade the winery. René's wife Nicole, along with their children Elisabeth, Bertrand, and Etienne, help run the estate today.

The Goutorbe family owns about 62 acres of vines, with a quarter of them located in the Grand Cru of Aÿ, and the rest in the Premier Crus of Mareuil-sur-Aÿ, Bisseuil, Avenay-Val d'Or, and Hautvillers. The vineyards are planted with 70 percent Pinot Noir, 25 percent Chardonnay, and 5 percent Pinot Meunier.

All parcels are vinified separately in stainless steel tanks. All champagnes age on lees in the bottles for at least three years before disgorgement, with vintage wines aging for at least five years. Goutorbe is a member of the *Club Trésor*.

THE WINES

CUVÉE TRADITION (NV)
Dosage: Brut
Price: $45

This entry-level brut is a blend of 70% Pinot Noir, 5% Pinot Meunier, and 25% Chardonnay. With about 15% reserve wine, this is the only Goutorbe wine that is not entirely composed of grapes from Premier and Grand Crus.

CUVÉE PRESTIGE (NV)
Dosage: Brut
Price: $50

A blend of 70% Pinot Noir, 5% Pinot Meunier, and 25% Chardonnay. With about 20% reserve wine, this wine is composed entirely of grapes from Premier and Grand Crus.

BLANC DE BLANCS (NV)
Dosage: Brut
Price: $50

This blanc de blancs is sourced exclusively from vineyards in Bisseuil.

ROSÉ GRAND CRU (NV)
Dosage: Brut
Price: $55

A blend of 75% Pinot Noir and 25% Chardonnay, this rosé is sourced entirely from vineyards in Aÿ. The color comes from still Pinot Noir, which comprises 12% of the cuvée. The wine spends 20 months on its lees.

BRUT MILLESIME (VINTAGE)
Dosage: Brut
Price: $65

Sourced entirely from Aÿ, this 75% Pinot Noir and 25% Chardonnay blend is aged on its lees for over 84 months.

SPECIAL CLUB MILLESIME (VINTAGE)
Dosage: Brut
Price: $85

Sourced from old vines in Aÿ, this blend of 70% Pinot Noir and 30% Chardonnay ages on its lees for over 84 months.

Henri Goutorbe
9 Bis Rue Jeanson
51160 Aÿ
www.champagne-henri-goutorbe.com
Tel: (+33) 3 26 55 21 70
info@champagne-henri-goutorbe.com
Accepts visitors Tues.-Fri.; Mon. and Sat. by appointment only.

MARC HÉBRART (R.M)

Jean-Paul Hébrart.

Production: About 110,000 bottles annually.

This estate dates back to 1964, when Marc Hébrart began producing champagne in the Marne Valley. In 1997, Marc retired and handed the estate's operations to his son Jean-Paul Hébrart, who had been making champagne under his own name.

Jean-Paul merged the two estates and today farms almost 37 acres spread over 75 different parcels. Most holdings are in the Vallée de la Marne; Hébrart has vines in Aÿ, Mareuil-sur-Aÿ, Avenay Val d'Or, Bisseuil, Dizy, and Hautvillers. But he also owns vines in the Montagne de Reims Premier Cru of Louvois and the Côtes des Blancs Grand Crus of Avize, Chouilly, and Oiry. About 70 percent of Hébrart's holdings are planted to Pinot Noir, the rest to Chardonnay.

In his vineyards, Hébrart farms sustainably, avoiding synthetic treatments as much as possible.

All parcels are vinified separately, generally in enameled-steel tanks, although Hébrart has started to utilize barrels for some cuvées. He allows malolactic fermentation to occur naturally, riddles all bottles by hand, and doses with *moût concentré rectifié*—concentrated and rectified grape must—rather than the more traditional *liqueur d'expédition*.

Hébrart is a member of the *Club Trésor*.

THE WINES

CUVÉE DE RESERVE (NV)
Dosage: Brut
Price: $45

A blend of 82% Pinot Noir sourced from Mareuil-sur-Aÿ, Avenay, Val d'Or and Bisseuil, and 18% Chardonnay from Mareuil-sur-Aÿ. About 40% of this wine is composed of reserves. This wine spends about 24 months on its lees.

BRUT SELECTION (NV)
Dosage: Brut
Price: $55

This wine is a blend of 65% old-vine Pinot Noir from Mareuil-sur-Aÿ and 35% Chardonnay from Chouilly and Oiry. Includes about 20% reserve wines. This wine ages for about 24 months.

BLANC DE BLANCS (NV)

Dosage: Brut

Price: $50

This 100% Chardonnay wine is sourced mostly from Mareuil-sur-Aÿ, with 20% of the grapes coming from Oiry and Chouilly. It is usually a blend of three different years and is aged *sur latte* for around 36 months.

ROSÉ (NV)

Dosage: Brut

Price: $55

Sourced entirely from Mareuil-sur-Aÿ, this rosé is made from equal parts Pinot Noir and Chardonnay. The base wine is blended with 8.5% still Pinot Noir that was fermented and aged in a barrel for one year, and the champagne ages *sur latte* for about 24 months.

SPECIAL CLUB (VINTAGE)

Dosage: Brut

Price: $85

A blend of 55% Pinot Noir and 45% Chardonnay, this wine is sourced from several parcels of various ages: 35% old-vine Pinot Noir and 25% old-vine Chardonnay from Mareuil-sur-Aÿ, 20% Pinot Noir from Aÿ, and 20% Chardonnay from Oiry and Chouilly. Aged for 48 months.

RIVE GAUCHE-RIVE DROITE (VINTAGE)

Dosage: Extra Brut

Price: $125

Equal parts Pinot Noir (from Aÿ) and Chardonnay (from Oiry and Chouilly), this wine is vinified in used barrels. It ages on its lees for nearly 6 years before disgorgement.

Marc Hébrart

18-20 Rue du Pont

51160 Mareuil-sur-Aÿ

Tel: (+33) 3 26 52 60 75

Visits by appointment only.

LAHERTE FRÈRES (N.M.)

Production: About 100,000 bottles annually.

In 1889, with about 12 acres in Chavot, a small village in the Coteaux Sud D'Épernay, Jean-Baptiste Laherte launched a champagne house. For several decades, though, the family sold its grapes to the local cooperative.

Fourth-generation proprietor Michel Laherte doubled the size of the estate and decided to start making his own champagne. When his sons Thierry and Christian Laherte took over the estate, they changed its name to Laherte Frères.

Today, Thierry's son Aurélien runs Laherte Frères. He joined the business in 2002 and took the reins in 2005.

The Lahertes own 26 acres of vines spread over 76 separate parcels. More than 50 of those parcels have been farmed organically since 2005 and are certified organic; the rest are farmed sustainably without the use of herbicides or pesticides. Interestingly, Laherte Frères is registered as a *négociant-manipulant*. The house has this designation because different members of the family own different parcels, so the grapes are technically "purchased" by the domaine. Most of the family's holdings are in the Coteaux Sud d'Épernay, where parcels are owned in Chavot, Épernay, Mancy, Morangis, Moussy, and Vaudancourt. In the Côte des Blancs, the Lahertes own parcels in Vertus and Voipreux. In the Vallée de la Marne, the Lahertes own parcels in Boursault and Le Breuil. Laherte also purchases fruit from a friend in the Montagne de Reims who biodynamically farms a small parcel of Pinot Noir.

Laherte's popularity has skyrocketed in recent years.

THE WINES

ULTRADITION BRUT NV
Dosage: Brut
Price: $40
A blend of 60 percent Pinot Meunier, 30 percent Chardonnay, and 10 percent Pinot Noir sourced from vineyards in the Côteaux sud d'Épernay, Côte des Blancs, and Vallée de la Marne, this wine is vinified in a combination of foudres, neutral barriques, and stainless steel tanks and goes through partial malolactic fermentation. About 40 percent of the cuvée is comprised of reserve wine, which is stored in barriques.

ULTRADITION BLANC DE BLANCS (NV)
Dosage: Brut
Price: $45
Sourced entirely from Chavot, Épernay, and Vaudancourt, this blanc de blancs is vinified in foudres and neutral barriques and goes through partial malolactic fermentation. About 50 percent of the cuvée is comprised of reserve wine, which is stored in barriques.

ULTRADITION ROSÉ (NV)
Dosage: Brut
Price: $45
A blend of 50 percent Pinot Meunier, 40 percent Pinot Noir, and 10 percent Chardonnay, this wine is vinified in a combination of foudres, neutral barriques, and stainless steel tanks and goes through partial malolactic fermentation. About 40 percent of the cuvée is comprised of reserve wine, which is stored in barriques. The color comes from

Laherte's still Pinot Meunier, which comprises 8-12 percent of the final cuvée.

BLANC DE BLANCS BRUT NATURE (NV)
Dosage: Brut Nature
Price: $50
Sourced from parcels on the southern slopes of Épernay and in the Côte des Blancs, this blanc de blancs is vinified in foudres and neutral barriques and goes through partial malolactic fermentation. About 50 percent of the cuvée is comprised of reserve wine, which is stored in barriques. It is finished without dosage.

MILLÉSIME (VINTAGE)
Dosage: Extra Brut
Price: $65
A blend of 85 percent Chardonnay and 15 percent Pinot Meunier sourced from old vines, this cuvée is vinified entirely in barriques, 40 percent of which are new. Malolactic fermentation is blocked.

ROSÉ DE SAIGNÉE LES BEAUDIERS (VINTAGE)
Dosage: Extra Brut
Price: $80
Sourced from three parcels of Pinot Meunier in "Les Beaudiers," a vineyard in Chavot, planted in 1953, 1958, and 1965. These grapes are de-stemmed and macerated for 12-16 hours and vinified in neutral barrique, without malolactic fermentation. This wine is produced each year and doesn't include any reserve wine, but a vintage date isn't listed on the label.

LES GRAPPES DORÉES (VINTAGE)

Dosage: Brut

Price: $60

A single-vineyard *blanc de blancs* sourced from Voipreux, a village in the southern Côte des Blancs, planted in 1961. This wine is vinified entirely in tank and goes through partial malolactic fermentation. About 30 percent of the cuvée is comprised of reserve wine, which is stored in barriques.

LES 7 (NV)

Dosage: Extra Brut

Price: $90

Sourced from single, horse-plowed parcel in Chavot that was co-planted to all Champagne's authorized grapes (Chardonnay, Pinot Meunier, Pinot Noir, Pinot Blanc, Petit Meslier, Pinot Gris, and Arbane) in 2003. Vinified in neutral barriques, malolactic fermentation is blocked. About 60 percent of each year's cuvée is comprised of a perpetual blend combining each vintage since the start in 2005.

LES VIGNES D'AUTREFOIS (VINTAGE)

Dosage: Extra Brut

Price: $65

Entirely Pinot Meunier, this single-vintage cuvée is sourced from four parcels in Chavot and two parcels in Mancy, all of which were planted between 1947 and 1953. Vinified in neutral barriques, malolactic fermentation is blocked.

LES EMPREINTES (VINTAGE)

Dosage: Extra Brut

Price: $70

Equal parts Chardonnay (sourced from a parcel in Chavot planted in 1957) and Pinot Noir (sourced from a parcel in Chavot planted in 1983), this single-vintage cuvée is vinified in neutral barriques and malolactic fermentation is blocked.

Laherte Frères
3 Rue des Jardins
51530 Chavot-Courcourt
www.champagne-laherte.com
Tel: (33) 3 26 54 32 09
contact@champagne-laherte.com
Visits by appointment only.

GEORGES LAVAL (R.M.)

About 15,000 bottles annually.

The Lavals have worked in Champagne's vineyards since 1697. But the family didn't begin producing wine commercially until 1971, when Georges Laval launched an eponymous domaine in Cumières, Champagne's westernmost Premier Cru. An organic pioneer, Laval has rejected the use of all synthetic fertilizers, herbicides, pesticides, and

Vincent Laval.

insecticides since day one. The Lavals own five acres of vines in Cumières, split over 7 parcels. (It also owns a half acre of Pinot Meunier in Chambrecy, a village in the western Montagne de Reims, but that fruit is sold off.)

Today, Vincent Laval, Georges's son, runs the estate. He joined the family business in 1991 and took over in 1996.

Laval is decidedly old-fashioned. In the vineyard, this means plowing by horse. In the cellar, this means utilizing a traditional, 2,000-kg vertical basket press. All vineyard and cellar work is done by hand, with the help of just three employees.

Laval relies on indigenous yeast for primary fermentation, which takes place in neutral oak barrels. Each vineyard parcel is vinified separately. He has never chaptalized and finishes all his wines without dosage, bottling without fining or filtration, and minimizing the use of sulfur.

THE WINES

CUMIÈRES PREMIER CRU (NV)
Dosage: Brut Nature
Price: $85

A blend that's typically comprised of about half Chardonnay, with the rest split between Pinot Noir and Pinot Meunier, sourced from all Laval's holdings in Cumières. The exact proportions change each year.

CUMIÈRES ROSÉ PREMIER CRU (NV)
Dosage: Brut Nature
Price: $125

A 50/50 blend of old-vine Pinot Noir and Pinot Meunier pressed by feet, this *saignée* champagne receives its color from a 20-hour maceration.

CHÊNES (VINTAGE)
Dosage: Brut Nature
Price: $170

A single-expression champagne, this *blanc de blancs* is sourced Les Chênes, a vineyard with just 16 inches of topsoil on top of solid chalk.

This mid-slope vineyard is in the eastern edge of Cumières, just before Hautvillers.

LES HAUTES-CHÈVRES (VINTAGE)
Dosage: Brut Nature
Price: $225

This *blanc de noirs* is 100% Pinot Meunier from Les Hautes-Chèvres, where vines were planted between 1930 and 1971. The dark topsoil here is thicker and more clayey than one might expect. (Note that earlier iterations of the wine contained some Pinot Noir.)

LES LONGUES VIOLES (VINTAGE)
Dosage: Brut Nature
Price: Not available.

Laval will release this new cuvée—a *blanc de noirs* from Pinot Noir vines planted in 1947, 1967, and 1983—in 2019. As a child, his family raved about the fruit from this vineyard. So about a decade ago, he decided to leave it alone, hoping that a return to nature would revitalize the soils. The inaugural release was harvested in 2012.

Georges Laval
16 Ruelle du Carrefour
51480 Cumières
www.georgeslaval.com
Tel: (33) 3 26 51 73 66
champagne@georgeslaval.com
Visits by appointment only.

CHRISTOPHE MIGNON (R.M.)

Production: About 15,000 bottles annually.

Christophe Mignon comes from a long lineage of impressive vignerons; his great-grandparents, who planted the 15.5 acres of vines that today comprise the Mignon estate, were once awarded a medal for their still red wine.

Mignon's holdings, which are split about equally between Le Breuil and Festigny south of the Marne River, are spread over 30 parcels. About 90 percent of his plantings are Pinot Meunier; the rest is split equally between Chardonnay and Pinot Noir.

Christophe Mignon.

In the vineyard, Mignon adheres to no set system but certainly takes a natural approach. His vineyards are packed with cover crops and he plows regularly. Like organic farmers, he doesn't use any synthetic chemicals. Unlike organic farmers, though, Mignon works to minimize the use of copper sulfate by instead using homemade phytotherapeutic preparations to help his vines resist disease. Like biodynamic farmers, Mignon follows the lunar calendar for all his work.

In the cellar, Mignon vinifies all his parcels separately in enameled-steel tanks. He relies on indigenous yeasts to launch primary fermentation for about half his production and inoculates with a strain cultivated by Fleury for the other half. Some wines go through malolactic fermentation, others don't; the decision depends on the vintage. His wines are finished with little to no dosage and he uses minimal amounts of sulfur.

Note that Mignon also produces 30,000 bottles of estate champagne under a different label, Eugène Prudhomme.

The Wines

Cuvée Christophe Mignon (NV)
Dosage: Brut Nature, Extra Brut (3 g/l),
Brut (6 g/l)
Price: $45

A 100% Pinot Meunier that combines two recent vintages in equal parts, aged 24 months *sur latte*. Mignon releases this wine with three different levels of dosage.

Rosé d'Assemblage (NV)
Dosage: Brut
Price: $50

A 100% Pinot Meunier that combines two recent vintages in equal parts, aged 24 months *sur latte*. The color comes from barrel-fermented Pinot Meunier, which comprises about 15 percent of the blend.

Cuvée Millésimée (Vintage)
Dosage: Brut Nature, Brut (6 g/l)
Price: $60

A 100% Pinot Meunier typically sourced from Mignon's oldest vines in both Festigny and Le Breuil. The vineyard sources can change each year. Mignon releases this wine with two different levels of dosage.

Rosé de Saignée (Vintage)
Dosage: Brut
Price: $55

Sourced from the Le Brousse vineyard in Le Breuil, this single-vintage Rosé of Pinot Meunier receives its dark color from a 15-20 hour maceration. This wine ages 30 months *sur latte*.

Cuvée Coup de Foudre (Vintage)
Dosage: Brut
Price: $50

A single-vintage blend of equal parts Pinot Meunier, Pinot Noir, and Chardonnay, this wine is vinified in enameled-steel and then aged for one year in a new, 1,700-liter oak foudre. This wine ages on its lees for 48 months before disgorgement.

Christophe Mignon
51700 Festigny
www.champagne-christophe-mignon.com
Tel: (33) 3 26 58 34 24
mignon.christophe@orange.fr
Visits by appointment.

MOUSSÉ FILS (N.M.)

Production: About 58,000 bottles annually.

The Moussé family has been making champagne since 1923. But the family has been growing grapes in the Vallée de la Marne village of Cuisles since 1750.

Today, fourth-generation vigneron Cédric Moussé oversees the estate and its 13.5 acres of vineyards, which are clustered closely together in Cuisles, Jonquery, Olizy-Violane, and Châtillon-sur-Marne. All his parcels are farmed sustainably, but not organically. While he doesn't use any herbicides, avoids chemical fertilizers, and embraces cover crops, he worries about the long-term impact of copper sulfates in the soil, so uses some pesticides early and late most seasons. He also uses organic, phytotherapeutic preparations to help his vines resist disease. About 80 percent of Moussé's vines are planted to Pinot Meunier, 15 percent to Pinot Noir, and 5 percent to Chardonnay.

In the cellar, all Moussé's wines go through malolactic fermentation. Most are vinified in stainless steel.

Moussé Fils joined the Club Trésors in 2005, becoming the first member to make a Spécial Club of 100% Pinot Meunier.

The Wines

L'Or d'Eugène (NV)

Dosage: Brut

A blanc de noirs comprised of 80% Pinot Meunier and 20% Pinot Noir, about half the wine is drawn from a perpetual blend started in 2003. It ages for two years before disgorgement.

Noire Reserve (NV)

Dosage: Brut

Price: $50

A non-vintage blend of 85% Pinot Meunier and 15% Pinot Noir, this champagne includes nearly 50% reserve wines. It ages *sur latte* for three years before disgorgement.

Opale (NV)

Dosage: Brut

Price: $60

Sourced from a single plot called Les Varosse in the village of Cuisles, this 100% Chardonnay ages for four years before disgorgement. Note that most of Cuisles is planted to Pinot Meunier, so this is quite an unique wine.

Rosé (NV)

Dosage: Brut

Price: $55

About 10% of this rosé d'assemblage is composed of still Pinot Meunier vinified in barrique for 15 months. The rest is typically composed of 90% Pinot Meunier and 10% Pinot Noir, although it is sometimes 100% Meunier. It ages for about two years before disgorgement.

Terre d'Illite (Vintage)

Dosage: Brut

Price: $60

Sourced from vineyards in Cuisles, this vintage champagne is a blend of 95% Pinot Meunier and 5% Pinot Noir, and spends 50 months on its lees before disgorgement.

Special Club (Vintage)

Dosage: Brut

Price: $95

Sourced from a single parcel in Cuisles, this vintage *blanc de noirs* is 100% Pinot Meunier and ages on its lees for 60 months.

Moussé Fils
5 Rue de Jonquery
51700 Cuisles
www.champagnemoussefils.com
Tel: (+33) 6 08 04 19 82
cedricmousse@gmail.com
Visits by appointment.

R. POUILLON & FILS (R.M.)

Fabrice Pouillon.

Production: About 60,000 bottles annually.

The Pouillons have grown grapes in Champagne for over a century. In 1947, Roger Pouillon decided to make his own champagne with the help of his uncle, well-known oenologist Louis Baulant, from a small parcel in Mutigny. Pouillon's production gradually expanded in the subsequent decades as grape contracts with *négociants* expired.

Today, the Pouillons make estate wines from 16 acres of vines split between 36 parcels in seven villages: Aÿ, Mareuil-sur-Aÿ, Mutigny, Avenay Val d'Or, Épernay, Festigny, and Tauxières-Mutry. About half the vineyards are planted to Pinot Noir, 30 percent to Chardonnay, and 20 percent to Pinot Meunier.

Since 1998, the estate has been run by third-generation proprietor and vigneron Fabrice Pouillon, who began moving toward organic viticulture almost immediately. In 2003, he began converting to biodynamics.

In the cellar, Pouillon handles each parcel separately, pressing the grapes with an ancient, wooden pneumatic press and vinifying each lot in enameled-steel tanks, where full malolactic fermentation takes place. The wines are aged in a combination of stainless steel vats, enameled-steel tanks, and neutral oak demi-muids and barriques. Fabrice Pouillon has quickly become one of Champagne's brightest stars.

THE WINES

RESERVE (NV)

Dosage: Brut
Price: $40

A blend of 70 percent Pinot Noir and equal parts Chardonnay and Pinot Meunier, sourced from parcels across five villages. Typically about 30 percent reserve wine.

BLANC DE BLANCS (NV)

Dosage: Brut
Price: $50

A 100-percent Chardonnay sourced from parcels in three villages, 85 percent of the base juice is fermented in steel tanks and 15% in aged barrels. Typically about 35 percent reserve wine.

ROSÉ (NV)

Dosage: Brut
Price: $50

Made entirely from Pinot Noir sourced from Mareuil-sur-Aÿ, this saignée champagne is typically a blend of two recent vintages.

SOLERA (NV)

Dosage: Brut
Price: $60

Equal parts Pinot Noir and Chardonnay, sourced entire from Mareuil-sur-Aÿ. Not technically a "solera," this wine is actually from a "perpetual blend"—a system of storing and aging wine that relies on a single tank that is continually replenished by each new harvest—started in 1997. Pouillon draws off and replaces 30 percent of this wine each year.

LES BLANCHIENS (VINTAGE)

Dosage: Brut Nature
Price: $75

Sourced from a single parcel in Aÿ that co-planted with equal parts Pinot Noir and Chardonnay.

LES VALNONS (VINTAGE)

Dosage: Extra Brut
Price: $75

A 100% Chardonnay from one of Aÿ's best slopes, this wine is particularly notable because 89 percent of Aÿ's vineyards—and virtually 100 percent of its top sites—are planted to Pinot Noir.

CHEMIN DU BOIS (VINTAGE)

Dosage: Extra Brut
Price: $80

Sourced from a single parcel of Pinot Noir in Mareuil-sur-Aÿ.

R. Pouillon & Fils
17 Rue d'Aÿ
51160 Mareuil-sur-Aÿ
www.champagne-pouillon.com
contact@champagne-pouillon.com
Tel: (33) 3 26 52 63 62
Visits by appointment.

TARLANT (R.M.)

Production: About 100,000 bottles annually.

In 1687, Pierre Tarlant planted grapevines in Gland, a small village in the Vallée de la Marne. Ever since, his family has been cultivating vines in Champagne. Nearly 100 years later, the Tarlants moved 18 miles east to Oeuilly, another village in the Vallée de la Marne, and began planting vines there.

Throughout the 19th century, the Tarlants made still wines for hotels and bars in nearby Paris.

In the early 20th century, Louis Adrien Tarlant, the mayor Oeuilly, helped craft the regulations that still dictate Champagne's boundaries and production methods. In 1928, ten years after returning home from World War I, Tarlant created his family's first estate champagne. It hit the market one year later as "Carte Blanche."

Today, the estate is run by brother-and-sister team Benoît and Melanie Tarlant, the 12th generation of Tarlant growers in Champagne. The estate's 35 acres of vineyards spread over 55 parcels in the villages of Oeuilly, Boursault, St-Agnan, and Celles-lès-Condé, and consist of Pinot Noir, Chardonnay, and Pinot Meunier. Small amounts of Pinot Blanc, Arbanne, and Petit Meslier are also planted.

In the vineyard, Benoît Tarlant eschews chemical pesticides and fertilizers and fills his parcels with grass as a cover crop. Each parcel is pressed and vinified separately. About half of Tarlant's production is barrel-fermented, and malolactic fermentation is blocked in all its wines. Most of Tarlant's champagnes are finished without dosage, a tradition started by Benoît's father Jean-Mary in the late-1970s.

Tarlant is one of the most transparent grower-producers in Champagne. All the estate's back labels include detailed information on assemblage, base wines, bottling date, disgorgement date, and dosage.

THE WINES

TRADITION (NV)
Dosage: Brut
Price: $50

A blend of 56% Pinot Noir, 39% Pinot Meunier, 5% Chardonnay, this wine is vinified in stainless steel. It includes about 30% reserve wine, which is stored in barrique.

ZERO (NV)
Dosage: Brut Nature
Price: $55

Equal parts Chardonnay, Pinot Meunier, and Pinot Noir, this wine is finished without dosage.

Rosé Zero (NV)

Dosage: Brut Nature

Price: $65

The base of this rosé d'assemblage is a blend of 85% Chardonnay and 15% Pinot Noir. The still wine that's added composes about 15 percent of the blend and is made up of both Pinot Noir and Pinot Meunier. This wine is finished without dosage.

Cuvée Louis (NV)

Dosage: Extra Brut

Price: $95

Benoît's homage to his great-great-grandfather Louis. Sourced exclusively from the "Les Crayons" vineyard in Oeuilly, this wine is a blend of 50% Chardonnay and 50% Pinot Noir. It is vinified in oak, where it ages for about eight months with regular lees stirring.

La Vigne Royale Extra Brut (Vintage)

Dosage: Extra Brut

Price: $170

A 100% Pinot Noir sourced from a single vineyard in Celles-lès-Condés, this wine is made entirely with Pinot Noir. It is vinified in oak, where it ages for about eight months with regular lees stirring, and then spends 8-12 years on its lees.

La Vigne d'Antan (Vintage)

Dosage: Extra Brut

Price: $200

A 100% Chardonnay sourced from ungrafted vines in the Les Sables vineyard in Oeuilly, which was planted between 1951 and 1960. It is vinified in oak, where it ages for about eight months with regular lees stirring, and then ages on its lees for about 6 years.

La Vigne d'Or Brut Nature (Vintage)

Dosage: Brut Nature

Price: $140

A 100% Pinot Meunier sourced from Pierre de Bellevue, a vineyard in Oeuilly planted more than 60 years ago. It is vinified in oak, where it ages for about eight months with regular lees stirring, and then ages on its lees for about 10 years. This wine is finished without dosage.

BAM! Brut Nature (NV)

Dosage: Brut Nature

Price: $150

BAM! is a blend of 18% Pinot Blanc, 18% Arbanne, and 64% Petit Meslier, all grape varieties that have almost disappeared from Champagne. A new cuvée, this wine is sourced from a single vineyard in Oeuilly and is typically a blend of two vintages.

Tarlant

21 Rue de la Coopérative

51480 Oeuilly

www.tarlant.com

Tel: (+33) 3 26 58 30 60

champagne@tarlant.com

Visits by appointment.

Section Four:

Côte des Blancs

Just south of Épernay, a 12-mile-long, chalk-covered ridge rises from the countryside. The hill is covered in 7,500 acres of vines, 97 percent of which are Chardonnay.

This hill is called the **Côte des Blancs**. And it's the most important sub-region of Champagne's smallest major growing area, which has the same name. While one might assume that the region was named for the white grapes that fill the hill's vineyards, the Côte des Blancs takes its moniker from the bright white color of the hill's soils. Indeed, the hillside was once known as the Côte Blanche.

Chalk is virtually everywhere in Champagne, obviously. On the Côte des Blancs itself, though, some vineyards are planted on less than 12 inches of topsoil. Near the surface, chalk mixes with sandstone, clay, and brown coal—but little separates the vines from pure chalk. The chalk provides a reliable source of water for grapes; it's porous enough to prevent vines from being waterlogged and absorbent enough to retain water for dry spells. Plus, since most vineyards on the hill face east and southeast, the chalk reflects sunlight so grapes bask and ripen in warmth.

The slope of the Côte des Blancs also helps drain cool, often humid air, thus reducing the risk of grape disease, protecting against spring frosts, and quickening ripening. It also sheds rain.

All six of the region's Grand Crus—and eight of its nine Premier Crus—lie close to or directly on this 12-mile-long ridge, which offers Champagne's most celebrated Chardonnay sites.

The region begins just southeast of Épernay in Chouilly and Oiry, two Grand Crus that sit across the Marne River from Aÿ and Mareuil-sur-Aÿ. Most vines in these villages are planted on slopes of a forest-covered hill called the *Butte de Saran*, away from the Marne's alluvial soils.

QUICK FACTS

16,000 planted acres
4,126 growers
Chardonnay: 84%
Pinot Meunier: 8%
Pinot Noir: 8%

SUB-REGIONS

Côte des Blancs
Val de Petit Morin
Vitryat
Côte de Sézanne

GRAND CRUS

Avize
Chouilly
Cramant
Le Mesnil-sur-Oger
Oger
Oiry

Mesnil-sur Oger.

PREMIER CRUS

Bergères-les-Vertus
Val-des-Marais
Coligny
Cuis
Grauves
Vertus
Villeneuve-Renneville-
  Chevigny
Voipreux
Étréchy

LEADING PRODUCERS

Agrapart
Etienne Calsac
Claude Cazals
Guy Charlemagne
Pascal Doquet
Veuve Fourny
Pierre Gimonnet
Larmandier-Bernier
A. R. Lenoble
Jean Milan
Pierre Moncuit
Pierre Péters
Jacques Selosse
Ulysse Collin
Varnier-Fannière
J. L. Vergnon
Waris-Hubert

The slope of the actual Côtes des Blancs begins to rise on the opposite side of the Butte de Saran in Cuis, a Premier Cru that was awarded 99 in the *Échelle des Crus* ranking. Once one moves a bit further south, the top Grand Crus of the Côtes des Blancs emerge, with vineyards planted on the actual slope of the hill in Cramant, Avize, Oger, and Le Mesnil-sur-Oger. All four of these Grand Crus are known for producing elegant, complex wines that age gracefully and offer aromas and flavors of chalk. Broadly speaking, the wines become more powerful as one moves south from Cramant to Mesnil, with wines from the former often praised for their delicacy and perfumed aromatics and wines from the latter for their richness, structure, and depth. As the slope of the actual Côtes des Blancs ends, one enters Vertus and Bergères-les-Vertus, two highly regarded Premier Crus.

There's more to the Côtes des Blancs than the actual slope, of course. The other notable sub-region is the Côte de Sézanne, a ridge that begins about 20 miles southwest of Bergères-les-Vertus. The subsoil of the Côte de Sézanne contains far less chalk than other parts of the Côtes des Blancs; it's packed with marl, clay, sandstone, and sand. Most vineyards in this region were planted in the 1960s, and although Chardonnay dominates, about 21 percent of the region is planted to Pinot Meunier and 15 percent to Pinot Noir. Thanks to its more southern location, the grapes in the Côte de Sézanne are typically riper, resulting in fatter, more exotically flavored wine.

PRODUCERS TO KNOW

Franck Bonville
Le Brun Servenay
Corbon
Demière-Ansiot
Diebolt-Vallois
José Dhondt
Dhondt-Grellet
Doyard
Pierre Callot
Vincent Couche
Gimonnet-Gonet
Grongnet
Eric Isselée
Legras & Haas
Alexandre Lenique
Lilbert Fils
Robert Moncuit
Perrot-Batteux
Michel Rocourt
Saint Chamant
Hubert Soreau
Suenen
Thierry Triolet
Vazart-Coquart
Vauversin
Vazart-Coquart

ICONIC WINES OF TERROIR

Agrapart et Fils: Cuvée Venus
Jacquesson: Avize Champ Caïn
Larmandier-Bernier: Les Chemins d'Avize
Pierre Péters: Cuvée Espéciale Les Chétillons
Salon: Cuvée S
Jacques Selosse: Substance
Ulysse Collin: Les Enfers

AGRAPART ET FILS (R.M.)

Production: About 90,000 bottles annually.

This domaine traces its roots to 1894, when Arthur Agrapart acquired a small estate in Avize and began making wine. About 60 years later, his grandson, Pierre, began acquiring additional vineyard parcels.

Since 1984, the estate has been run by Fabrice and Pascal, fourth-generation vignerons. Over the past 30 years, the two brothers have gained international recognition for their wines—and today, young growers across Champagne revere them.

The family owns more than 27 acres of vineyards spread over 60 separate parcels, most of which lie in the Grand Cru villages of Avize, Cramant, Oiry, and Oger. The average vine age is about 40 years.

The brothers ferment each parcel separately to maximize blending options. While the domaine isn't technically organic or biodynamic, the brothers eschew pesticides and rely on indigenous yeasts and natural methods in the cellar. Dosages are low across the entire lineup and riddling is performed manually. While some stainless steel is used, the top wines are fermented in neutral, 600-liter oak barrels. Across the lineup, their wines are marked by pure fruit and fresh acid. The back labels of all Agrapart's wines list both the bottling date and the disgorgement date.

Pascal Agrapart.

THE WINES

AGRAPART 7 CRUS (NV)

Dosage: Brut

Price: $50

A non-vintage blanc de blancs sourced from vineyards in seven different villages, this wine is typically blended from two different years, with half of the older vintage aged in oak barrels.

TERROIRS (NV)

Dosage: Extra Brut

Price: $65

Also blended from two different years, with half of the older vintage aged in oak barrels, this wine is made exclusively from Grand Cru Chardonnay.

LES DEMOISELLES ROSÉ (NV)

Dosage: Brut

Price: $70

Agrapart's rosé is simply the Terroirs blended with still Pinot Noir from Cumières, purchased from René Geoffroy.

COMPLANTEE (NV)

Dosage: Extra Brut

Price: $75

In 2003, the domaine planted a single parcel of the La Fosse vineyard in Avize with Pinot Blanc, Arbane, and Petit Meslier—three "heirloom" varieties—alongside Chardonnay, Pinot Noir, and Pinot Meunier. The concept? To prove that over time, terroir trumps variety. The grapes are co-harvested and co-fermented.

MINERAL (VINTAGE)

Dosage: Extra Brut

Price: $100

Sourced from 40-year old Chardonnay vines in Le Champ Bouton in Avize and Bionnes in Cramant, two vineyards in neighboring villages that both boast a hard, chalky soil.

L'AVIZOISE (VINTAGE)

Dosage: Extra Brut

Price: $120

Sourced from 50-year-old Chardonnay vines in Les Robarts and La Voie d'Épernay, two adjoining vineyards marked by clay soils in Avize.

CUVÉE VENUS (VINTAGE)

Dosage: Brut Nature

Price: $165

Sourced from less than one acre of 60-year-old Chardonnay vines in La Fosse that is worked by horse rather than tractor. Since tractors tend to compact soil, the brothers hope that this parcel will benefit from better aeration. Like Mineral, this parcel is a known for its hard, chalky soil.

Agrapart et Fils

57 Avenue Jean Jaurès

51190 Avize

www.champagne-agrapart.com

Tel: (+33) 3 26 57 51 38

champagne.agrapart@wanadoo.fr

No visits or direct sales.

ETIENNE CALSAC (R.M.)

Production: About 14,000 bottles annually.

In 2010, at the age of 26, Etienne Calsac took over his grandparents' 7 acres of vineyards. Calsac's family had been growing grapes for several generations, but the focus was always on selling the grapes to *négociants*. That all changed when Calsac took over the operation with a new vision and philosophy firmly grounded in organic viticulture.

Calsac studied in Avize and traveled to the United States, New Zealand, and Canada to learn more about winemaking before coming home and re-settling in Champagne.

Calsac's vineyards are spread over three villages: Avize and Gravues in the Côte de Blancs and Bisseuil in the Marne Valley. In Avize, he has a walled vineyard called "Clos des Maladries."

Calsac's vineyards are packed with cover crops and mostly plowed by horse. Each parcel is vinified separately.

THE WINES

L'ÉCHAPPÉE BELLE (NV)
Dosage: Brut / Extra Brut
Price: $40

A blend of 95% Chardonnay, which is mainly sourced from Grauves, and 5% Pinot Noir, which appears in this blend as reserve wine. The wine ages for 36 months before disgorgement. This wine is made with two different levels of dosage.

INFINIMENT BLANC (NV)
Dosage: Brut
Price: $55

A blanc de blancs sourced from very chalky vineyards in Bisseuil and Avize. About 15% of this champagne was vinified in neutral barriques. The wine spends 36 months on its lees before disgorgement.

ROSÉ DE CRAIE (NV)
Dosage: Brut
Price: $60

A rosé d'assemblage of 86% Chardonnay from Bisseuil and Avize and 14% still Pinot Noir from the Montagne de Reims. About 10% of this champagne was vinified in neutral barriques. The wine ages for 36 months before disgorgement.

Etienne Calsac
128 Allée Augustin Lorite,
51190 Avize
www.champagne-etienne-calsac.com
Tel: (+33) 6 11 83 69 49
etienne@champagne-etienne-calsac.com
Visits by appointment only.

CLAUDE CAZALS (R.M.)

Production: About 90,000 bottles annually.

The Cazals family has been in Champagne since 1897, when cooper Ernest Cazals came to deliver barrels and decided to settle in Le Mesnil-sur-Oger. Ernest's son Olivier and grandson Claude carried on the family business. In 1968, Claude invented and patented the gyropalette, an automatic remuage machine that removes yeast deposits from many champagne bottles at a time, which is still used by some champagne producers today. After Claude's death in 1996, his daughter Delphine took over the responsibility of running the domaine.

This estate owns 22 acres of Chardonnay vineyards in the southern Côte des Blancs, split between the Grand Crus of Oger and Le Mesnil-sur-Oger and the Premier Crus of Vertus and Villeneuve-Renneville-Chevigny.

One of its most priced plots is "Clos Cazals," a nine-acre walled vineyard in Oger that was planted by Olivier in 1947. In 1995, Delphine convinced her father, Claude to make a single-vineyard, single-vintage champagne from the grapes grown in "Clos Cazals," a nine-acre, walled vineyard behind their home, and this cuvée is now the estate's most coveted wine.

THE WINES

CARTE BLANCHE (NV)
Dosage: Brut
Price: $35
This entry-level, non-vintage blanc de blancs sourced from across all Cazals' vineyards.

CARTE D'OR (NV)
Dosage: Brut
Price: $40
This non-vintage blanc de blancs is sourced exclusively from parcels in Oger and Le Mesnil-sur-Oger.

CUVÉE VIVE (NV)
Dosage: Extra Brut
Price: $40
This non-vintage blanc de blancs is similar to the Carte d'Or, but finished with less dosage.

MILLÉSIME (VINTAGE)
Dosage: Brut
Price: $70
Produced only in exceptional years, this vintage offering is sourced from old vines in Le Mesnil-sur-Oger and Oger.

CLOS CAZALS GRAND CRU BLANC DE BLANCS (VINTAGE)
Dosage: Extra Brut
Price: $125
Produced only in exceptional years, this vintage offering is sourced entirely from Clos Cazals, a nine-acre walled vineyard in Oger that was planted in 1947. It ages for six years on its lees before disgorgement.

Champagne Claude Cazals
28, rue du Grand Mont
51190 Le Mesnil-sur-Oger
www.champagne-claude-cazals.net
Tel: (33) 3 26 57 52 26
contact@champagne-claude-cazals.net
Visit by appointment only.

GUY CHARLEMAGNE (S.R.)

Production: 130,000 bottles per year.

Headquartered directly across the street from Salon in Le Mesnil-sur-Oger, this domaine was established in 1892 by Gustave Charlemagne. Like most growers, though, he sold his grapes to *négociants*.

In the mid-1930s, his son Louis took over and began producing his own champagne. His son Guy took over in 1953 and set about boosting the winery's reputation and expanding its size by purchasing additional vineyard plots. Today, Guy's son Philippe runs the estate.

The two men own 37 acres of vines, about 60 percent of which are in the Grand Crus of Le Mesnil-sur-Oger and Oger. Of the remaining vines, most are in the Côte de Sézanne, but small plots are owned in the Côte des Blancs villages of Cuis and Mancy. The average age of its vines is more than 40 years old. Because Guy owns some vines and Philippe owns others, the winery is registered as a *"société de récoltant."*

Most fermentation takes place in stainless steel, but 30 percent of Charlemagne's top wine, Mesnillésime, ferments in barrique. (The barrels range from 2- to 18-years old, so are mostly neutral.) All wines undergo malolactic fermentation, save for the barrel-fermented component of the Mesnillésime.

The Wines

Brut Nature (NV)
Dosage: Brut Nature
Price: $45

A blend of 70% Chardonnay and 30% Pinot Noir, sourced entirely from vineyards in the Côte de Sézanne and finished without dosage.

Brut Classic (NV)
Dosage: Brut
Price: $30

Equal parts Chardonnay and Pinot Noir, sourced entirely from vineyards in the Côte de Sézanne.

Brut Reserve (NV)

Dosage: Brut

Price: $50

A blanc de blancs sourced entirely from Le Mesnil-sur-Oger and Oger.

Brut Rosé (NV)

Dosage: Brut

Price: $50

A saignée rosé of pure Pinot Noir from vineyards in Mancy and Cuis.

Cuvée Charlemagne (Vintage)

Dosage: Brut

Price: $50

A blanc de blancs sourced entirely from the estate's best plots in Le Mesnil-sur-Oger

and Oger. It ages on its lees for 3-4 years prior to disgorgement.

Mesnillesime (Vintage)

Dosage: Brut

Price: $60

Charlemagne's prestige cuvée, sourced entirely from 70-year-old vines in Le Mesnil-sur-Oger and Oger. About 30 percent of the grapes in this wine are vinified in barriques ranging in age from 2-18 years. This component of the blend does not go through malolactic fermentation. This wine ages on its lees for six years before disgorgement.

Guy Charlemagne

4 Rue de la Brèche d'Oger

51190 Le Mesnil-sur-Oger

Tel: (33) 3 26 57 52 98

www.champagne-guy-charlemagne.com

Visits by appointment.

PASCAL DOQUET (S.R.)

Production: About 75,000 bottles annually.

Pascal Doquet grew up surrounded by wine and vineyards. His maternal grandfather, André Jeanmaire, ran a small champagne house—and as a teenager, Doquet apprenticed there. That brand was sold in the 1970s, but in 1974, Doquet's parents, Nicole and Michel, launched a house of their own: Doquet-Jeanmaire.

Pascal Doquet began working alongside his parents in 1982, and assumed full control of the estate in 1995. They officially retired in 2004 and divided their vineyard holdings among all their children.

So Pascal Doquet renamed the estate and registered as a société récoltant. (This designation is what allows him to source from his family without registering as a *négociant*.)

Today, Doquet farms 22 acres of vines in the Côte des Blancs, with 4 acres in the Grand Cru of Le Mesnil-sur-Oger, 9 acres in the Premier Crus of Vertus and Bergères-lès-Vertus, and 9 acres in at the eastern end of the subregion, in Bassu and Bassuet. About 95% of his vines are planted to Chardonnay, the rest to Pinot Noir.

Doquet's devotion to his vineyards is almost fanatical. He tends the vines almost entirely by hand, allows natural cover to grow freely between rows, plows with a special, lightweight tractor, and has been certified as organic since 2010.

In the cellar, Doquet vinifies each plot individually and relies on native yeasts. Non-vintage wines are vinified in enameled-steel and vintage wines in barrel. Most wines go through malolactic fermentation, but he is not dogmatic about it. He ages his wine far longer than most producers.

THE WINES

HORIZON (NV)
Dosage: Brut
Price: $45

A blanc de blancs sourced mostly from vines in Bassu and Bassuet that were planted in 1970. This champagne is vinified in enameled-steel tanks, where it rests for six months before moving to bottle. Once in the bottle, it ages on its lees for about three years before disgorgement.

PREMIER CRU BLANC DE BLANCS (NV)
Dosage: Brut / Extra Brut / Brut Nature
Price: $40

A blanc de blancs sourced from Vertus and Bergères-les-Vertus, this champagne is vinified in enameled-steel tanks, where it rests for six months before moving to bottle. Once in the bottle, it ages *sur latte* for about three years before disgorgement. This wine is released as a Brut, and Extra Brut, and without any dosage.

GRAND CRU BLANC DE BLANCS
Dosage: Brut / Extra Brut

A blanc de blancs sourced from Le Mesnil-sur-Oger, this champagne is mostly vinified in enameled-steel tanks, although a small percentage of the cuvée is vinified in barrique. This wine ages for about seven

years before disgorgement. This wine is released with two different levels of dosage.

PREMIER CRU ROSÉ (NV)
Dosage: Brut / Extra Brut
Price: $55

This wine is composed of 85% Pinot Noir from a vineyard called La Barre, on the southern end of Vertus, and a parcel on a hill called Le Mont Aimé, on the southern end of Bergères-les-Vertus. This fruit is macerated, saignée-style, but then moved to barrique, where it's treated as a reserve wine. From these barriques, Doquet draws off his wine, adding some Chardonnay. This wine is released with two different levels of dosage.

LE MONT AIMÉ COEUR DE TERROIR (VINTAGE)
Dosage: Brut
Price: $70

Harvested from Le Mont Aimé, an unusual terroir on the southern end of Bergères-les-Vertus that features sandy and stony chalk soils, this blanc de blancs is mostly vinified in enameled-steel tanks, although a small percentage of the cuvée is vinified in barrique. This wine ages for about seven years before disgorgement.

VERTUS COEUR DE TERROIR (VINTAGE)
Dosage: Brut
Price: $70

Harvested from Vertus, this blanc de blancs is vinified in two-thirds enameled-steel tanks, one-third in barrique. This wine ages for about seven years before disgorgement.

LE MESNIL SUR OGER COEUR DE TERROIR (VINTAGE)
Dosage: Brut
Price: $100

Harvested from Le Mesnil Sur Oger—including vines that were planted in 1929—this blanc de blancs is vinified in enameled-steel tanks and barrique. This wine for about seven years before disgorgement.

Pascal Doquet
44 Chemin du Moulin de la Censé Bize
51130 Vertus
www.champagne-doquet.com
Tel: 03.26.52.16.50
contact@champagne-doquet.com

VEUVE FOURNY ET FILS (N.M.)

Production: About 190,000 bottles annually.

In 1856, the Fourny family began tending vines in Vertus. About 70 years later, Albert Fourny, a third-generation grower, began making his own champagne.

The effort was successful, so he began expanding the family's holdings. His son Roger followed in his footsteps—and was so successful that in 1979, he had to re-register as a *négociant-manipulant* to purchase grapes from family and friends in Vertus. In 1980, though, tragedy struck. Roger Fourny died in an accident.

Fourny's widow took the reins, as her sons, Charles and Emmanuel, were just 10 and 11 at the time. In 1993, the two brothers took over the estate.

Today, they own 21 acres of vines, spread across 40 parcels in Vertus. To supplement production, they continue to purchase about 12 acres worth of grapes each year from family and friends in Vertus.

In the vineyard, the brothers farm sustainably—but not 100 percent organically. In the late-1990s, their first foray into organic production backfired when mildew ruined half of the crop.

In the cellar, the brothers vinify all their parcels separately in either stainless steal or neutral barrique. Lees aging is longer than most growers, ranging from 2.5 years for their basic cuvée to nine years for their prestige cuvée. Most wines go through partial malolactic.

THE WINES

GRANDE RÉSERVE (NV)
Dosage: Brut
Price: $45

Vinified in vats and oak casks, blend of 80% Chardonnay and 20% Pinot Noir is blended from three consecutive vintages along with 40% reserve wine.

ROSÉ (NV)
Dosage: Brut
Price: $50

A blend of 85% Chardonnay and 15% still, old-vine Pinot Noir, with about 30% reserve wine. This wine is vinified in neutral barrique before aging *sur latte* for 2 years.

BLANC DE BLANCS (NV)
Dosage: Brut / Brut Nature / Extra Dry
Price: $50

Vinified in vats and oak casks, this wine is blended from three consecutive vintages along with 20% reserve wine. Most of the production is bottled as brut, some is finished with 17 grams of sugar per liter and sold as "Extra Dry" and some is finished without dosage and sold as "Brut Nature de Veuve Fourny & Fils."

CUVÉE "R" (NV)
Dosage: Extra Brut
Price: $65

A blend of 90% Chardonnay, 5% Pinot Noir, and 5% Pinot Meunier, this wine is vinified 18 months in oak casks and aged in bottles for at least four years. Typically, this is a blend of two different vintages and doesn't include reserve wine.

ROSÉ LES ROUGESMONTS (VINTAGE)
Dosage: Extra Brute
Price: $55

A saigneé rosé Pinot Noir, this wine is vinified 12 months in oak casks and aged in bottles for at least four years.

MONTS DE VERTUS (VINTAGE)
Dosage: Extra Brut
Price: $75

A blanc de blancs sourced exclusively from 70-plus-year-old vines in Vertus, this wine ages in a barrique for one year before bottling. Once bottled, it ages for 5 years before disgorgement.

CUVÉE DU CLOS FAUBOURG NOTRE DAME MILLÉSIMÉ (VINTAGE)
Dosage: Extra Brut
Price: $140

Fourny's tête de cuvée is sourced entirely from a 0.75-acre walled vineyard in Vertus—called Clos Faubourg Notre Dame—that was planted more than 60 years ago. Only released in exceptional years, this wine is vinified in neutral barrique and aged for 9 years before disgorgement.

Veuve Fourny et Fils
5 Rue du Mesnil
51130 Vertus
www.champagne-veuve-fourny.com
Tel: (33) 3 26 52 16 30
info@champagne-veuve-fourny.com
Visits by appointment.

PIERRE GIMONNET ET FILS (R.M.)

Production: About 250,000 bottles annually.

The Gimonnets have been growing grapes in Champagne since 1750 and making wine since 1935, when Pierre Gimonnet began bottling estate Champagne in Cuis, a village at the foot of the Côte des Blancs.

Today, Pierre's grandsons, Didier and Olivier run the estate. Most vineyard work is handled by Olivier and most cellar work is handled by Didier. The brothers sustainably farm 64 acres of vineyards, about half which are in the Premier Cru village of Cuis. Most of their other holdings are the Grand Cru villages of Cramant and Chouilly, although the brothers also own five acres in the Premier Cru of Vertus, two in the Grand Cru village of Oger, and half-acre parcels in both Aÿ and Mareuil-sur-Aÿ. Almost all their grapes are Chardonnay, with their oldest fruit coming off vines planted in 1911. Their average vines are 40 years old.

In the cellar, Gimonnet eschews oak, as he believes it overpowers Chardonnay's delicacy. So both primary fermentation and malolactic take place in stainless steel tanks. Inspired by the traditions of Champagne, Gimonnet has always been obsessed with blending. So even though he vinifies all parcels separately, his reserve wine is always a blend. Despite owning some of Champagne's greatest vineyard sites—including parcels in Cramant planted in 1911 and 1913—Gimonnet refused to make a single-village wine until 2011. He has since made several, but still calls these singular offerings an experiment.

Without question, Gimonnet offers some of the purest, most polished wines of terroir in Champagne.

THE WINES

CUIS IER CRU (NV)
Dosage: Brut
Price: $50

A blanc de blancs from Cuis, this wine is released after just 18 months *sur latte*.

ROSÉ DE BLANCS (NV)
Dosage: Brut
Price: $60

A rosé d'assemblage, 88% of this wine is comprised of Chardonnay from Chouilly, Cramant, Oger, Cuis, and Vertus. The rest is comprised of still Pinot Noir from a grower in Bouzy.

FLEURON (VINTAGE)
Dosage: Brut
Price: $70

About 80 percent of this blanc de blancs is comprised of Chardonnay from Cramant and Chouilly. The remainder is from Cuis and Oger.

OENOPHILE (VINTAGE)
Dosage: Brut Nature
Price: $70

This wine is identical to the Fleuron, but it's released later and finished without dosage.

GASTRONOME (VINTAGE)
Dosage: Brut
Price: $65

Blended from Cramant, Chouilly, Cuis, and Oger, this blanc de blancs has fewer bubbles than the typical champagne, as it's bottled with 4 atmospheres of pressure rather than the standard 6.

PARADOXE (VINTAGE)
Dosage: Brut
Price: $60

Comprised of equal parts Pinot Noir and Chardonnay, Gimonnnet created this cuvée after purchasing small parcels in Mareuil-sur-Aÿ and Aÿ in 2001 and 2003, respectively.

SPECIAL CLUB (VINTAGE)
Dosage: Brut
Price: $100

More than half the Chardonnay in Gimonnet's prestige cuvée always comes from Cramant, where the estate has its oldest vines.

Pierre Gimonnet et Fils
1 Rue de la République
51530 Cuis, France
www.champagne-gimonnet.com
Tel: (33) 3 26 59 78 70
info@champagne-gimonnet.com
Visits accepted; appointments recommended.

LARMANDIER-BERNIER (R.M.)

Pierre Larmandier.

About 140,000 bottles annually.

The Larmandiers and Berniers have worked in Champagne's vineyards since the French Revolution. The two families linked in 1971 when Philippe Larmandier married Elisabeth Bernier. Today, their son, Pierre, and his wife, Sophie, run the house. They own 36 acres in the Côte des Blancs, split between Vertus, Cramant, Chouilly, Oger, and Avize. About 90 percent of their holdings are planted to Chardonnay, the rest to Pinot Noir. The average vine age is 35 years old.

When Pierre took over the property in 1988, he quickly began focusing terroir, even creating a single-vineyard cuvée—Vieille Vigne du Levant—in his first official harvest. Larmandier ceased use of all synthetic chemical applications in his vineyards in 1992 and has been certified organic since 2003.

In the cellar, Larmandier is similarly thoughtful. Each vineyard is vinified separately, and since 1999 he has relied on indigenous yeast for primary fermentation. Most fermentation takes place in neutral barriques and foudres, although some stainless steel tanks and enamel-lined tanks are used.

Larmandier is one of the few vignerons in Champagne who performs *bâtonnage*, which is the practice stirring the lees while a wine is aging. This technique is common in Burgundy, where it's praised for imparting richness. But it's controversial in Champagne, as some producers believe it takes away from a wine's delicacy. Bâtonnage isn't practiced with all Larmandier's wines and it's always very light; the decision depends on what the fruit demands.

Dosage is minimal; using *moût concentré rectifié*, or concentrated and rectified grape must, rather than the more traditional *liqueur d'expédition*, all Larmandier's wines receive less than five grams of sugar per liter. One cuvée—Terre de Vertus—is finished without dosage. All wines are hand riddled and hand disgorged.

THE WINES

LATITUDE (NV)
Dosage: Extra Brut
Price: $55

A blanc de blancs from the warm, rich soils of southern Vertus. About 70 percent of this wine comes from a single vintage and is fermented in stainless steel tanks. The rest comes from reserve wines, which are aged in a combination of neutral barriques and foudres.

LONGITUDE IER CRU (NV)
Dosage: Extra Brut
Price: $55

The vineyards for this blanc de blancs, where there's very little top soil, form a line close to the 4th meridian. About 60 percent of this wine comes from a single vintage and is fermented in stainless steel tanks. The rest comes from reserve wines, which are aged in a combination of neutral barriques and foudres.

ROSÉ DE SAIGNÉE IER CRU (NV)
Dosage: Extra Brut
Price: $70

Made from the oldest Pinot Noir vines in Vertus, this *saignée* champagne receives its color from a 2-3 day maceration. It's vinified in enamel-lined stainless steel tanks.

TERRE DE VERTUS IER CRU (VINTAGE)
Dosage: Brut Nature
Price: $65

A vintage blanc de blancs from Larmandier-Bernier's two top vineyards in Vertus: Les Barillers and Les Faucherets, which are located on the middle slopes of the village. Vinified in a combination of stainless steel vats and neutral oak, this wine is typically aged for at least four years prior to disgorgement.

Vieille Vigne du Levant Grand Cru (Vintage)

Dosage: Extra Brut
Price: $90

A single-expression blanc de blancs from the oldest vines in Cramant, which range from 50-70 years old. Vinified entirely in neutral oak, this wine is typically aged for at least four years prior to disgorgement.

Les Chemins d'Avize Grand Cru (Vintage)

Dosage: Extra Brut
Price: $115

Sourced from two small parcels in Avize—Chemin de Plivot and Chemin de Flavigny—that were previously blended into Longitude. Vinified entirely in neutral oak.

Larmandier-Bernier

19 Avenue du Général de Gaulle

51130 Vertus

www.larmandier.fr

Tel: (33) 3 26 52 13 24

champagne@larmandier.fr

Visits by appointment only.

A. R. LENOBLE (N.M.)

Anne Malassagne, one of the proprietors of A. R. Lenoble.

Production: About 320,000 bottles annually.

When he founded this estate in 1920, the Alsace-born Armand-Raphaël Graser had trouble imagining his own name on the label. Adding his initials to the invented moniker Lenoble, Graser christened his company with a name as elegant and refined as the champagne he sought to create.

The estate remains family-owned and independently operated to this day, under the leadership of Anne and Antoine Malassagne, Graser's great-grandchildren. Its 44.5 acres is spread among three areas: Chouilly (25 acres), where Chardonnay dominates; Bisseuil (14.5 acres), where Pinot Noir dominates; and Damery (5 acres), where Pinot Meunier dominates.

In the vineyard, Lenoble farms sustainably. The estate refuses to use chemical fertilizers, rarely uses herbicides, and keeps the use of pesticides to an absolute minimum. It takes biodiversity seriously, packing its vineyards with trees, flowers, and even bees from which it cultivates honey. In recognition for its commitment to environmentally-sound growing practices, Lenoble was the second-ever Champagne estate to earn the Haute Valeur Environnementale certification.

Note that Lenoble is a *négociant*. While the estate uses its own fruit for most of its lineup, it purchases Pinot Meunier for it three least-expensive offerings.

Recently, A. R. Lenoble has found itself in the middle of debate about labeling transparency. While its newest labels detail *cépage* (the precise breakdown of the blend), dosage, harvest date, and bottling date (i.e., when it goes *sur latte*), disgorgement isn't provided. Lenoble believes that the bottling date is much more informative—and worries that "disgorgement" could be misinterpreted by consumers.

THE WINES

CUVÉE INTENSE (NV)
Dosage: Brut
Price: $45

A blend of 30% Chardonnay, 30% Pinot Noir, and 35% Pinot Meunier. About 65% of this wine comes from the base vintage, the rest from reserves. About 20 percent of this wine is vinified in barrique.

DOSAGE ZÉRO (NV)
Dosage: Brut nature
Price: $45

The Dosage Zéro begins with the same blend as the Cuvée Intense, but is aged an additional year on its lees.

CUVÉE RICHE (NV)
Dosage: Demi-sec
Price: $40

The Cuvée Riche starts with the same blend as the Cuvée Intense and Dosage Zero, but with a far more generous dosage of 32g.

ROSÉ TERROIRS (NV)
Dosage: Brut
Price: $55

This rosé d'assemblage is comprised of 88% Chardonnay from Chouilly and

12% still Pinot Noir from Bisseuil. About 65% of this wine comes from the base vintage, the rest from reserves. About 20 percent of this wine is vinified in barrique.

GRAND CRU BLANC DE BLANCS CHOUILLY (NV)
Dosage: Brut
Price: $55

Comprised entirely of Chardonnay from the Grand Cru of Chouilly. About 65% of this wine comes from the base vintage, the rest from reserves. About 20 percent of this wine is vinified in barrique.

L'EPURÉE (NV)
Dosage: Brut
Price: $45

Comprised entirely of Chardonnay from Chouilly, what sets this offering apart is that it doesn't undergo malolactic fermentation, and is dosed at a slightly lower level.

BLANC DE NOIRS PREMIER CRU (VINTAGE)

Dosage: Brut

Price: $75

Comprised entirely of Pinot Noir from Bisseuil grapes, about 30 percent of this wine is vinified in barrique.

GENTILHOMME (VINTAGE)

Dosage: Brut

Price: $105

The grapes for this vintage-dated wine are sourced from prime parcels, averaging 25 years of age, below the Butte de Saran, including one of the most celebrated areas in Chouilly, Montaigu. It's entirely vinified in oak.

LES AVENTURES (NV)

Dosage: Brut

Price: $105

A barrel-fermented blanc de blancs sourced from a one-acre vineyard in Chouilly called Les Aventures. This wine is typically a blend of two or three vintages.

A. R. Lenoble

35-37 Rue Paul Douce

51480 Damery

www.champagne-arlenoble.com

Tel: (+33) 3 26 58 42 60

contact@champagne-arlenoble.com

Visits by appointment only.

JEAN MILAN (N.M.)

Production: About 130,000 bottles annually.

Founded in 1864 by Charles Milan in the Grand Cru Côtes de Blanc village of Oger—and named after Charles's son—Jean Milan remains a family owned and run estate some five generations later. For decades, Milan supplied grapes for Grand Marques such as Pol Roger, Krug, and Veuve Clicquot. The estate has since become a celebrated producer in its own right, known for offerings that showcase Oger's distinct terroir.

Today, Caroline Milan and her brother Jean-Charles—the great-great-grandchildren of Charles—uphold the same level of craftsmanship and tradition that has long characterized the estate. The two own 15 acres of vines, entirely in Oger. And they recently changed from a récoltant-manipulant designation to a *négociant-manipulant* designation to boost production, and they have since taken great care to source their grapes almost exclusively from carefully selected parcels throughout Oger. All of the estate's offerings, save its rosé, are blanc de blancs, usually comprised of two vintages. All the estate's offerings, save for one of its prestige cuvées, are vinified in stainless steel.

THE WINES

SPÉCIAL (NV)

Dosage: Brut

Price: $50

This blanc de blancs blends two vintages and ages for three years before disgorgement.

MILLENAIRE (NV)

Dosage: Brut

Price: $60

Identical to the Spécial, but aged for four years before disgorgement.

CARTE BLANCHE (NV)

Dosage: Brut

Price: $60

Identical to the Spécial and Millenaire, but aged for five years before disgorgement.

TRANSPARENCE SELECTION (VINTAGE)

Dosage: Brut Nature

Price: $75

First made in 2006, this vintage wine ages on its lees under cork instead of crown cap. It ages for about three years before disgorgement.

JEAN MILAN GLAMOUR ROSÉ (NV)

Dosage: Brut

Price: $60

This rosé d'assemblage includes about 10% still Pinot Noir, purchased from a grower in Avenay Val d'Or. The rest is composed of Oger Chardonnay.

JEAN MILAN GRANDE RESERVE 1864 (NV)

Dosage: Brut

Price: $85

This blanc de blancs is made entirely from Oger Chardonnay grapes, fermented and aged in oak barrels, and usually spends about seven years on its lees.

JEAN MILAN SYMPHORINE (VINTAGE)

Dosage: Brut

Price: $75

One of Milan's two prestige cuvées, this stands as a pure example of Oger terroir, made from extremely ripe grapes grown on the estate's oldest and best parcels: Les Barbettes, Beaudures, Les Chênets and Les Zalieux.

JEAN MILAN TERRES DE NOEL (VINTAGE)

Dosage: Brut

Price: $90

The estate's second prestige cuvée is made exclusively from the more-than-70-year-old vines on a single parcel known as Terres de Noel. This blanc de blancs goes through malolactic fermentation and spends some 40 months on its lees.

Jean Milan

8 Rue d'Avize

51190 Oger

www.champagne-milan.com

Tel: (+33) 3 26 57 50 09

info@champagne-milan.com

Monday-Saturday from 10:00 a.m. till 12:00 p.m. and 2:00 p.m. till 6:00 p.m.

Sunday from 10:00 a.m. till 12:00 p.m.

PIERRE MONCUIT (R.M.)

Production: About 180,000 bottles annually.

Managed by the brother-sister team of Yves and Nicole Moncuit since 1977, this domaine dates to the late 1880s. Yves handles the business and marketing aspects of the business, while Nicole handles the vineyards and winemaking. Roughly 37 of the family's 49 acres—spread across 20 parcels—are located in the Grand Cru Le Mesnil-sur-Oger. The rest of its vineyards lie in Sézanne.

Moncuit's champagnes distinguish themselves in several ways. Notably, Moncuit doesn't blend the fruit from Le Mesnil with the fruit from Sézanne. Her entry-level cuvée is entirely Sézanne fruit. Similarly, Moncuit doesn't use reserve wines—she believes in showcasing the uniqueness of each growing season. Moncuit's vines are among the oldest in Le Mesnil; she hasn't replanted any parcels in more than 30 years. All champagnes are vinified in stainless steel and undergo malolactic fermentation.

With Nicole's daughter Valerie assuming greater responsibilities around the estate, there's little doubt that Moncuit will continue to furnish some of Le Mesnil's finest champagnes for decades to come.

Yves and Valerie Moncuit. Photo by Luisa Bonachea.

The Wines

Hugues de Coulmet (Vintage)

Dosage: Brut

Price: $40

Sourced entirely from Sézanne, this blanc de blancs is vinified entirely in stainless steel and goes through full malolactic. It ages for two years. Although this wine is always from a single vintage, it is labeled as a non-vintage wine.

Delos (Vintage)

Dosage: Brut / Extra Brut

Price: $50

Sourced entirely from Les Mesnil-sur-Oger, this blanc de blancs is vinified entirely in stainless steel and goes through full malolactic. It ages on its lees for three years. This wine is released with two different levels of dosage. Although this wine is always from a single vintage, it is labeled as a non-vintage wine.

Rosé (NV)

Dosage: Brut

Price: $45

About 80-85% of this wine is composed of Chardonnay from Les Mesnil-sur-Oger. The color comes from still Ambonnay Pinot Noir. It ages on its lees for three years. Although this wine is always from a single vintage, it is labeled as a non-vintage wine.

Cuvée Nicole Moncuit Vieilles Vignes (Vintage)

Dosage: Brut

Price: $80

While all Moncuit's champagnes are from a single vintage, this is the only cuvée with the vintage listed on the label. Only produced in exceptional vintages, this champagne is sourced from 100-year old vines on a tiny parcel in Le Mesnil-sur-Oger. It spends nine years on its lees.

Pierre Moncuit
11 Rue Persault Maheu
51190 Le Mesnil-Sur-Oger
www.pierre-moncuit.fr
Tel: (33) 3 26 57 52 65
contact@pierre-moncuit.fr
Visits by appointment.

PIERRE PÉTERS (R.M.)

Fabienne Péters.

Production: 160,000 bottles.

While the first Pierre Péters vintage is dated 1944, the Péters family has been involved in Champagne's winemaking trade for over 170 years. Gaspard Péters married into a family of growers based in Le Mesnil-sur-Oger back in 1840. Decades later, his grandson Camille Péters began bottling his own champagne, eventually leaving the business to his son Pierre.

The estate has since been handed down to Pierre's grandson Rodolphe, who oversees the estate's 47 acres of Chardonnay. Spread over 63 parcels, the vast majority of Péters's holdings are in the Grand Crus of Le Mesnil-sur-Oger, Oger, Avize and Cramant. More than 60% of his holdings are in Le Mesnil.

While Péters isn't rigid about organic viticulture, he refuses to use insecticides in his vineyards and is a big believer in cover crops. In the cellar, Péters is careful to press his grapes slowly and gently and vinifies all his wines in stainless steel. Since 1988, he has stored its reserve wines as a perpetual blend in resin-lined concrete vats.

Thanks to Péters's relatively sizeable production, his wines are found in many markets. So his basic offering—labeled as Cuvée de Réserve—offers a wonderful introduction to grower champagne.

THE WINES

CUVÉE DE RÉSERVE (NV)
Dosage: Brut
Price: $60

Sourced entirely from the Grand Crus of Les Mesnil-sur-Oger, Oger, Avize and Cramant, this blanc de blancs typically includes about 40-50% reserve wine. Prior to disgorgement, it ages on its lees for two years.

EXTRA BRUT (VINTAGE)
Dosage: Extra Brut
Price: $60

Although a vintage isn't listed on the label, this single-vintage wine is identical to L'Esprit, but only spends two years on its lees and is finished with a lower dosage.

L'ESPRIT (VINTAGE)
Dosage: Brut
Price: $80

The estate's vintage *blanc de blancs* is sourced from four parcels: Les Montmartins in Le Mesnil, Les Plantes d'Oger in Oger, La Fosse in Avize, and Chemin de Châlons in Cramant. Prior to disgorgement, it ages on its lees for four years.

Réserve Oubliée (NV)

Dosage: Brut
Price: $115

This blanc de blancs is made from Péters's perpetual cuvée, which was created in 1988. After it's drawn out for release, it spends about 15 months on its lees.

Cuvée Espéciale Les Chétillons (Vintage)

Dosage: Brut
Price: $125

A vintage blanc de blancs sourced exclusively from three parcels of Les Chétillons, an esteemed vineyard in Le Mesnil. Prior to disgorgement, it ages on its lees for six years.

Pierre Peters Rosé for Albane (NV)

Dosage: Brut
Price: $$70

An unconventional rosé, Péters' co-ferments purchased Pinot Meunier with Chardonnay to create a saignée. This saignée only makes up 40% of the final cuvée, as it is then blended with Chardonnay from Le Mesnil, along with a small amount of reserve wine. Prior to disgorgement, it ages on its lees for two years.

Pierre Péters

26 rue des Lombards

51190 Le Mesnil sur Oger

www.champagne-peters.com

Tel: (+33) 03 26 57 50 32

Visits by appointment.

JACQUES SELOSSE (R.M.)

Production: About 60,000 bottles annually.

It isn't hyperbole to argue that Anselme Selosse has had a larger impact in Champagne than anyone since Dom Pérignon.

For Selosse, every wine has a higher purpose: It must translate place, clearly expressing the characteristics of the soils and climate in which it's

Anselme Selosse and his son, Guillaume.

grown. This concept isn't unique, of course. But when Selosse took over his father's winery in 1974, such talking points were not yet clichéd. In Champagne, especially, few producers cared about such things.

Jacques Selosse, Anselme's father, launched his eponymous domaine in 1949. That year, he stopped selling grapes and began bottling his own wines. Like most growers, Selosse continued to sell some fruit from his holdings, counting Lanson as one of his more notable clients, for several years. But eventually, Selosse's project became viable on its own.

Anselme returned home to take over his father's estate in 1974 after attending oenology school and working alongside the legendary vignerons at Domaine Coche-Dury, Domaine Leflaive, and Domaine des Comtes Lafon in Burgundy. While working in Burgundy, Selosse learned to care about the quality of the fruit underneath a wine. He learned, too, that the quality of that fruit was entirely dependent on the soil from which it came. Those growers in Champagne who maximized yields by utilizing fertilizers, herbicides, insecticides, and fungicides didn't have healthy fruit, so certainly couldn't make quality wine.

Shortly after taking over the domaine, Selosse converted to organic farming and managing his yields with a focus on quality. He started to push ripeness to its physiological extreme, a difficult feat in France's northernmost wine region. In the cellar, Selosse switched to wild yeasts for primary fermentation. This was common in Burgundy, but quite unusual in Champagne. He refused to add sugar to his wines prior to fermentation, even though most producers in the region regularly relied on chaptalization to spike alcohol content. He worked to avoid sulfur and other additives that might compromise the unique character of his grapes. He kept dosage to a minimum. All these practices continue today.

To be sure, Selosse gave due respect to many old ways of doing things. This is most evident in his creation of a solera for his main cuvée, "Substance," in 1986, which enabled him to produce a wine without vintage variation. In 1994, Selosse started a perpetual blend of Aÿ Pinot Noir to offer a contrast to this offering. His use of such systems are both a nod to tradition and a revolutionary innovation.

Today, Selosse farms 18.5 acres of vines. Most are in the Côte des Blancs and planted to Chardonnay, split between Avize, Cramant, Oger, and Le Mesnil-sur-Oger. Some are in Aÿ, Ambonnay, and Mareuil-sur-Aÿ, where his vines are planted to Pinot Noir. His son Guillaume, who recently returned to his family's estate, is expected to take over the operations in 2018.

The Wines

Initial (NV)
Dosage: Brut
Price: $185

A blanc de blancs of three recent vintages from lower-slope vines in Avize, Oger, and Cramant.

Version Originale (NV)
Dosage: Extra Brut
Price: $240

A blanc de blancs of three older vintages from hillside vines in Avize, Oger, and Cramant.

Rosé (NV)
Dosage: Brut
Price: $285

Chardonnay from a pair of older vintages, blended with a small amount of still Pinot Noir purchased from Egly-Ouriet in Ambonnay.

Exquise Sec (NV)
Dosage: Demi-Sec
Price: $250

Typically a blend of three vintages, with a base wine of Chardonnay sourced entirely from Oger. Dosed at 25 g/l.

Substance (NV)
Dosage: Extra Brut
Price: $350

A solera of Avize Chardonnay created in 1986.

La Côte Faron (NV)
Dosage: Extra Brut
Price: $395

A perpetual blend of Aÿ Pinot Noir started in 1994. This wine was formerly known as Contraste.

Les Carelles (NV)
Dosage: Extra Brut
Price: $395

A perpetual blend of Le Mesnil Chardonnay started in 2003.

Sous le Mont (NV)
Dosage: Extra Brut
Price: $400

A perpetual blend of Mareuil Pinot Noir started in 2005. This is sourced from a vineyard not far from Philipponnat's Clos des Goisses.

Le Bout du Clos (NV)
Dosage: Extra Brut
Price: $400

A perpetual blend of Ambonnay Pinot Noir started in 2004.

Les Chantereines (NV)
Dosage: Extra Brut
Price: $800

A perpetual blend of Chardonnay from a steep, east-facing parcel in Avize started in 2004.

CHEMIN DE CHÂLONS (NV)
Dosage: Extra Brut
Price: $800
    A perpetual blend of Chardonnay from Cramant started in 2004.

MILLÉSIME (VINTAGE)
Dosage: Extra Brut
Price: $750
    Sourced from the same two parcels in Avize each year, Les Chantereines and Les Maladries.

Jacques Selosse
59 Rue de Cramant
51190 Avize
www.selosse-lesavises.com
Tel: (33) 326 577 006
hotel@selosse-lesavises.com
Visits very limited and by appointment only.

ULYSSE COLLIN (R.M.)

Production: About 45,000 bottles annually.

    Based in Congy, a village that sits 8 miles south of Vertus in between the Côte des Blancs and the Côte des Sézanne, Olivier Collin traces his family's winegrowing history to 1703.

    His family has probably been producing and selling its own wine since the winegrower riots of 1911. For most of the 20th century, though, the Collin family sold the grapes from its 21.5 acres of vines to large *négociants*.

Olivier Collin of Champagne Ulysse Collin.

In 2001, Olivier Collin spent two months interning for Anselme Selosse. Inspired to produce his own wine, he quickly began cleansing and revitalizing his family's soils. And in 2003, he took back a three-acre parcel of Chardonnay vines in a vineyard called "Les Pierrières" that had been leased to Pommery.

That first effort was a failure, though. Severe frost destroyed most of his crop.

In 2004, Collin succeeded with the production of 5,400 bottles of "Les Pierrières." Production doubled in 2005 and in 2006 he added on a second wine. Today, Collin produces five different wines from four different vineyards. Collin will soon release a new wine, currently dubbed "Jardin de Ulysses," from a 0.75-acre parcel of vines that's co-planted to Pinot Noir, Chardonnay, and Pinot Meunier. While he produces a wine with each vintage, he has been blending in an increasing amount of reserve wine each year.

Collin considers himself a natural winemaker. He relies on indigenous yeasts for initial fermentation, which takes place in old barrels, and he doesn't interfere with malolactic fermentation. His wines are neither fined nor filtered. His champagnes are all extra brut, topped with only about 1-2 grams of sugar per liter. In the vineyard, his approach is sustainable but he isn't a dogmatist. In 2012, he farmed one of his vineyards organically and lost 80 percent of his crop. While Collin still sells some of his fruit, he has been taking back more and more of his family's holdings each year.

THE WINES

LES PIERRIÈRES (NV)
Dosage: Extra Brut
Price: $90

A blanc de blancs from a 3-acre parcel of vines Vert-Toulon, a village that sits four miles east of Congy. The vines, which have south and southwest exposure, are planted on a mix of chalk and black flint.

LES MAILLONS (NV)
Dosage: Extra Brut
Price: $95

A blanc de noirs from a 6-acre plot of 45-year-old Pinot Noir planted on a mix of chalk and heavy clay in Barbonne-Fayel, a village in the Côte de Sézanne.

LES MAILLONS ROSÉ (NV)
Dosage: Extra Brut
Price: $100

A saignée rosé from Les Maillons that is macerated for 18 hours and aged in neutral oak for 12 months.

LES ROISES (NV)
Dosage: Extra Brut
Price: $110

A blanc de blancs a from a 1.5-acre parcel of 60-year-old Chardonnay vines in Congy planted on clay topsoils and pure chalk subsoils. The vines are afflicted with "court-noué" a disease that stifles vigor, and "millerandage," which reduces yields and causes berries to ripen irregularly. These two maladies are thought to result in more concentrated, amplified wines.

LES ENFERS (NV)
Dosage: Extra Brut
Price: $300

Collin's smallest production wine, this blanc de blancs comes from a 1.4 acre parcel of 60-year-old Chardonnay vines that sits right next to Les Roises. These vines sit on very little topsoil, though, so are essentially planted on pure chalk.

Ulysse Collin
19/21 Rue des Vignerons
51270 Congy, France
Phone: (+33) 3 26 59 35 48
champagne-ulysse.collin@orange.fr
Visits by appointment.

VARNIER-FANNIÈRE (R.M.)

Production: About 36,000 bottles annually.

The Fannière family began tending vineyards in Avize in 1860, but for almost 100 years, it sold those grapes to *négociants* like Möet, Pommery, and Roederer.

In 1947, Jean Fannière decided to produce his own champagne. Success came quickly. By 1959, when his son-in-law Guy Varnier was taking charge of the company, the company was selling about 10,000 bottles each year.

Varnier added his name to the company's label and boosted production by acquiring parcels in the Grand Crus of Cramant and Oger. Since 1989, Guy's son Denis has run the estate.

Today, Varnier-Fannière owns 10 acres of vines, with an average vine age approaching 50, in Avize, Oiry, Oger, and Cramant. The estate focuses exclusively on Chardonnay, purchasing still Pinot Noir for its rosé from a grower in Ambonnay.

In the cellar, Varnier presses all his grapes with the same Coquard winepress used by his grandfather. All his wines are vinified in stainless steel, where they go through full malolactic fermentation. And he bottles with a bit less atmospheric pressure than most producers.

THE WINES

GRAND CRU (NV)

Dosage: Brut / Brut Nature
Price: $60

This non-vintage blanc de blancs is typically sourced from all four villages where Varnier farms. Typically a blend of two different vintages, this wine ages on its lees for two years before disgorgement. Most of the production is bottled as brut, but a small percentage of this wine is sold as "Zero" and finished without dosage.

CUVÉE SAINT DENIS (NV)

Dosage: Brut
Price: $70

Sourced from Clos du Grand Père, a parcel of 80-year-old Chardonnay vines in Avize, this blanc de blancs ages on its lees for 48 months before disgorgement.

ROSÉ (NV)

Dosage: Brut / Brut Nature
Price: $60

An assemblage of 90% Chardonnay and 10% still Pinot Noir purchased from Paul Dethune, a grower in Ambonnay. This rosé ages on its lees for 36 months before disgorgement. Most of the production is bottled as brut, but a small percentage of this wine is sold as "Zero" and finished without dosage.

CUVÉE DE JEAN FANNIÈRE ORIGINE (NV)

Dosage: Extra Brut
Price: $70

Dedicated to the estate's founder, Jean Fannière, this blanc de blancs is typically sourced from old vines in Avize, Cramant, and Oger. Typically a blend of two different vintages, this wine ages on its lees for over four years before disgorgement.

GRAND VINTAGE (VINTAGE)

Dosage: Brut
Price: $115

Sourced from Varnier's oldest parcels, which are in Cramant and Avize, this blanc de blancs is only made in exceptional years. It ages for five years on its lees before disgorgement.

Varnier-Fannière

23 Rempart du Midi
51190 Avize
www.varnier-fanniere.com
Tel: (+33) 3 26 57 53 36
contact@varnier-fanniere.com
Visits by appointment.

J. L. VERGNON (R.M.)

Production: About 50,000 bottles annually.

The Vergnon estate traces its origins to the mid-20th century, when Maison Regnault Frères, a wine retailer, began producing champagne in the Grand Cru Le Mesnil-sur-Oger. In 1950, Elisabeth Regnault, gave the estate to her son, Jean-Louis.

For the next 35 years, Jean-Louis Vergnon sold his grapes to the local cooperative. In 1985, recognizing the quality of his fruit, Vergnon began making his own champagne.

Today, the Vergnon vineyards are spread across 13 acres in the Côte des Blancs, with holdings in Le Mesnil-sur-Oger, Oger, Avize, Vertus, and Villeneuve-Renneville-Chevigny.

In 2002, the Vergnon family brought on Christophe Constant to run the estate—and the results have been transformative. Constant harvests ripe to avoid ever needing to chaptalize his wines or rely on malolactic fermentation to soften them. Dosage, when performed, is always light. Although most wines are vinified in stainless steel, Constant has recently started vinifying in large, 300- and 400-liter barrels. Constant farms sustainably, avoiding pesticides and filling his vineyards with cover crops.

Many wine enthusiasts consider Vergnon one of the best-kept secrets in Champagne, so the wines will surely skyrocket in popularity in the years ahead.

THE WINES

CONVERSATION (NV)
Dosage: Brut
Price: $50

Sourced from the Grand Crus of Le Mesnil-sur-Oger, Oger, and Avize, this blanc de blancs contains 25 percent reserve wine and is vinified in stainless steel. It ages for three years prior to disgorgement.

MURMURE (NV)
Dosage: Brut Nature
Price: $50

Sourced entirely from the Premier Cru of Vertus, this blanc de blancs ages for three years prior to disgorgement and is finished without dosage.

ELOQUENCE (NV)
Dosage: Extra Brut
Price: $55

Almost identical to the Conversation in composition, but finished with a lower dosage.

ROSÉMOTION (NV)
Dosage: Extra Brut
Price: $65

Grand Cru Chardonnay blended with red wine. This rosé d'assemblage includes about 12% still Pinot Noir, purchased from a grower in Aÿ. The rest is composed of Chardonnay sourced from the Grand Crus of Le Mesnil-sur-Oger, Oger, and Avize.

Vinified entirely in stainless steel, it ages for three years prior to disgorgement.

EXPRESSION (VINTAGE)
Dosage: Extra Brut
Price: $70

Sourced entirely from Oger, this wine goes through malolactic fermentation, unlike most Vergnon cuvées. It ages for at least three years before disgorgement.

CONFIDENCE (VINTAGE)
Dosage: Brut Nature
Price: $100

Sourced from the estate's oldest—and best—parcel in Le Mesnil-sur-Oger, this champagne reliest on indigenous yeast for primary fermentation and is vinified in 300-liter barrels with 1-3 years of age. It ages for at least three years before disgorgement, and is finished without dosage.

J.L. Vergnon
1 Grande Rue
51190 Le Mesnil sur Oger
contact@champagne-jl-vergnon.com
Tel: 03.26.57.53.86
www.champagne-l-vergnon.com

WARIS-HUBERT (R.M.)

Production: About 60,000 bottles annually.

Avize is a village with fewer than 2,000 residents. So when residents Stéphanie Hubert and Olivier Waris—both fourth-generation growers—wed in 1997, many likely predicted that the two would join their plots and establish a champagne house.

Waris-Hubert has over 28 acres of vines. Most are in the Côte des Blancs, where the estate has holdings in Grauves, Sézanne, and the Grand Crus of Avize, Oger, Cramant, and Chouilly. Waris-Hubert also owns vines in the Vallée de la Marne, with holdings in the Grand Cru Aÿ and the Premier Cru of Bisseuil.

Together, Stéphanie and Olivier oversee every step of production—from farming their vineyards to bottling their champagne. In the cellar, each parcel is vinified separately in stainless steel and go through malolactic fermentation.

THE WINES

GRAND CRU CHARDONNAY (NV)
Dosage: Brut / Brut Nature
Price: $60

Sourced entirely from Cramant and Avize, this blanc de blancs is vinified in stainless steel, where it stays for 6 months. This wine comes with two different levels of dosage. The "Brut" is aged for 3 years and dosed at 7 g/l. The "Dosage Zero" is aged for 18 months and finished without dosage.

PINOT NOIR (NV)
Dosage: Brut
Price: $60

This blanc de noirs is a 100% Pinot Noir sourced from Sézanne and Aÿ. It is vinified in stainless steel, where it stays for 6 months, and aged for 2 years.

ROSÉ (NV)
Dosage: Brut
Price: $60

A blend of 85% Chardonnay from Avize and 15% still Pinot Noir from Bouzy, this rosé is vinified in stainless steel, where it stays for 6 months, and aged for 18 months.

MILLÉSIME (VINTAGE)
Dosage: Brut
Price: $65

Sourced from vines in Avize planted in the early 1970s, this vintage champagne is vinified in stainless steel, where it stays for 6 months. This wine ages for about 5 years.

EQUINOXE (VINTAGE)
Dosage: Brut
Price: $100

Sourced from Avize, this vintage champagne is vinified entirely in oak and only goes through partial malolactic. This wine spends about 5 years on its lees. The cork is held tight with an old-fashioned string closure.

Waris-Hubert
14 Rue d'Oger
51190 Avize
Tel: (+33) 3 26 58 29 93
www.champagne-waris-hubert.fr
contact@champagne-waris-hubert.fr
Visits by appointment.

Section Five:

The Aube

A vineyard outside of Avirey Lingey in The Aube.
Photo by Luisa Bonachea.

Champagne's ancient capital, Troyes, sits about 65 miles south of Épernay. Once the epicenter of Champagne's textile industry, the city is still packed with cobblestone streets, colorful half-timbered houses, and other reminders of medieval times.

Today, Troyes serves as the commercial center of the Aube, Champagne's southernmost growing region.

Humid air from the Atlantic Ocean and the warm, dryer air of continental Europe impact the Aube's climate. These influences, combined with its southern location, bring higher temperatures to the region and thus riper grapes. The region also sees more rain than the rest of Champagne, which sometimes poses a problem in its largest growing area, the Côte des Bar.

Beginning about 20 miles southeast of Troyes, the Côte des Bar connects the region's two major riverside towns, Bar-sur-Seine, which sits on the Seine, and Bar-sur-Aube, which sits on the Aube. The sub-region around the Aube is called Bar sur Aubois and the sub-region around the Seine is called Bar Séquanais. Vineyards in both sub-regions are planted along the many streams that feed into the rivers, typically on the steep slopes that fill the landscape.

The soils here don't contain much chalk. Like the soils in Chablis, Burgundy's northernmost sub-region, they're Kimmeridgian marl topped by limestone. Rocky vineyards in the Côte des Bar handle rainfall well, as the loose soil eases drainage. In the lesser vineyards of the sub-region, though, the soil sometimes struggles to absorb water, which can damage vines. But whereas producers in Chablis focus on Chardonnay, producers in the Côte des Bar focus on Pinot Noir.

QUICK FACTS

19,000 planted acres
2,427 growers
Pinot Noir: 86%
Chardonnay: 10%
Pinot Meunier: 4%

SUB-REGIONS

Bar sur Aubois
Bar Séquanais
Montgueux

LEADING PRODUCERS

Cédric Bouchard
Marie-Courtin
Dosnon
Fleury
Bertrand Gautherot
    [Vouette et Sorbée]
Olivier Horiot
Jacques Lassaigne
Serge Mathieu
Ruppert-Leroy

PRODUCERS TO KNOW

Vincent Couche
Colette Bonnet
Devaux
Charles Dufour
R. Dumont & Fils
Nathalie Falmet
Pierre Gerbais
Coessens Largillier
Moutard
Piollot Père et Fils
Jean Velut
Val Frison

ICONIC WINES OF TERROIR

Cédric Bouchard: Creux d'Enfer
Jacques Lassaigne: Millésime
Marie Courtin: Concordance
Vouette et Sorbée Fidèle

Today, about 86 percent of the Aube is planted to Pinot Noir, 10 percent to Chardonnay, and 4 percent to Pinot Meunier. Here, these grapes tend to produce full-bodied, fruity champagnes.

Although the Aube was included in Champagne's official 1927 boundaries, it has always had a complicated relationship with the appellation. Its climate and soil are quite different from the northern growing districts, of course, and it's geographically isolated. These differences motivated many growers in the villages surrounding Reims and Épernay to push for the Aube's exclusion from Champagne in the opening years of the 20th century. Moreover, up until the end of the Second World War, the region was planted mostly to Gamay, the grape of Beaujolais.

So it's no wonder why, for most of modern history, Champagne's savvy marketers ignored the Aube—even though its grapes were extensively used in many non-vintage champagnes. Today, though, the Aube is in the midst of a renaissance. In the Côte des Bar, especially, young vignerons are exploring the region's soils, slopes, and microclimates to prove that the region has exceptional terroir.

The Côte des Bar is also notable for Riceys, a series of three neighboring villages—Riceys-Haut, Riceys Haute-Rive, and Riceys-Bas—that together form a small appellation for a still, obscure rosé called "Rosé des Riceys."

The other major sub-region of the Aube, Montgueux, sits six miles west of Troyes on top of a 900-foot outcrop of chalk. With southeast-facing slopes and soil that's nearly identical to the hillside of the Côte des Blancs, the sub-region has been prized for its Chardonnay since it was planted in the 1950s.

Vineyards of Champagne Marie Courtin.

CÉDRIC BOUCHARD / ROSES DE JEANNE (R.M.)

Production: About 15,000 bottles annually.

Cédric Bouchard believes that great wines are singular: single varieties harvested in single years in single vineyards. He no doubt developed this belief in the 1990s while working as a caviste in Paris, where he became enchanted by natural wine. Bouchard began pursuing this vision in 2000 when his father agreed to let him farm a two-acre vineyard—Les Ursules—in his childhood village of Celles-sur-Ource.

In the vineyard, Bouchard farms naturally. In the cellar, he intervenes minimally. In 2002, he released his first champagne: a blanc de noirs branded as "Roses de Jeanne" as an homage to his grandmother.

That year, he also began working with a miniscule parcel (just 0.08 acres) of Pinot Noir called "Creux d'Enfer," from which he made a saignée rosé. That same year, he also planted a small plot of Chardonnay in a parcel he named "La Haute Lemble." In 2003, he began making wine from a fourth vineyard: a four-acre parcel owned by his father in nearby Polisot called "Val Vilaine." He branded this single-expression cuvée as "Inflorescence."

Bouchard has gradually expanded his production in the years since, adding a fifth champagne under the Inflorescence brand in 2004 and sixth under the Roses de Jeanne brand in 2005. In 2007, he planted a seventh site.

In 2012, after taking charge of his father's vineyard, Bouchard retired the Inflorescence brand. Today, he crafts seven distinct wines from seven different sites. All are branded as Roses de Jeanne.

Bouchard vinifies all his wine in stainless steel and enameled-steel, relying on indigenous yeast for primary fermentation and letting malolactic fermentation run its natural course. Bouchard sees bubbles as an accessory, so catalyzes the second, in-bottle fermentation with a liqueur de tirage that results in 4.5 atmospheres of pressure rather than the standard 6. Although his wines are finished without dosage, all are labeled as brut.

The Wines

Les Ursules (Vintage)
Dosage: Brut Nature
Price: $100

From a two-acre parcel of Pinot Noir mostly planted in 1974, this this blanc de noirs ages for 28 months on its lees.

Creux d'Enfer (Vintage)
Dosage: Brut Nature
Price: $190

From just 0.08 acres of Pinot Noir planted in 1994, the grapes for this saignée are crushed by foot. Aged for 38 months on its lees.

Côte de Val Vilaine (Vintage)
Dosage: Brut Nature
Price: $75

From a 3.5-acre parcel of Pinot Noir planted in 1974, this this blanc de noirs ages for 28 months on its lees. This wine was formerly called Inflorescence.

Côte de Béchalin (Vintage)
Dosage: Brut Nature
Price: $100

From a 1.8-acre vineyard of Pinot Noir, this blanc de noirs ages for 80 months on its lees. Bouchard began making wine from this vineyard, which was owned by a family friend, in 2004. He purchased it in 2007. This wine was formerly known as La Parcelle and bottled under the Inflorescence label.

La Haute Lemble (Vintage)
Dosage: Brut Nature
Price: $120

From a quarter-acre parcel of Chardonnay planted in 2002, the grapes for this blanc de blancs are crushed by foot. Aged for 46 months on its lees.

La Bolorée (Vintage)
Dosage: Brut Nature
Price: $160

From a half-acre parcel of Pinot Blanc planted in 1960, this blanc de blancs ages for 38 months on its lees.

Presle (Vintage)
Dosage: Brut Nature
Price: $150

From a half-acre parcel planted with 10 different clones of Pinot Noir in 2007, this blanc de noirs ages for 36 months on its lees.

Roses de Jeanne
4 Rue du Creaux-Michel
10110 Celles-sur-Ource
Tel: (33) 3 25 29 69 78
Visits by appointment only.

MARIE COURTIN (R.M.)

Production: About 20,000 bottles annually.

At the tail end of 2000, Dominique Moreau was offered the chance to lease 2.5 acres of vines in Polisot, a small village in the Côte des Bar, from a retiring grower. Those vines had been planted by her father-in-law in the late-1960s and early 1970s, so she jumped at the opportunity.

Moreau soon acquired those vines along with some adjoining parcels, and today owns six continuous acres inside a 7.5 acre vineyard. Her husband, the proprietor of Piollot Père et Fils, owns the other 1.5 acres. Most of Moreau's vines are Pinot Noir, although one-third of an acre is planted to Chardonnay and a handful of vines are Pinot Blanc. She has been farming organically since day one and certified since 2010.

Moreau named her winery Marie Courtin as an homage to her great-grandmother. Her first harvest took place in 2006 with just two wines. Since then, her production—and reputation—have grown. Without question, she is one of the Aube's superstars.

In the cellar, Moreau keeps things simple. With Pinot Noir, whole bunches are pressed in a traditional coquard basket and the juice is then left to settle for about 24 hours. With Chardonnay, Moreau utilizes a modern pneumatic press. She relies on indigenous yeast for primary fermentation and vinification takes place in either old cement tanks or neutral oak, depending on the cuvée, and full malolactic takes place. Moreau inoculates second fermentation with a yeast that she developed from her own fruit in 2003. Bottling takes place after about a year, and all her wines age for about 30 months. All her wines are finished without dosage. While early releases were made entirely from a single vintage, Moreau now blends in a bit of reserve wines to her cuvées.

Dominiuqe Moreau. Photo by Luisa Bonachea.

THE WINES

RESONANCE (NV)
Dosage: Extra Brut
Price: $55

    A blanc de noirs sourced from the top of her vineyard's slope, where there is little topsoil. This wine is vinified in old concrete tanks. Finished without dosage.

EFFLORESCENCE (NV)
Dosage: Extra Brut
Price: $70

    While this blanc de noirs comes from the same parcel as Resonance, it is vinified and aged in neutral barrique before being bottled. Also finished without dosage.

ÉLOQUENCE (NV)
Dosage: Extra Brut
Price: $80

    This blanc de blancs is sourced from Moreau's small parcel of Chardonnay, which was planted in the 1990s. About half is vinified in oak, the other half in enameled-steel tanks. This is typically a blend of two harvests. Finished without dosage.

CONCORDANCE (NV)
Dosage: Extra Brut
Price: $95

    A blanc de noirs sourced from Moreau's oldest Pinot Noir vines, which were planted in 1968. This wine is aged for three years before disgorgement, where it's finished without dosage.

INDULGENCE (NV)
Dosage: Extra Brut
Price: $95

    A rosé of pinot noir, this saignée champagne receives its color from a 4-day maceration. This wine is aged for three years before disgorgement

Marie Courtin
8 Rue de Tonnerre
10110 Polisot
Tel: (33) 3 25 38 57 45
dqs.moreau@orange.fr
Visits by appointment only.

DOSNON (N.M.)

Production: About 40,000 bottles annually.

    Dosnon is scratching out its own niche as a relatively new champagne house focused on mineral-driven, low-dosage champagne. Based in the Côte des Bar village of Avirey-Lingey, this artisanal *négociant* was established in 2008 as a partnership between Davy Dosnon, who spent his teenage years working alongside his grandfather on two acres of vines in Avirey-Lingey and later worked Rossignol-Trapet in Burgundy, and Simon-Charles Lepage. The partnership split in 2012 after a business dispute.

    Today, Dosnon owns just over five acres of vines spread over six parcels but sources from vineyards across the Aube. Virtually all his vines are planted in hard, Kimmeridgian limestone soils, quite similar to those in Chablis. He is assisted by Nicolas Laugerotte.

The wines are all fermented and aged in old Puligny-Montrachet barriques. They undergo malolactic fermentation, and no wines are fined or filtered. The different parcels are vinified separately.

Davy Dosnon and his colleague, Nicolas Laugerotte. Photo by Luisa Bonachea.

THE WINES

RÉCOLTE BRUTE (NV)

Dosage: Extra Brut
Price: $40

A blend of 70% Pinot Noir and 30% Chardonnay, this wine is fermented and aged in old barrels and blended with 40% reserve wine.

RÉCOLTE NOIRE (NV)

Dosage: Brut / Brut Zero
Price: $45

This 100% Pinot Noir uses a current vintage and blends in 40% reserve wine. A small amount is hand labeled and finished without dosage.

RÉCOLTE BLANCHE (NV)

Dosage: Brut
Price: $45

A blanc de blancs that shows Chardonnay's interpretation of the village's hard limestone soil, this wine also contains 40% reserve wine.

RÉCOLTE ROSÉ (NV)

Dosage: Brut
Price: $50

Dosnon's rosé takes its color from still Pinot Meunier from Polisy, which comprises about 5% of the cuvée. The rest is entirely Pinot Noir.

GRANDE CUVÉE ALLIAE (VINTAGE)

Dosage: Brut Nature
Price: $85

Equal parts Chardonnay and Pinot Noir, this wine vinifies in barriques (10% of which are new) for 10 months. It spends about 4.5 years on its lees before disgorgement and is finished without dosage.

GRANDE EPHEMERE (VINTAGE)

Dosage: Extra Brut
Price: $65

A 100% Pinot Meunier that vinifies in barriques for 10 months. It spends 4.5 years on its lees before disgorgement.

Dosnon
4 Bis Rue du Bas de Lingey
10340 Avirey Lingey
Phone: (+33) 3 25 29 19 24
nicolas@champagne-dosnon.com
www.champagne-dosnon.com
Visits by appointment only.

FLEURY (N.M.)

About 180,000 bottles annually.

Robert Fleury began producing wine from his family's vineyards in Courteron, a village about 30 miles south of Troyes, in 1929. His son, Jean-Pierre, took over in 1962. Inspired, in part, by Rachel Carson's *Silent Spring*, he quickly adopted an ecologically conscious approach to farming. In 1970, he began studying biodynamics and incorporating some of its methods. He converted 7.5 acres of vineyards to biodynamic viticulture in 1989—a first for Champagne—and converted the rest of his holdings in 1992.

Today, Jean-Pierre's son, Jean-Sébastien, runs the estate and is taking the natural approach even further. Some plots are now plowed with horses and he's introduced a sulfur-free cuvée to the family's offerings.

The family's 37 acres are spread over about a dozen parcels in Courteron. While most of its holdings are planted to Pinot Noir, the family also farms Chardonnay and small amounts of Pinot Blanc and Pinot Gris. Note that Fleury is technically a *négociant*. Its own vineyards provide enough fruit for 65 percent of production; the rest is purchased from two neighbors who also farm biodynamically.

In the cellar, Fleury has relied exclusively on indigenous yeasts for primary fermentation since 1996. (In fact, Jean-Pierre even isolated his cellar's yeast and now sells it commercially as a biodynamic yeast strain.) Its wines are fermented in either barrels or enameled-steel tanks, and reserve wines are stored in neutral barriques or foudres. While most wines see full malolactic fermentation, conversion is sometimes blocked in vintage offerings. Very little sulfur is used.

THE WINES

BLANC DE NOIRS (NV)
Dosage: Brut
Price: $40

Fleury's entry-level offering is comprised entirely of Pinot Noir, mostly from two recent harvests which are vinified in enameled-steel tanks.

FLEUR DE L'EUROPE (NV)
Dosage: Brut
Price: $55

Typically comprised of 85 percent Pinot Noir and 15 percent Chardonnay. This wine always has a generous percentage of reserve wine (25+ percent), which is stored in neutral barriques. The base wine, which is comprised of two harvests, is vinified in enameled-steel tanks.

Rosé de Saignée (NV)

Dosage: Brut
Price: $50

Made entirely from Pinot Noir, this saignée champagne receives its color from an 18-hour maceration. It's vinified in enamel-lined stainless steel tanks.

Cuvée Robert Fleury (Vintage)

Dosage: Extra Brut
Price: $55

Typically comprised of old-vine Chardonnay, Pinot Noir, Pinot Blanc, and Pinot Meunier, vinified entirely in neutral oak.

Millesime (Vintage)

Dosage: Extra Brut
Price: $75

Typically a blend of about 80 percent Pinot Noir and 25 percent Chardonnay. The vinification of the Pinot Noir is split evenly between enameled-steel tanks and neutral oak. The Chardonnay is vinified entirely in enameled-steel tanks. This wine is typically aged for about ten years on its lees under natural cork.

Cépages Blancs (Vintage)

Dosage: Extra Brut
Price: $90

This blanc de blancs is typically a blend of about 85 percent Chardonnay and 15 percent Pinot Blanc. About 80 percent of the base wine is vinified in enameled-steel tanks, the rest in neutral oak.

Notes Blanches (Vintage)

Dosage: Brut Nature
Price: $60

A single-vintage Pinot Blanc sourced from a single parcel planted in the early 1980s, this wine is vinified entirely in neutral oak.

Sonate No. 9 (Vintage)

Dosage: Extra Brut
Price: $125

A blend of 90 percent Pinot Noir and 10 percent Chardonnay that's vinified without any added sulfur, this wine is sourced entirely from the Val Prune vineyard, which was the first holding converted to biodynamics. While finished without dosage, this wine is labeled as Extra Brut because it sometimes contains a touch of residual sugar leftover from initial fermentation.

Boléro (Vintage)

Dosage: Extra Brut
Price: $50

A blanc de noirs comprised entirely of Pinot Noir, vinified in enameled-steel tanks and aged 7 years on its lees under natural cork.

Fleury
43 Grande Rue
10250 Courteron
www.champagne-fleury.fr
Tel: (33) 3 25 38 20 28
champagne@champagne-fleury.fr
Visits by appointment only.

BERTRAND GAUTHEROT [VOUETTE ET SORBÉE] (R.M.)

Production: About 30,000 bottles annually.

Bertrand Gautherot grew up on a farm in Buxières-sur-Arce that was packed with life; his family raised sheep, cultivated honey, and grew grains, stone fruits, grapes, and more. They made wine for personal consumption, but sold most of their grapes off to the local cooperative. As a teenager helping his father tend the vines, Gautherot hoped to one day run the cooperative.

In 1993, after working for a few years in industrial plastic design, Gautherot returned home to take over the family vineyards. Worried about chemicals leeching into the water supply, he eliminated the use of herbicides, pesticides, and other chemical treatments in his vineyards in 1996. And by 1998, he was certified as both organic and biodynamic.

In 2001, at the urging of his friend Anselme Selosse, Gautherot began making his own champagne: a single-vintage Pinot Noir, barrel-fermented with native yeasts. Gautherot allowed malolactic fermentation to take place and finished his wine without dosage. While gearing up to release his first offering, he established his domaine, calling it "Vouette et Sorbée" after two of his parcels: Vouette, a one-acre plot where the clay and limestone soil date back to the Upper Jurassic age; and Sorbée, a higher-elevation, 2.5-acre site where the kimmeridgian soil dates back to the Portlandian age. The soils in Gautherot's third parcel, Biaunes, closely resemble Vouette's, but the climate is colder and wetter.

In 2004, Gautherot released 3,000 bottles of champagne, called "Fidèle." Wine enthusiasts snapped it up, so production steadily increased. In 2008, Gautherot's final contract with a *négociant*, Duval-Leroy, ended. In 2011, he stopped selling grapes to the local cooperative.

Today, Gautherot farms 12.5 acres of vines which he uses to make three distinctive champagnes and a handful of micro-production, experimental cuvées.

Two of his three wines are always from a single vintage, but they can't be released as vintage champagnes because they don't spend three years on their lees. On his back labels, Gautherot details the disgorgement date and the harvest year.

THE WINES

FIDÈLE (NV)

Dosage: Brut Nature

Price: $75

Gautherot's primary cuvée, Fidèle is a blanc de noirs sourced from all three of his plots. About 90-95 percent of the wine always comes from a single vintage; the rest draws from a perpetual blend started in 2001. It's barrel-fermented with native yeasts, undergoes full malolactic fermentation, and is finished without dosage.

BLANC D'ARGILE (VINTAGE)

Dosage: Brut Nature

Price: $95

This single-vintage blanc de blancs comes entirely from the Biaunes vineyard. Like all of Gautherot's wines, it's barrel-fermented with native yeasts, undergoes full malolactic fermentation, and is finished without dosage.

SAIGNÉE DE SORBÉE (VINTAGE)

Dosage: Brut Nature

Price: $95

A single-vintage saignée of Pinot Noir from the Sorbée vineyard. Like all of Gautherot's wines, it's barrel-fermented with native yeasts, undergoes full malolactic fermentation, and is finished without dosage.

Bertrand Gautherot

Vouette et Sorbée

8 Rue de Vaux

10110 Buxières-sur-Arce

www.vouette-et-sorbee.com

Tel: (33) 9 79 70 32 70

vouette-et-sorbee@orange.fr

No visits.

OLIVIER HORIOT

Production: About 6,000 bottles annually.

Olivier Horiot is the only vigneron in Champagne more famous for his still wines than his fizzy ones. But this makes sense. When he took charge of his family's 16 acres of vines in Les Riceys in 2000, he quickly turned his attention to the still rosé for which his region is famous.

Horiot also turned his attention to the soil, working to eliminate the use of synthetic pesticides, herbicides, and fertilizers quickly and completely. In 2002, Horiot converted the five acres of vines used for his wines to

Olivier Horiot.

biodynamics. He then turned his attention to his other 12 acres, converting his remaining parcels to biodynamics by 2006. (Those other grapes are sold to the local cooperative, which is run by his father and *négociants*.)

In 2004, Horiot introduced a number of champagnes to his portfolio. But still wines continue to comprise about 70 percent of his annual production. Notably, Horiot makes a rosé, a still red, a blanc de noirs, and a saignée rosé champagne from the same vineyard. He relies on indigenous yeast to for primary fermentation in all his wines.

THE WINES

ROSÉ DES RICEYS "EN BARMONT" (VINTAGE)
Price: $40

100% Pinot Noir. Sourced from the vineyard of Barmont, a warm site where grapes easily ripen, Horiot typically presses about 10 percent of each cuvée by foot before adding whole bunches. The wine then macerates "semi-carbonically"—in other words, the juice begins to ferment while still inside the grape—for about a week. Horiot then transfers the wine to neutral barriques, where wines are left on their lees for about a year, to finish fermentation.

COTEAUX CHAMPENOIS: RICEYS ROUGE "EN BARMONT" (VINTAGE)
Price: $50

A still red comprised entirely of Pinot Noir from the Barmont vineyard.

ROSÉ DES RICEYS "EN VALINGRAIN" (VINTAGE)
Price: $40

This wine is made identically to "En Barmont," but the grapes are instead sourced from the slightly cooler Valingrain vineyard.

COTEAUX CHAMPENOIS: RICEYS BLANC "EN VALINGRAIN" (VINTAGE)
Price: $60

A still white comprised of both Chardonnay and Pinot Blanc from the Valingrain vineyard.

BLANC DE NOIRS "EN BARMONT" SÈVE (NV)
Dosage: Extra Brut
Price: $50

A blanc de noirs comprised entirely of Pinot Noir from the Barmont vineyard. Fermented and aged for one year in neutral barrique, this wine is then aged for four years on its lees.

ROSÉ DE SAIGNÉE "EN BARMONT" SÈVE (NV)
Dosage: Extra Brut
Price: $50

This rosé de saignée of Pinot Noir from the Barmont vineyard receives its color from a four-day, semi-carbonic maceration. Fermented and aged for one year in neutral barrique, this wine is then aged for four years on its lees.

5 SENS (VINTAGE)
Dosage: Brut Nature
Price: $60

A blend of equal parts Chardonnay, Pinot Noir, Pinot Meunier, Pinot Blanc, and Arbanne fermented and aged separately for one year in neutral barrique before assemblage. This wine is finished without dosage.

MÉTISSE (VINTAGE)
Dosage: Extra Brut
Price: $50
   About 80% Pinot Noir and 20% Pinot Blanc, this champagne is fermented and aged for one year in neutral barrique and then aged for four years on its lees.

ARBANE (VINTAGE)
Dosage: Extra Brut
Price: $60
   Comprised entirely of Arbane, this this champagne is fermented and aged for one year in neutral barrique and then aged for four years on its lees.

Olivier Horiot
25 Rue de Bise
10340 Les Riceys
www.horiot.fr
Tel: (33) 3 25 29 32 16
champagne@horiot.fr

JACQUES LASSAIGNE (N.M.)

Production: About 55,000 bottles annually.

   With soil that's nearly identical to what's found in the Côte des Blancs, Montgueux has been prized for its Chardonnay since it was planted in the 1950s. Jacques Lassaigne was one of the first growers there. He produced some champagne, but like most small growers, he sold the majority of grapes to large *négociants*.

   In 1999, Jacques' son Emmanuel took over the estate and quickly worked to invigorate the vineyard, eliminating the use synthetic fertilizers, herbicides, pesticides, and insecticides. (While he farms organically, he hasn't gone through the certification process.) Emmanuel has also worked to boost estate champagne production, allowing contracts with *négociants* to expire.

   Fascinated by Montgueux's terroir, he began vinifying his parcels separately. While this practice is common among top growers today, it was quite rare at the turn of the century, especially in Montgueux.

   Lassaigne has 12 acres of vines, with an average age of about 40, on the eastern edge of the Montgueux's southeast facing slope. Now a *négociant* himself, he supplements his production with about 2.5 acres worth of fruit from neighboring vineyards where he has total control. His fruit—and thus, his production—is entirely Chardonnay. (Lassaigne had a small amount of Pinot Noir—used in a cuvée called "Les Papilles Insolites" and a rosé—but those vines have been ripped out.)

In the cellar, Lassaigne relies on indigenous yeast for primary fermentation, which takes place in stainless steel or neutral barrique. All bottles are disgorged by hand.

The Wines

Les Vignes de Montgueux (NV)
Dosage: Extra Brut
Price: $50

Typically comprised of two recent vintages, this non-vintage blanc de blancs is vinified in stainless steel.

Le Cotet (NV)
Dosage: Extra Brut
Price: $75

From a single-vineyard planted on a topsoil of clay and silex in the mid-1960s, about 10 percent of this wine is vinified in neutral oak. The base wine typically comprises about 90 percent of the cuvée.

La Colline Inspirée (Vintage)
Dosage: Extra Brut
Price: $80

Sourced from three old-vine parcels in Montgueux—Paluets, Cotet, and Grande Côte—and vinified entirely in neutral barrique. The base wine typically comprises about 75 percent of the cuvée.

Millésime (Vintage)
Dosage: Brut Nature
Price: $90

Lassaigne's vintage wine, which is made every year, is vinified in tank and finished without dosage.

Jacques Lassaigne
7 Chemin du Coteau
10300 Montguex
www.montgueux.com
Tel: (33) 3 25 74 84 83
e.lassaigne@montgueux.com
Visits by appointment only.

SERGE MATHIEU (R.M.)

Production: About 100,000 bottles annually.

The Mathieu family has worked in Aube's vineyards since the 18th century. Historical records show the Mathieus acquiring parcels in Avirey-Lingey in 1760, 1850, 1894, and throughout the 20th century.

For most of its history, though, the Mathieus sold their grapes to *négociants*. That changed in 1970 when seventh-generation proprietor Serge Mathieu—who had started working alongside his father 12 years earlier—decided to vinify his own grapes. Production has rapidly expanded in the years since.

Serge Mathieu's daughter, Isabelle, has been integral to the estate since 1987, when she joined and began running marketing and much of the business. In 1998, Isabelle's husband, Michel Jacob, joined the firm, taking over vineyard management immediately and gradually taking the reins in the cellar as well.

Today, the domaine owns 28 acres of vines in Avirey-Lingey spread over 20 parcels. The largest parcel—a 7.5-acre vineyard called La Bressoire—is adjacent to the winery and planted entirely to Pinot Noir. Fifteen parcels planted to both Pinot Noir and Chardonnay sit on a slope called "Bagneux." Four other parcels planted to Pinot Noir and Chardonnay sit on a hill called Couins. About 80 percent of Mathieu's holdings are Pinot Noir; the rest are Chardonnay.

Jacob is gradually phasing out the use of chemical applications in all his vineyards. But he admits to prioritizing pragmatism over dogmatism, so his farming is better described as sustainable.

In the cellar, Jacob vinifies and ages his wines in stainless and enameled-steel vats. All wines complete malolactic fermentation and are aged for 3-5 years before disgorgement, dosage, and release.

TRADITION (NV)
Dosage: Brut
Price: $45

A Blanc de Noirs typically comprised of two different vintages. It spends three years on its lees before disgorgement.

PRESTIGE (NV)
Dosage: Brut
Price: $50

A blend of about two-thirds Pinot Noir and one-third Chardonnay, this wine is also typically comprised of two different vintages. It ages for four years.

ROSÉ (NV)
Dosage: Brut
Price: $45

Typically from a single year, this rosé receives its color from still Pinot Noir, which typically comprises about 13 percent of the cuvée. The base wine is typically 100 percent Pinot Noir, but Chardonnay is sometimes included.

TÊTE DE CUVÉE SELECT (NV)
Dosage: Brut
Price: $50

A blend of about equal parts Pinot Noir and Chardonnay, this wine ages for four years on its lees. Dosage is typically very light.

MILLÉSIMÉ (VINTAGE)
Dosage: Brut
Price: $55

A vintage blanc de noirs that ages for 5-6 years on its lees and an additional year in bottle before release. The dosage is typically very light.

Serge Mathieu
6 Rue des Vignes
10340 Avirey-Lingey
www.champagne-serge-mathieu.fr
Tel: (33) 3 25 29 32 58
information@champagne-serge-mathieu.fr
No visits.

RUPPERT-LEROY (R.M.)

Production: About 10,000 bottles annually.

Gerard Ruppert settled in Essoyes, a village at the southeastern extreme of the Aube just three miles from Burgundy, in 1975. He had just completed a doctorate in philosophy, but rather than pursue a life in academia, Ruppert was drawn to the land. With his purchase, he planned to start a small farm and raise sheep.

Ruppert soon planted one acre of his property to grapes, farming organically even though such practices were quite unusual at the time, especially in Champagne. As the years went on, he planted more vines, eventually growing his holdings to 10 acres, split equally between Pinot Noir and Chardonnay. For several decades, though, Ruppert simply sold his grapes to the local cooperative.

In 2009, ready to retire, Ruppert offered his vines to his three children. Only one child—his daughter Bénédicte—was interested in continuing his work. Bénédicte and her husband Emmanuel promptly quit their jobs as physical education teachers to take charge in the vineyard. They decided to take things a step further, choosing to make their own wines and begin converting to biodynamics. Thanks to decades of organic viticulture, their soils were already healthy—and the wines became a hit, with trendy restaurants in Paris snatching them up.

Today, all Ruppert-Leroy's wines are from a single vintage and a single vineyard, bottled without dosage. Note that the vintage isn't noted on the label, as the wines don't spend long enough on their lees to qualify as vintage champagnes.

THE WINES

FOSSE-GRELY (VINTAGE)
Dosage: Brut Nature
Price: $60

Equal parts Pinot Noir and Chardonnay from the red clay and limestone soils of Fosse-Grely, a six-acre parcel planted around 30 years ago. Vinified in stainless steel, where it ages for nine months with malolactic fermentation neither encouraged nor discouraged. This wine spends 22 months on its lees.

FOSSE-GRELY "AUTREMENT" (VINTAGE)
Dosage: Brut Nature
Price: $70

A blanc de noirs from Fosse-Grely that sees no sulfur at any point in the winemaking process. It is otherwise treated identically to the regular Fosse-Grely bottling.

COGNAUX (VINTAGE)
Dosage: Brut Nature
Price: $65

A 100-percent Pinot Noir from a one-acre plot planted 15-30 years ago on Kimmeridgian clay, fermented and aged for nine months in tank and neutral oak. Malolactic fermentation neither encouraged nor discouraged. This wine spends 22 months on its lees.

SAIGNÉE DES COGNAUX (VINTAGE)
Dosage: Brut Nature
Price: $65

This rosé de saignée from Cognaux experiences a four-day, semi-carbonic maceration for its color. It is otherwise treated identically to Cognaux.

MARTIN-FONTAINE (VINTAGE)
Dosage: Brut Nature
Price: $75

A 100-percent Chardonnay from a 2.5-acre plot planted 20 years ago on Kimmeridgian clay, fermented and aged for nine months in tank and neutral oak. Malolactic fermentation neither encouraged nor discouraged. This wine spends 22 months on its lees.

Ruppert-Leroy
10360 Essoyes
www.champagne-ruppert-leroy.com
Tel: (33) 3 25 29 81 31
ruppertleroy@orange.fr
Visits by appointment.

GLOSSARY

-A-

Appellation d'origine contrôlée: Translated as "controlled designation of origin," this certification is granted to products with geographical indications, like wines and cheeses. In Champagne, AOC regulations dictate the region's boundaries, approved grape varieties, vineyard practices, the winemaking processes, and even labelling and packaging.

Assemblage: Blending; the process of combining wines from different grapes from different vineyards from different vintages to create a perfect blend.

-B-

Barrique: A standard oak barrel. Historically, champagne barrels were 205 liters, but most producers have moved to the 228-liter barrels that are produced in Burgundy, as this size has become the global standard.

Base: The still wine that exists before a secondary fermentation is initiated.

Bâtonnage: The practice of stirring the lees while a wine is aging. This technique is common in Burgundy, where it's praised for imparting richness. But it's controversial in Champagne, as some producers believe it takes away from a wine's delicacy.

Biodynamic: A form of alternative agriculture and winemaking derived from a series of lectures given in 1924 by philosopher Rudolf Steiner.

Blanc de Blancs: Translated as "white from whites," this designation is used when a champagne is made completely of white grapes. Almost always, a blanc de blancs is 100 percent Chardonnay.

Blanc de Noirs: Translated as "white from blacks," this designation is used when a champagne is made completely of Pinot Noir and/or Pinot Meunier, Champagne's only approved dark-skinned grapes.

Brut: The most common style of champagne, this term can be used on labels for wines with 0-12 grams per liter of residual sugar.

Brut Nature: A wine without any dosage. This term can be used on labels for wines with 0-3 grams per liter of residual sugar. Wines without dosage are sometimes labeled as "Zero Dosage."

Brut Zero: See "Brut Nature."

-C-

Cépage: The percentage of each variety in the composition of a blended wine.

Chaptalization: The practice of adding sugar to a wine prior to fermentation to spike alcohol content.

Clos: A walled vineyard. Today, this phrase is sometimes used to describe notable vineyards without walls.

Club de Viticulteurs Champenois: See "Club Trésor."

Club Trésor: An exclusive group of the region's small growers devoted to producing high quality wines. Each member makes a "Special Club" champagne.

Comité Interprofessional du Vin de Champagne: A trade association of all Champagne's growers and producers, first established during World War II.

Cooperative-manipulant: Translated as "cooperative-producer," this designation, abbreviated as "CM," is reserved for cooperatives where many growers join together to share resources and produce wine under a single brand.

Coteaux Champenois: An AOC designation for still wines from Champagne.

-D-

Demi-Muid: A large oak barrel that holds 500 to 600 liters of wine.

Demi-Sec: A very sweet champagne, this term can be used on labels for wines with 32-50 grams per liter of residual sugar.

Disgorgement: The removal of lees and other sediments that remain in a bottle after the second fermentation, which gives champagne its bubbles.

Dégorgement: See "disgorgement."

Dégorgement à la glace: The process of dipping the neck of a pre-disgorged bottle into a shallow pool of below-freezing liquid to turn the sediment into a frosty pellet, thus allowing for its expelling with virtually no loss of wine.

Dosage: The process of sweetening a champagne after disgorgement. The level of dosage determines a champagne's sweetness level (e.g. Extra Brut, Brut, etc.) This step is only required if a winemaker wants to sweeten his wines, and these days, it's fashionably avoided.

Doux: The sweetest style of champagne, this term can be used on labels for wines with more than 50 grams per liter of residual sugar.

Dry: Confusingly, this term is used for sweet champagnes with 17-32 grams per liter of residual sugar.

-E-

Échelle des Crus: A grape pricing scale based on locality, established in 1911. In 1911, the government rated each village in Champagne, assigning a quality rating of 22.55 to 100. Twelve villages were awarded "Grand Cru" status, so were awarded 100 percent of the price. About three dozen villages were ranked between 90 and 99 and awarded "Premier Cru" status. Those in villages ranked between 22.5 and 89 couldn't designate their grapes as "Grand Cru" or "Premier Cru" and were paid according to their specific ranking. The scale was later adjusted to a Cru floor of 80. This pricing system persisted until 1992. The ratings were officially abolished in 2007, but the terms Grand Cru and Premier Cru are still used by those who source grapes and produce wine from Champagne's top villages.

Extra Brut: An extremely dry style of champagne, this term can be used on labels for wines with 0-6 grams per liter of residual sugar.

Extra Dry: A noticeably sweet champagne, this term can be used on labels for wines with 12-17 grams per liter of residual sugar.

-F-

Filtration: The removal of suspended particles in wine.

Fine de la Marne: An oak-aged high quality brandy produced by distilling leftover wine and wine lees.

Fining: The clarification of wine.

Foudre: A giant oak vat that typically holds 2,200 to 5,500 liters of wine.

-G-

Grand Cru: See Échelle des Crus.

Grande Marque: Translated as "big brand." In 1882, 22 of Champagne's leading producers joined to form the "Syndicat du commerce des vins de Champagne." By the end of the 19th century, the group had grown to 60 and members called themselves grandes marques. This group disbanded in the late 1990s. But today, the phrase "grandes marques" is still used informally to reference Champagne's biggest brands.

-I-

Institut National des Appellations d'Origine: A powerful regulatory body tasked with enforcing appellation d'origine controlee rules. This group recently changed its name to the "institut national de l'origine et de la qualité."

-L-

Lieu-Dit: Translated as "place name," this term refers to a named parcel of vines.

Liqueur de tirage: A mixture of sugar and yeast that launches secondary fermentation.

Lees: The dead yeast deposits that are left over after fermentation.

Liqueur d'expédition: A sweet liquid—typically comprised of still wine and cane sugar, and sometimes brandy—that is used to top off champagne after disgorgement, in a process called "dosage." This is only required if a winemaker wants to sweeten his wines.

-M-

Malolactic Fermentation: A winemaking process that converts tart-tasting malic acid, naturally present in grape must, to softer-tasting lactic acid. This process can occur naturally, but can also be initiated or blocked by a winemaker. It's relatively common in Champagne to balance high acidity levels.

Marc de Champagne: An oak-aged brandy produced by distilling the seeds, skins, and stalks that are left after grapes are pressed.

Marque d'acheteur: Translated as "buyer's brand," this designation, abbreviated as "MA," is reserved for those that sell champagne as their own even though they didn't produce it themselves.

Méthode Champenoise: See "Méthode Traditionelle." This term was banned by the European Union in 1985.

Méthode Traditionelle: Translated as "traditional method," this term describes the technique of creating a sparkling wine by launching a second fermentation inside a bottle.

Millésime: See "vintage."

Moût concentré rectifié: A sweet liquid comprised of concentrated and rectified grape must that is used to top off champagne after disgorgement, in a process called "dosage." Like liqueur d'expédition, which is much more common, this is only required if a winemaker wants to sweeten his wines.

-N-

Natural wine: While there's no formal set of standards for "natural" wine producers most adhere to the following set of rough rules: Grapes are grown organically or biodynamically; Grapes are harvested by hand; Primary fermentation relies on indigenous yeasts; Acidification, chaptalization, and other cellar manipulations are rejected; The use of sulfur dioxide is limited.

Négociant-distributeur: Translated as merchant-distributor, this designation, abbreviated as "ND," is reserved for those that purchase finished champagne to label and distribute on their own.

Négociant-manipulant: Translated as merchant-producer, this designation, abbreviated as "NM," is reserved for those who buy more than 6 percent of their fruit.

Non-vintage: More than 85 percent of all champagne produced contains grapes harvested over multiple years.

-O-

Organic: A form of agriculture that prohibits the use of synthetic fertilizers, herbicides, and pesticides. If a vineyard is certified as organic, it is typically inspected once each year. Note that while many grapes are now grown organically, very few wines are labeled as organic because in the United States, only wines without added sulfur dioxide can be labeled as organic.

-P-

Perpetual Blend: A system of storing and aging wine that relies on a single tank that is continually replenished by each new harvest. Like a solera, this process creates a multi-vintage blend that always includes some wine from every year since it was created. See "solera."

Pétillant-naturel: Translated as "naturally sparkling," this term is used to describe a wine that is fizzy because it was bottled before primary fermentation has finished.

Phylloxera: A pest that feeds on the roots of vitis vinifera, the European grapevine, stunting growth or killing it. This grape pest destroyed most vineyards in Europe in the second half of the 19th century.

Premier Cru: See "Échelle des Crus."

Pressed Juice: With white wine production, the initial crushing process releases only about 65 percent of a berry's juice. The remaining juice is extracted through the use of a "press"—and as extraction becomes more aggressive, the resulting juice becomes more astringent and bitter.

Prestige Cuvée: A producer's top wine. Typically from a single vintage and coming from meticulously selected sites, barrels, or grapes, these wines almost always spend five years or more on the lees. Most come in fancy bottles. Some well-known examples include Moët & Chandon's Dom Pérignon, Pol Roger's Sir Winston Churchill, Louis Roederer's Cristal, and Taittinger's Comtes de Champagne.

Pupitre: A riddling rack comprised of two heavy, rectangular boards that together form an inverted "V." Traditionally, each side holds 60 bottles at a 45-degree angle.

-R-

Ratafia de Champagne: A blend of brandy and unfermented grape juice, typically from later pressings.

Récoltant-coopérateur: Translated as grower-cooperator, this designation, abbreviated as "RC," is used when a cooperative handles the winemaking for an individual grower who sells the resulting wine under his own brand.

Récoltant-manipulant: Translated as "grower-producer," this designation, abbreviated as "RM," is reserved for those who rely on estate fruit for 95 percent or more of their production. Colloquially, these are called "grower champagnes."

Remuage: See "riddling."

Reserve Wine: Older, still wine that is blended with the youngest vintage to create a base for the production of non-vintage champagne.

Riddling: Forcing the lees and other sediments that remain in a champagne bottle after the second fermentation, by gravity, to the bottle's neck. During this process, a wine moves from *sur latte* (on its side) to *sur pointe* (on its neck).

Rosé d'Assemblage: A rosé that is created by blending a small amount of still red wine into a clear champagne to dye the juice pink.

Rosé des Riceys: An AOC designation for still rosé from in and around Riceys, a village in the Aube.

Rosé de Saignée: A rosé that is created by leaving the juice from dark-skinned grapes in contact with its skins for a short period of time, typically a few hours to a few days.

-S-

Sabrage: The ceremonial art of opening champagne with a sword.

Saignée: See "Rosé de Saignée."

Single-expression champagne: A single-vineyard, single variety, single-vintage champagne.

Société de récoltants: Translated as union of growers, this designation, abbreviated as "SR," is reserved for those who pool resources to make wine under one or several labels.

Solera: A process for aging wine by fractional blending. Developed by Sherry producers in Spain, a solera typically includes several rows of small oak barrels stacked on top of one another, grouped by vintages. The oldest barrels are on the bottom and the youngest on top. Wines are always bottled from the oldest barrels, which are then refilled from the barrels that sit on top of them. Since no barrel is ever drained, some of the earlier wines always remain in each barrel. In Champagne, the most notable solera holds Anselme Selosse's "Substance," which was created in 1986. See "perpetual blend."

Sucre-oenomètre: A device that measures the amount of sugar in a wine.

Sur latte: Storing a bottle on its side. This phrase is used to describe already bottled, but not yet disgorged champagne that is ageing on its lees. Colloquially, this phrase is sometimes used pejoratively to describe bulk, not-yet-finished champagne that is purchased by large *négociants* to label as their own. In Champagne, confusingly, the majority of sur lie ageing takes place *sur latte*.

Sur lie: Translated as "on the lees." By law, non-vintage champagne must age for 12 months on the lees. Vintage-dated champagne must age for three years. Many houses age their top cuvées for much longer. In Champagne, confusingly, the majority of sur lie ageing takes place *sur latte*.

Sur pointe: Storing of a bottle upside down, on its neck. Wines are stored in this fashion after riddling but before disgorgement.

Sustainable: Producers that advertise themselves as "sustainable" typically eschew synthetic fertilizers, herbicides, and pesticides but have the flexibility to use such treatments if needed. Technically, sustainable viticulture has no formal definition.

-T-

Terroir: The term that is used to capture all the influences—climate, soil, elevation, and more—that shape a wine's final expression. Those who obsess over terroir believe that great wines have an obligation to translate time and place, clearly expressing the characteristics of their vintage and the soils and climate in which they're grown.

Tête de Cuvée: See "prestige cuvée."

-V-

Vigneron: Translated as "winegrower," this term is used as a synonym for grower-producer.

Vin clair: A still wine that is used to create a base for a champagne's final blend. Typically, many different vin clairs comprise a base.

Vintage: If a vintage is listed on the label, 100 percent of the wine inside came from that particular year's harvest.

-Z-

Zero Dosage: See "Brut Nature."

SELECTED BIBLIOGRAPHY

Baxevanis, John J. *The Wines of Champagne, Burgundy, Eastern and Southern France*. Rowman & Littlefield Publishers, 1987.

Clarke, Oz. *Landscapes of Wine: A Grand Tour of the World's Greatest Wine Regions and Vineyards*. Webster International Publishers, 2007.

Charters, Steve. *The Business of Champagne: A Delicate Balance*. Routledge, 2011.

Colman, Tyler. *Wine Politics: How Governments, Environmentalists, Mobsters, and Critics Influence the Wines We Drink*. University of California Press, 2010.

Edwards, Michael. *The Finest Wines of Champagne: A Guide to the Best Cuvées, Houses, and Growers*. University of California Press, 2009.

Forbes, Patrick. *Champagne: The Wine, the Land and the People*. David & Charles, 1967.

Gately, Iain. *Drink: A Cultural History of Alcohol*. Avery, 2009.

Gergaud, Olivier. *Anchoring and Property Prices: The Influence of Echelle Des Crus Ratings on Land Sales in the Champagne Region of France*. American Association Of Wine Economists, December 2015.

Guy, Kolleen M. *When Champagne Became French: Wine and the Making of a National Identity*. Johns Hopkins University Press, 2007.

Hagen, Rainer and Hagen, Rose-Marie. *What Great Paintings Say, Volume 1*. Taschen 2002.

Hughes, Stefan. *Catchers of the Light: The Forgotten Lives of the Men and Women Who First Photographed the Heavens*. ArtDeCiel Publishing, 2012.

Jackson, Ronald S. *Wine Science: Principles and Applications*. Academic Press, 2014.

Johnson, Hugh. *Vintage: The Story of Wine*. Simon and Schuster, 1989.

Joseph, Ryan. *The History of Champagne in Hip-Hop*. First We Feast, December 22, 2014.

Kissack, Chris. www.TheWineDoctor.com.

Kladstrup, Don and Petie. *Champagne: How the World's Most Glamorous Wine Triumphed Over War and Hard Times*. William Morrow, 2005.

Liem, Peter. www.ChampagneGuide.net.

Lloyd, Nick. *Hundred Days: The Campaign That Ended World War I*. Basic Books, 2014.

Lukacs, Paul. *Inventing Wine: A New History of One of the World's Most Ancient Pleasures*. W. W. Norton & Company, 2013.

Mazzeo, Tilar J. *The Widow Clicquot: The Story of a Champagne Empire and the Woman who Ruled It*. HarperBusiness, 2009.

Martin, Scott C. *The SAGE Encyclopedia of Alcohol: Social, Cultural, and Historical Perspectives*. SAGE Publications, 2015.

Michelin Guides. *The Americans in the Great War, Vol. 1: The Second Battle of the Marne*. 1919.

O'Connell, Daniel. *The Inner Man (1891)*. Applewood Books, 2008.

Parker, Thomas. *Tasting French Terroir: The History of an Idea*. University of California Press, 2015.

Pevitt, Christine. *Philippe, Duc D'Orleans Regent of France*. Atlantic Monthly Press, 1997.

Risser, Nicole Dombrowski. *France under Fire: German Invasion, Civilian Flight and Family Survival*. Cambridge University Press, 2015.

Robinson, Jancis. *The Oxford Companion to Wine (3rd Edition)*. Oxford University Press, 2006.

Spinage, C. A. *Cattle Plague: A History*. Springer Science & Business Media, 2003.

Stevenson, Tom. *Christie's World Encyclopedia of Champagne & Sparkling Wine*. Sterling Epicure, 2014.

Sumption, Jonathan. *The Hundred Years War, Volume 2: Trial by Fire*. University of Pennsylvania Press, 2001.

The Temperance Society. *Temperance: A Monthly Journal of the Church Temperance Society, Volumes 1-3*. 1908.

Tucker, Spencer C. *The Encyclopedia of World War I: A Political, Social, and Military History*. ABC-CLIO, 2005.

Tungate, Mark. *Luxury World: The Past, Present and Future of Luxury Brands*. Kogan Page, 2009.

Ulwencreutz, Lars. *Ulwencreutz's Royal Families in Europe V*. Lulu.com, 2013.

Vine, Richard. *The Curious World of Wine: Facts, Legends, and Lore About the Drink We Love*. TarcherPerigee, 2012.

Vizetelly, Henry. *A History of Champagne: With Notes on the Other Sparkling Wines of France*. Southeran, 1882.

Wagner, John A. *Encyclopedia of the Hundred Years War*. Greenwood, 2006.

Wheeler, Edward Jewitt and Crane, Frank. *Current Opinion: Volume 50*. Current Literature Publishing Company, 1912.

Wickes, Margaret L. *A Toast to the Good Life: Exploring the Regulation of Champagne*. LEDA at Harvard Law School, 2003.

Wilson, James E. *Terroir: The Role of Geology, Climate and Culture in the Making of French Wines*. Wine Appreciation Guild, 1998.

ACKNOWLEDGEMENTS

This project began in August 2013 over lunch with Kevin Sidders, a friend who had recently left banking to start VinConnect, a company that lets American consumers buy direct from top European wineries. While we ate, Kevin asked if I could suggest a straightforward guide to Champagne to help him prepare for his first visit to the region.

I could think of fantastic guides to other storied places, like Burgundy and Bordeaux. I could name books about Champagne's history. But I couldn't think of an approachable guide to Champagne. I didn't set out to write this book that day, but I started thinking about it. So if it weren't for Kevin, this book wouldn't exist.

Thanks are owed to John Brooks, a retired Air Force major general who now spends his days writing about wine. In November 2014, just a few months after I returned from my first trip to Champagne, John invited me to dinner with wine importer Terry Theise. That evening inspired me to move forward with this project.

Huge thanks to my agent, Keith Urbahn, for believing in this book from day one, sharpening my proposal, and finding a publisher.

Thanks are due to my wine squad: Scott Claffee, Warren Leonard, Michael Lewis, Tim O'Rourke, and Jeremiah Paskus. There's never a shortage of champagne with these guys.

Thanks are also owed to Sam Ryan and Robby Schrum—great colleagues and even better friends—for so strongly supporting my wine writing habit.

On the text itself, thanks to Tom Natan, Daniel Petroski, and Darryl Priest for offering feedback on early drafts. I'm grateful for Shelby Vittek and Isaac Baker, who helped draft some of the producer profiles. I'm deeply indebted to Tom Ryan—to whom I owe several cases of champagne—for his editing. I couldn't have met any deadlines without this crew.

My four-legged confidant, Morris Norris, provided companionship throughout the process. While I could easily blame Morris for any mistakes—it's hard to type with paws—all errors, omissions, and oversights are mine.

Finally, I'm forever grateful to Amy Norris, my partner in everything. She makes every moment of every day worth celebrating.